AN OCEAN OF INSPIRATION

Nicole,
hope you enjoyed seeing wild dolphins today. Keep exploring!

AN OCEAN OF
INSPIRATION

The John Olguin Story

By

Stefan E. Harzen,

Barbara J. Brunnick

and Mike Schaadt

Edited by Xavier Hermosillo

RMB

Rocky Mountain Books
www.rmbooks.com

Library and Archives Canada Cataloguing in Publication

Harzen, Stefan
An ocean of inspiration : the John Olguin story / by Stefan E. Harzen, Barbara J. Brunnick, and Mike Schaadt ; edited by Xavier Hermosillo.

Includes bibliographical references.
Issued also in electronic format. (ISBN 978-1-926855-81-3)
ISBN 978-1-926855-80-6

1. Olguin, John, 1921-2011.
2. Cabrillo Marine Aquarium—Employees—Biography.
3. Marine organisms—California, Southern.
4. Whale watching industry—California, Southern—History.
5. San Pedro (Los Angeles, Calif—Biography.
I. Brunnick, Barbara J. II. Schaadt, Mike III. Hermosillo, Xavier IV. Title.

QH91.3.O45H37 2011   597.092   C2011-906017-5

Front cover photo: *John Olguin in 1980.* Photo Courtesy John Olguin Private Archive

Printed in the United States of America

We don't own anything.
We are just borrowing it.
Whatever you think is valuable,
whether it is a new car,
a house or jewels.
It's not really yours.
Let's not waste time on anything
that does not help others or is not joyful.

JOHN OLGUIN

Contents

Introduction   9

Acknowledgments   15

Prologue   17

Turning Lemons into Lemonade   27

Adventures of an American Hero   59

San Pedro   81

Father of the Cabrillo Marine Museum   99

The Ringmaster   139

Trailblazer   159

Godfather to a Generation   197

The Community Organizer   235

The Family Man   255

Turning the Tables on Retirement   287

Postscript   303

Authors' Reflections   307

Community Reaction   311

Bibliography and Further Reading   323

Introduction

We have all found ourselves, at some moment in life, looking for a little bit of inspiration around us, something to help us live a better, more positive and more productive life. We look for a person or an idea that can help us deal with the difficulties that challenge us in school, at work, in relationships with others, or in life in general. We feel adrift sometimes, alone in a sea of uncertainty, hoping that things will get better, sooner than later. Then that miracle comes along – not an obvious one, but a miracle nevertheless – that somehow draws us in and has an unforgettable impact on us, despite our doubts or our inability to see that the help we seek in life is right in front of us. It may not look like inspiration or a miracle at first; little gifts of life like this can sometimes look more like warts than treasures, more like dirty rocks than precious gems, until we find that ocean of inspiration that will change our lives forever.

You have no doubt heard or read stories about someone who achieved great success despite being born dirt poor, or born with a physical disability, or who was the product of an abusive father, perhaps someone whose first language was not English, and who never obtained a college degree. Several success stories involve someone with half a dozen or more brothers and sisters, crammed into a two-bedroom house, part of a family that moved around almost every two years because of the dysfunction in the family, and that strained under a father who couldn't hold onto a job. If you were this struggling person and you had to work at a young age to help feed your family, and every time you tried to get a job or make a move that made life more bearable, you were told "NO" over and over again, what would you do?

You're about to meet an extraordinary man: John Olguin (pronounced *Ohl-geen*), who faced every single one of those obstacles, including a heavy lisp, yet he went on to become a war hero, develop a museum/aquarium that is now rated as one of the best in the world, become a mentor to thousands, and much, much more. He never took "No" for an answer; he always found a way to get things done, no matter what the obstacles. And on top of everything else, he was a nice guy who never let his ego get in the way of his mission of personal and professional generosity, humanity, love of people and children, his hometown of San Pedro, California, and his wife and children. This is what drove John to do all the things he did so successfully, overcoming obstacles that would have shattered others. People like John truly only come along once in a lifetime.

Self-made success is not new in America. Bill Gates (Harvard University) started Microsoft in his garage; William Hewlett and David Packard (both Stanford University) started what is now HP, a multinational information technology company, in their garage; and long-time television queen Oprah Winfrey, who was born into poverty in Mississippi, yet secured a full scholarship to Tennessee State University, became the richest African American of the 20th century. Other significant success stories have included the YouTube, Facebook, and Twitter blockbusters, and all of these ventures were either motivated by profit or became huge multi-million and multi-billon dollar giants.

John Olguin was never in it for the money and he didn't get rich for all his hard work. He was a newspaper delivery boy in his early teens, became a beach lifeguard, fell in love

with the ocean, and started sharing his enthusiasm with anyone who would listen. For John, life was not only about his
love of teaching young children that the ocean and its creatures were special and worthy of discovery and well-being, he
also wanted his young followers to pass on that knowledge to
others. He wanted to help young people find careers in the
field of conservation and marine science, but most importantly he wanted to help them find their own passion and total
success in all aspects of their lives. He went beyond the call of
duty and helped his museum volunteers get into prestigious
colleges and universities, and he partnered his students with
world-renowned scientists in hard-to-get-into programs who
respected John's recommendations. Not every Whalewatch
student became a scientist, but hundreds of scientists today
can be traced back to John. Many others became lawyers,
doctors, teachers, artists, entrepreneurs – you name it, John
helped make it happen over his career and his lifetime.

If you didn't have a dream, John would help you create one
and then enable you to achieve it. He was committed to helping his audiences avoid the kind of difficult childhood he had
suffered, and he cultivated and shaped people around him
with his ideas, his values and his passions. He was a face-to-
face, hands-on Pied Piper, with a magic voice that enthralled
all who had the good fortune to be within the sound of it.

If John had texted or Tweeted his invitations to whale
watching, lectures, or other opportunities, it would not have
had the kind of impact he had telling fish stories with his
body, because his body language spoke volumes for kids in
ways that technology cannot.

You had to be in the room with John to absorb his contagious energy and excitement. As John was inviting kids to
get on the Whalewatch boats, or go grunion hunting on the

beach, he didn't have to worry about today's litigious environment, where we're killing off learning opportunities for kids by requiring the signing of legal releases, making Saturday trips complex legal test cases. Simplicity in our society during John's time made his success possible and his dreams were easier to achieve then, as opposed to now. He and his students, as well as their supportive parents, took the risk that learning about nature, human dynamics, and the ocean's inhabitants could develop future leaders, museum and aquarium directors, and entrants into a variety of fields of endeavor.

John became one of the early founders of ecotourism by adding hands-on education to the up-close experience of being with nature's creatures on the Whalewatch trips. He turned curious middle school and high school students into the teachers of the younger schoolchildren who visited the Cabrillo Beach Museum. John trained them so well and got them and their audiences so excited and motivated with his fantastic storytelling that what began as simple trips to watch whales became a dual career as a lifeguard and an untrained, but passionate, sea life museum director.

John Olguin was also one of the original environmentalists, whose love for nature, the beaches he served as a lifeguard, the funky ocean museum he turned into an outright sensation, the wild "jellyfish" dances he performed for kids, his legendary and unforgettable storytelling all created an awareness of the bodies of water surrounding our communities and hugging the coast. The deep, mysterious ocean was now an open book for children to study and enjoy.

And imagine how powerful John's tutoring and mentoring must have been that it inspired a young volunteer-turned-scientist, John Ljubenkov, to honor John Olguin by naming a new species of anemone (a marine animal having a columnar body and one or more circles of tentacles surrounding the mouth) after him. It is called *Edwardsia olguini* and it is one of many examples of John's impact on his students and museum volunteers.

John was an outdoors person on and off duty, through and through, as was his wife, Muriel. You'll see how their bedroom was outdoors - yes, they slept under the stars through most of their 62 years of marriage, 365 days a year, come rain or shine. They stayed physically fit by rowing from San Pedro to Catalina Island through the dangerous 24 miles (one way) of the shipping channel that brings the world's commerce to the ports of Los Angeles and Long Beach, the largest port complex in the U.S. and the third largest in the world.

It's not often that a person from such humble beginnings, with no formal college education, lives a life that has such a significant impact on the dreams of children, business, war, science, and on education at any age, aspiring careers in all fields, and on the early stages of a worldwide movement to learn about the oceans around us and the magnificent creatures that inhabit them and fascinate us.

In addition to the honor of editing this book, I had the pleasure of knowing John since we were both born in San Pedro and I learned of his passion for the ocean as a child. He also impacted my life by motivating my daughter, through her years as a young docent and Sea Ranger, to become an outdoor educator and teach preschoolers to senior citizens about the ocean's creatures, as well as the rest of nature's beauty and its sustainability. My wife works at Cabrillo Marine Aquarium and has coordinated school visits for thousands of children to the aquarium from throughout Southern California, as well as from parts of Arizona and Nevada. I saw the power of John's enthusiasm and persuasion firsthand.

Enjoy meeting John Olguin and getting a glimpse into his magnificent life, then share this amazing story with the important people in your life.

Xavier Hermosillo
Editor

Acknowledgments

Writing a biography about someone whose life spans almost ninety years, and who touched so many lives around the world, would have been impossible without the support and assistance of the many who shared part of his journey. In particular, this book would not have been possible without the day-to-day commitment, passion, dedication, and tenacity of Barbara J. Brunnick, my wife and one of the many thousands of John Olguin-inspired success stories in marine science and other important fields. Our co-author, Mike Schaadt, the current director of the Cabrillo Marine Aquarium, brings to this story more than 22 years of having worked for John, and alongside him, before taking the reins of John's dream at the beach in 2006. This biography of John's life is the result of a wonderful collaboration among us and with our editor, Xavier Hermosillo, whose intimate knowledge of San Pedro and its people proved invaluable. Of course, he knew John, too.

Stefan Harzen

We were most fortunate that John was still around when we began to write this book in 2000. He agreed to spend countless hours conducting interviews and going over materials contained in his personal archive. Likewise, we had the privilege of spending many hours with his wife of 62 years, Muriel, and their three children, Monica, Viola and John Cabrillo. John's brother Leonard also shared his invaluable accounts, insights and recollections, which greatly added to the fabric of John's life story.

Many others contributed to this book. An attempt to list

all those who contributed is quite impossible. Nevertheless, we list here those who come to mind as having contributed something special to this project. To those we have left out, we apologize most profusely.

We wish to thank Sarah Callender for researching John's Army records, and Ed Mastro for gathering and preparing many of the photographs. We are deeply indebted to the late Bill Oleson and Bill Samaras, for illuminating the private side of John's life and for sharing their intimate knowledge of the history of both San Pedro and the Cabrillo Marine Aquarium. And for sharing memories and personal stories, we are grateful to: Dana Nolan, Susanne Lawrenz-Miller, Larry Fukuhara, Helen Anderson, Bud Williams, Hatsuye Endo Ogawa, Marion P. Morgan, David A. Bond, Hubert Bernatz, Billy Schmidt, Bob Evans, Betsy Barnhart, Bernice Fish-Jessop, Judy and Glenn Scoble, Tom Porterhouse, Patricia S. Johnston, Bill O'Sullivan, Pete Lee, Claude Morris, and Geoff Agisim.

In addition, Robin Makowski, Ted Cranford, Alisa Schulman-Janiger, Bob Talbot, Joe and Martha McKinzie, Monica Olguin, Russ Buchan and Kristen Heather also helped with the manuscript. We are especially grateful to Shauna Rusnak for her guidance and support in editing and improving the manuscript and bringing it across the finish line, and Don Gorman of Rocky Mountain Books who embraced this story and sounded like John when he encouraged us to write it.

Finally, the three of us wish to thank our spouses, families and friends for their patience as we spent time researching and writing this book. Their support of our endeavors remains a constant in our lives and we are forever grateful to all of them.

PROLOGUE

*A*pril 4, 1987, was a pleasant spring day and for most people in San Pedro, California, it was a Saturday like any other. But for one citizen, and a famous one at that, it would officially mark the end of a fifty year career that shaped, and was shaped by, the community of San Pedro. It was expected by many to be "Retirement Day" for this lucky man, but it would turn out to be more of a "Transition Day" into a new life that would seemingly go on forever, touch the lives of tens of thousands, and make history.

Born into a poor Mexican family, this man became a lifeguard, who saw his duties as not only on, but also off the beach; he dedicated his life to helping others and making his community a better place. He was a man of great resilience and perseverance, who turned a small seashell collection on Cabrillo Beach into the world-renowned Cabrillo Marine Museum. A uniquely gifted educator, he created the now-famous grunion- and whale-watching programs. He was a mentor and godfather to a million careers, including some world-renowned marine scientists, photographers, writers and artists. A naturalist and explorer, this man was driven by a never-ending desire to learn more about the world; his rowing adventures with his wife, Muriel, and their three children are the stuff of legends. As a storyteller, he could capture any audience and make everyone feel as if they had been there with him. He was a man who, as you shall see, changed the world and who continues to be an inspiration to all those who ever had the good fortune to meet him. This man was John Olguin.

In the early evening of that Saturday in 1987, a dark limousine drove into the San Pedro hills and pulled up in front of a modest home with a small garage stuffed with too many things to park a car and a front door rarely used. Most friends and family entered through a sliding-glass door that led into a close space with a desk, which was adjacent to an equally small kitchen. Walking through the kitchen, you would see that the living and family rooms had walls covered with artwork, photographs and mementos. Next to the large dining table, a piano sat near a set of glass doors that revealed a sizable deck with a spectacular view of the Pacific Ocean and the Port of Los Angeles. On a clear day, the view afforded glimpses of whales passing by, and there was no better place to gaze at the stars on still nights under the Southern California sky. This atypical yet beautiful place was the home of John and his wife, Muriel.

The most unusual feature of this home, designed and built in 1952 by the Olguins, was undoubtedly the large bed on the porch that rested under a canopy to provide some protection from the elements. Since returning from a camping trip in 1965, John and Muriel slept in this beautiful bedroom every night; it was an ideal choice for two people who had always loved the outdoors more than anything. Senses would awaken with the smell of plants and flowers, the breeze rising up from the ocean, and the sounds of their famous peacock chiming in with the chatter of birds and the barks of sea lions below. The frequent throbbing of ships going past was often met by the soft glow of the sun as it set over the horizon, seemingly sinking into the ocean. Nothing could be more soothing and rejuvenating. John and Muriel slept under the stars, rain or shine, all of their lives.

The United States Air Force Color Guard accompanied John and Muriel on the five-minute limousine drive from their home to Fort MacArthur, home to the U.S. Air Force since 1982. Situated on Pacific Avenue overlooking the ocean, the fort appropriately stands right above the Cabrillo Marine Museum. After a brief welcome by the commanding officer of Fort MacArthur, the distinguished group made their way to the Officers' Club where about three hundred people, including the Olguins' children, Viola, Monica and John, were waiting. Family, friends, co-workers, collaborators and dignitaries had all gathered to honor and pay tribute to a man whose life was intrinsically intertwined with, and influenced by, his hometown of San Pedro, as much as he influenced the town's own history.

After fifty years of working for the City of Los Angeles, beginning as a lifeguard in 1937 and later serving as a director for nearly forty years at the Cabrillo Marine Museum – renamed the Cabrillo Marine Aquarium in 1993 – John was retiring. It was indeed an occasion to celebrate and reminisce. Individuals shared memorable moments of this remarkable man who, throughout his entire life, had earned great respect and recognition.

As far back as Grade 10, John received the American Legion Award for Leadership. During World War II, he was awarded a Silver Star medal, the third highest military decoration that honors valor in the face of the enemy. A 1974 Career Service Award of the City of Los Angeles was followed by his election as San Pedro's Citizen of the Year in 1978. In 1986, John was the recipient of the KNBC TV Spirit

Award of Southern California, which was quickly followed by the status of Honorary Mayor of San Pedro in 1987.

John's long list of distinctions truly goes on and on. In 1999, the *Los Angeles Times* named him the Citizen of the Century. Then in 2000, he represented San Pedro in the L.A. Visitors and Convention Bureau ad campaign, with his portrait displayed all over the Greater Los Angeles area. While most would think the combination of those two distinctions would be as grand as it gets, John's unmatched commitment to the community was met with the legacy of being named the Citizen of the Millennium by the Rotary Club of San Pedro in 2009. The title of Citizen of the Millennium was bestowed in recognition of John's lasting contributions to preserving the natural resources of San Pedro for future generations, and his role in establishing the Cabrillo Marine Museum, the Los Angeles Maritime Museum, the Point Fermin Marine Life Refuge and the Cabrillo Whalewatch Program.

John had a rare gift: an uncanny ability to communicate well with all people, regardless of age, race or creed. No matter who or what they were, everyone was attracted to his boundless enthusiasm. Whether by a story about his own rowing adventures, or about the wonders of the world, he captivated friends and strangers alike. John worked with anyone and, more importantly, he treated everyone with the same openness and honesty, no matter what their standing. He worked just as successfully with Los Angeles Mayor Tom Bradley on the future of the harbor area and world-renowned architect Frank Gehry on the new building for the museum that opened in 1981, as he did with boat builder Bill Oleson on the restoration of the Point Fermin Lighthouse and the return of its famous antique lens. He afforded the same attention to those who wanted to help him as to those who sought out his help.

John was a master of person-to-person networking. His network included thousands of San Pedro citizens who worked with him, benefited from his endeavors and came to his rescue when he needed help. He could seek out anyone's strengths and put them to good use, at just the right task. With his gentle power of persuasion and an absence of negative ways, John was widely known as an honest, trusting, inquisitive and accepting person. A charismatic man with boundless energy, he was generous to a fault with his time. Always very demanding, he was equally supportive in every way. If things did not turn out well, John learned from the experience without becoming a skeptic or cynic.

Many of John's admirable characteristics were nurtured by his relatively challenging youth. Growing up during the Depression, John experienced the difficulties of being poor and going to sleep hungry firsthand. As one of nine children, he had to work as a young boy to help support his family. However, unlike most children, he was innately resourceful from a very young age. Whatever he did, he applied himself completely. Whether as a shoeshine boy, delivering milk and newspapers, being a lifeguard, or serving in the military, John always tried to be the best he could be and, in most cases, he succeeded at being extraordinary.

Another facet of John's youth that shaped his life was his role as one of the original beach boys who hung out at Cabrillo Beach and other hot spots around the Palos Verdes Peninsula. Becoming a lifeguard in 1937, at age sixteen, he worked his way up to the rank of captain by 1948. He served as the head of the lifeguards on Cabrillo Beach until his retirement in 1963, when he assumed the full-time and paid position of director of the Cabrillo Marine Museum. In his heart and the way he lived, John remained a lifeguard all his life; if he was not looking out over the water, his eyes were scanning across the community of San Pedro. With an exceptional level of awareness, John always seemed to notice when people were struggling and, as reliably as when he was on the beach, John would rush to lend a helping hand.

Building on the work of his predecessor, Dr. William Lloyd, the first director of the Cabrillo Marine Museum, it was John's vision, exuberance and perseverance – combined with ingenuity and a little horse-trading – that turned what was mainly a seashell collection and exhibit into an interactive museum and education facility. For decades, volunteer speaking engagements filled John's calendar, slowly producing a projector here and a microscope there. Shrewd trades of duplicate collector's items, and many "loans" that were never recalled by their donors, all helped to assemble the museum's collection.

John did not take no for an answer and, if necessary, he would circumvent and bend the rules right up to the breaking point to accomplish his objectives. He was, after all, in his hometown of San Pedro, and that gave him a lot of room and opportunity to wheel and deal for the good of the museum. He knew everyone and everyone knew him. Hardly anyone, including his supervisors and the city management, was as well connected as John. In the early days, when the City of Los Angeles did not provide a lot of support, the people of his hometown did. They believed in John's vision and understood its importance. They were committed to helping John get things done. Together they would say, "If it's good for the museum, let's do it. If it's good for the children, let's do it." In fact, John Olguin's rallying cry, which is now firmly embedded in the annals of local history, stems from those days and sentiments: "Do it! Do it!"

And so they did. With community investment over the years, the Cabrillo Marine Museum became an important institution in San Pedro and in the City of Los Angeles. It also became a major facet of the city's Department of Recreation and Parks. In the early 1950s, John and the museum gained world fame when he turned the natural phenomenon of the grunion run into an educational and community event that brought hundreds, and often thousands, of people to Cabrillo Beach at night.

John diversified the programming further in 1971 when he created the world's first whale watching program with the particular aim of having youth get a closer look at gray whales. By the mid-1980s, more than a million children and adults had participated in the Cabrillo Whalewatch program. John had unwittingly revolutionized how people would interact with sea life for decades to come. Beyond acting as a springboard for many careers in the sciences and arts for his excited young whale watching fans, the trips also proved that watching whales was more profitable than whaling, which viewed the beautiful ocean giants as mere sources of meat and other by-products that could be sold. This transition suggested that ecotourism, an unknown term back then, could possibly save species and subsequently entire ecosystems from destruction. Watching whales changed the way that people thought about the ocean and the world around them, and established John Olguin as one of the greatest environmentalists of our time.

Over the years, more than two million people participated in the grunion run and Cabrillo Whalewatch alone. These and other programs that John developed with the help of volunteers in the 1960s and 1970s are of monumental scale now, bringing more than three hundred thousand visitors to the museum every year.

Beyond these programs, John was involved in many other causes: he was one of the founders of the Los Angeles Maritime Museum and was instrumental in restoring the Point Fermin Lighthouse and securing its place on the National Register of Historic Places. For decades, John dedicated his time and energy to a great variety of social initiatives that benefited people both at home and worldwide. From providing food baskets to the poor on Thanksgiving and helping to create a care center for San Pedro senior citizens, to participating in the Hunger Walk/Run with proceeds benefiting the hungry all over the world, John Olguin seemed to "Do It" all.

With his humble and caring ways, and totally without guile, John had a major influence on a great number of people's professional and personal lives. Not that John did not love publicity or attention, but he always channeled it toward things that benefited the museum or the entire San Pedro community. Without him, some people would have lost their businesses, some would not have met their future spouses, and many would have just not done as well in life overall. Like the ocean, John touched the lives of countless people, his influence felt around the globe as he moved in and out of people's lives.

After several years of rumors, it was now official: John was retiring. Yet, everybody knew that even retirement could not make John change his ways. He certainly would not be going anywhere far. Occasionally John would say that he was moving on, but he did so with a twinkle in his eye. "My next move is to Green Hills," he would say, referring to the large local cemetery in San Pedro on Western Avenue. "Beautiful view lots. I'll be able to see the whales migrate until eternity," he would add. After moving on to his so-called retirement, John continued to organize Whalewatch trips and other fundraisers to support the Cabrillo Marine Aquarium and many social causes in San Pedro. Always eager to learn new things and share the stories with anyone who would listen, his determination to explore new frontiers never faded. Quite to the contrary, in retirement his determination found new life.

John's life is a great love story. He always did what he loved to do and learned to love the things he had to do. He genuinely loved people, especially children, and had a special gift for communicating with them. He was capable of easily captivating their young minds and making them believe that only they possessed the means to unlock the secrets of life. And, of course, he had a boundless love for the ocean that he conveyed as one of those precious secrets.

All that said, John found the eternal love of his life in Muriel: an artist, teacher and philanthropist in her own right. Together, they not only helped shape the incredible community of San Pedro, but they also found time to explore the world. Their preferred mode of transportation, whenever possible, was a rowboat. The couple lived their lives in the same manner that they ventured out to sea: pulling the oars – not hard, just steady – and leaning back to use their own weight to draw through the water. That's what got them the mileage. As John used to say, "five miles to a peanut butter sandwich!"

By his final decade, John looked like a perfect fit for the part in Hemingway's *The Old Man and the Sea* and he continued to inspire many with his remarkable life. Perhaps the greatest irony of his life is that it began with John as a poor Mexican kid who, for years, could not speak English without a lisp. Yet John grew out of his speech impediment and went on to become one of the greatest and most talented storytellers to captivate an audience, whether in Japanese, Tagalog,

Fijian or even some Greek. As he moved through his life –
growing into his roles as a man, father, grandfather, museum
director, educator, a sort of patron saint of sea life, and a tireless community leader – he never ceased to commit himself
to learning more and helping others. Through his determination and generosity, John Olguin had a far greater influence on marine science, education and the community of San
Pedro than anyone could have ever imagined possible.

TURNING LEMONS INTO LEMONADE

*A*merica has always prided itself on providing unparalleled opportunities of vertical mobility. No matter what the circumstances at birth, American children are taught from a very early age that they are the masters of their own fate; they can become anything they want to be. That is the essence of the American Dream and there are only two things required: an unwavering belief in oneself and an entrepreneurial spirit that seeks to lead rather than follow. John Olguin had plenty of both.

John was born on February 18, 1921, in San Pedro, California, into the family of Roy and Josephine Olguin. The Olguin family already had two sons, Roy Jr. and Gus, and lived at 745 24th Street, between Gaffey Street and Cabrillo Avenue. That year, February 18 was a rainy day and the doctor had trouble getting up the rutted and muddy street to get to Josephine. However, he did make it on time and John came into this world without notable problems. With two boys already in the family, Josephine had hoped that her wish for a daughter would finally be granted. And so, John's birth was a bit of a disappointment, although that disappointment was short-lived.

John was born into a family that was deeply rooted in the Mexican culture, as his father in particular was not prepared to adopt the American way of life. At home, Spanish was the only language allowed, and John's father was determined to instill order and discipline in his children. For instance, no one could eat until he was ready. Everyone had to sit around the table, hands clasped, and wait for him to sit down. Only once he had picked up a glass of water, taken a sip and put it back down, could his family begin to eat. He was very strict with the older children, who would later remember him as a disciplinarian and old patriarch. For the younger ones, he would be mostly absent.

Over the years, Roy and Josephine frequently moved from one rental place to another. In 1922, they moved from 24th Street to the corner of Second and Beacon streets. Within a year, they moved again to a sandy-street section below Harbor Boulevard. It was a district called Mexican Hollywood, whose habitants were equally as poor as they had great hopes and maybe expectations. They had lived there for only three months when Juanita, John's maternal grandmother, who lived in neighboring Wilmington at the time, suffered a stroke. In order to take care of her, the family picked up their lives again and moved to a small house near Colon Street, right across the tracks from their grandmother. It was there in 1923, that a Pacific Electric streetcar killed John's two-year-old sister, Lucille.

After John's grandmother died in 1925, Josephine and Roy decided to move to Seaside Avenue on Terminal Island, part of what was then called East San Pedro. It was an area in transition whose residents, mostly well-to-do people, were leaving. They had built their homes on a sand pit across the street from Brighton Beach, a beautiful location that rivaled Coronado Island in San Diego. But then the local authorities dredged the harbor again and deposited the sand in front of all of the beautiful homes, whose residents now had to walk a quarter- or a half-mile to get to the water. Many homeowners did not like the walk and ended up selling their houses, with a lot of the new owners turning them into rental properties.

The rent was very cheap because the only way to get onto the island was via the Henry Ford Bridge or by ferry. All of a sudden, these houses became available to poor people and John and his family found themselves in a two-story home on Seaside Avenue, with a fireplace and half a dozen bedrooms. The house was surrounded by a fence and had a garden. There was, however, only one paved street in the neighborhood, all of the other roads were sand. At the end of the street was Seaside Elementary School, John's grammar school. When the morning bell rang, John would go right out the back gate, through a hole in the fence and straight into the school. The school's principal, Ms. Mar, was the first schoolteacher John ever had. She would later also teach John's children.

As John's father was often unable to make enough money to support his family, the responsibility to make ends meet fell on the shoulders of his wife. Josephine was working the early-morning shift, from 5 a.m. to 2 p.m., at the French Sardine Company so she could be home when the children returned from school at 3 p.m. It was always Josephine, a very supportive and loving woman, who held the family together. Like in most other families, the older boys – Roy, Gus and John – had to work to support the family. It soon became clear that John, even at a very young age, had some unusual gifts: a great way with people, an entrepreneurial spirit and an unyielding power of persuasion.

Around the same time, Pacific Electric settled on the deadly accident of John's sister, Lucille, and his father decided to move the entire family again. This time they would move to

San Francisco to start life over. John was 5 years old and, for the first time, he would leave San Pedro. His father had gone ahead and found a rental house at 1314½ Jessie Street in San Francisco, so it was time for the rest of the family to follow. Josephine, with the five kids in tow, took the *SS Yale* on an overnight trip that left San Pedro at 6 p.m. and arrived in San Francisco the next morning. One can imagine the excitement with which they arrived in the big city, with everyone looking forward to a better, more stable life. For a while, they lived on Jessie Street, where Albert, the youngest of the six brothers, was born. Unfortunately, the stable life was not to be. Roy Sr. continued to have the same difficulties holding onto a job and soon the Olguin family, on the verge of being destitute, was forced to move again.

While living in San Francisco, John attended Marshall Elementary School for about a year and a half. Later, he remembered the stark differences between Seaside and Marshall elementary schools. In San Pedro, the playground and the entire grounds were sandy, but in San Francisco, it was all asphalt. John had never played on asphalt and he missed the sand and the beach. Seaside had a wooden fence but at Marshall the fence was made of iron and made him feel as if he was in prison.

Unfortunately, the situation at home was not much better. It was late November and John had been playing with some neighbor kids in the backyard. When he went back inside, he found his mother sitting at the kitchen table crying. He was soon to learn that there was no food in the house for Thanksgiving Day, not even the usual rice and beans that they ate every day. John tried to comfort his mother by telling her that he would find some food.

There he was, an ambitious six-year-old child who wanted

to help his mother, yet not knowing where to turn nor what to do to find food as he walked down the street. Good fortune does seem to come to those who dare to dream. Soon, John found himself at a church. When he walked through its big doors, it was crowded with people sitting in the pews. At the front, he saw rows of food baskets filled with turkey, stuffing, sweet potatoes, pumpkin pie and other delicacies.

John sat down and listened. Whenever a name was called, someone would get up, walk to the front, receive a basket and walk out of the church. Sometimes there would be a smile, but mostly just expressions of relief; there would be food on the table for Thanksgiving dinner. They kept calling out names until the room was almost empty and then John heard the words, "That's it." John's name was not on the list. Of course, nobody had known that little Johnny would be there, so his name could not have been called.

John was not about to go home empty-handed. He walked up to the man who had been calling out names for hours and told him that he needed food for his family of ten. The church people tried to send John on his way, but he kept pleading his case. Eventually, they took a couple of baskets and drove John home to see whether or not he was telling the truth. When they arrived, John took the strangers to his mother and said with his strong lisp, "Here is where I live and there is nothing to eat in this house." John opened all of the cupboards and they were all empty. He then took the strangers to his backyard where his siblings were playing with some of the neighbor's kids and, bending the truth just a little bit, he said, "And these are all my brothers and sisters." Nothing else needed to be said. The church people went back to the car and brought in the baskets.

His mother cooked the turkey and a complete Thanksgiving

dinner. Once the family was seated, she cut off one of the turkey's legs, a whole leg, and put it on John's plate. Every year after that, John always got a leg of the turkey. Even after he was married, his mother would call him up and tell him to come over and get his turkey leg: "I am saving it for you." The tradition continued until Josephine's death in 1976.

In 1928, after two years of barely surviving in San Francisco and Josephine being homesick, Roy Sr. relocated the family back to San Pedro. They moved into a house at 455 – 8th Street. John was happy to be back in his hometown and continuing Grade 2 at Cabrillo Elementary School. By then, the Port of Los Angeles had become the largest man-made harbor on the West Coast. It had surpassed San Francisco as the busiest seaport and ranked second in the entire country in foreign-export tonnage. At its peak in 1928, a total of 26.5 million tons of cargo went through the Port, a record that would last for almost forty years. No one could have anticipated that, within two years, this era would come to an abrupt end as the world slid into the devastating Great Depression.

Those were difficult times and life was tough for almost everyone. John and his family were no exception. School for the Olguin kids started at 8 a.m., but they rose at 6:30 a.m. in order to make their beds, mop the room, make their own breakfast and clean the kitchen before they left for school. Like many children in those days, John and his brothers had to work in the afternoons to help support their family. But unlike most, John was innately resourceful from a very young age and always had a positive outlook. He would try to be the best he could be and, in most cases, he succeeded in being extraordinary.

Starting kindergarten at 5 years old had brought with it a major challenge for John: speaking English. Around his father, Spanish was the only language allowed, so John had very little knowledge of the English language and had to start from scratch. He remembered it feeling as though he had landed in a foreign country. Learning the new language was even more difficult for John due to his lisp. After taking so much of other kids laughing at him, an intimidated John decided that he would not speak again. He kept his commitment so well that his teachers actually began to think that he had a learning disability.

It was not until John was in Grade 4, at 8 years old, that he really began to speak again, and he credited his teacher, Mrs. Gustavson, with helping him to overcome his speech impediment. In a strange way, John was also helped to speak by his love for the ocean. Having spent so many days in the water, he was nicknamed "the human fish." When John won a swim meet at a local pool, he was featured in the newspaper and Mrs. Gustavson asked him to get up in front of the class and talk about it. John started talking quietly, then all of the sudden his enthusiasm overwhelmed his embarrassment and he began to speak freely. Mrs. Gustavson immediately made sure John went to speech school twice a week. He always remembered practicing "sixty-one, sixty-two, sixty-three," while sticking his tongue out at three but keeping it behind his teeth on the 'sixty.' Eventually, John overcame the lisp and, as his friends often joke, he did not stop talking ever since.

John would come home from school in the mid-afternoon each day and pick up his shoeshine box before he went to visit his customers. He had a regular route, visiting different people on different days. For instance, every Saturday John shined shoes for Mr. Bauer who owned the Bauer and Button Radio Store between 8th and 7th streets on Pacific Avenue. He also shined shoes on Wednesdays at five o'clock for Mr. Rugiford, who was the owner of the Seaboard Motors car dealership on the corner of 4th and Pacific. In addition to his regular customers, John also worked in a barbershop sweeping up hair, so they would let him shine the shoes of the customers that were getting a haircut.

John looked for any opportunity to shine shoes, so when five hundred police officers were sent to support the San Pedro Police Department with the longshoremen's strike, John went to talk to the chief of police. Not a bit afraid, this Tom Thumb stood in front of the chief, who did not want to have any shoeshine boys at the station. John resisted all attempts by the chief to get rid of him and said, "Wait, my father is not working, I have five brothers. What I make buys our food. If I cannot shine shoes, we don't eat!"

The chief relented, called the lieutenant over and said, "I don't want anyone here to shine shoes except Johnny here. Only him, nobody else."

John thanked him and ran out to buy a bottle of shining cream to shine badges, buttons, gun holsters, belts, shoes, and anything else that would generate some money. By the time he was done, John had made $5, which was a lot of money back then. It was more than his father made and was enough to provide food for his family for the better part of a week.

While attending grammar school, John may have stood out by saying very little if anything, but his years at Dana Junior High School in San Pedro were different. No longer afraid to speak, John transformed himself into a leader with undeniably superior communication skills. Dana Junior High School ("Dana") opened on May 4, 1928, named after author Richard Henry Dana, whose book *Two Years Before the Mast* told the story of a common sailor's journey from Boston to San Pedro in 1834. The school was on Cabrillo Avenue, between 14th and 17th streets, and accommodated the junior high school grades that had previously been housed in San Pedro High School. Dana started out with an enrollment of 625, but reached 1,500 as early as 1930.

It was 1934 and John was 13 years old. His father was still living with the family, but he continued to move from one job to the next. One day he would sell fruit, the next work at the cannery, and then he started to work in the wholesale meat business. The Depression had made everything worse. Yet, while many experienced it as a time of suffering and hardship, John was able to draw on some innate joy and turn the struggle into something positive. He was doing his part to support his family, which felt good. When John landed a job in the cafeteria at Dana, lunch suddenly became the best meal of the day. The work was not too hard, so it left him plenty of energy for his first business endeavor.

One of his teachers had a new car and she would give him five cents every time he wiped off the windshield at lunchtime. John cleaned it every day, making twenty-five cents per week. Then, he convinced another teacher and another, until soon he was wiping off most of the cars between his time working in the cafeteria and going to school. Eventually, John had enough work that he hired one of his friends to help him, paying him a share of the monies he took in. In the end, his friend did most of the work while John continued to work in the cafeteria and manage everything else.

The same year, John began to deliver the local paper, the *San Pedro News-Pilot.* John had wanted to be a paperboy for a long time because it provided a steady income and a chance to see more of the world. Back then, anyone bringing in two new subscriptions to the *News-Pilot* would get a free trip to an amusement park in Santa Monica or to the mountains to see the snow. John had never seen snow. He could see the mountains from San Pedro, but he had never been near them and he really wanted to go. Financially supporting his family as best he could was important to John, but he really wanted to get out of town and see more of the world. He recognized that to accomplish his dream, he had to get people to subscribe to the newspaper so he could go on one of those trips.

John began to deliver his papers and, to the great delight of his supervisor Mr. Manard, he quickly developed a deliberate strategy. Like all paperboys, he would get extra newspapers and give them to people. He would leave the paper on people's doorsteps a few times, then go back and ask them to subscribe for at least thirty days. Some agreed, some did not, but John quickly became the No. 1 carrier. Within his first two years, John achieved his goals and went on trips to Catalina Island, to the mountains to see the snow, and to San Diego, Santa Monica, Los Angeles and Hollywood. Not bad for a 13-year-old kid.

One of the recipients of John's unsolicited newspapers was a man who lived along John's route and had a reputation for being unfriendly and difficult. John had left a few newspapers on his doorstep, hoping he might become interested in subscribing. The next time he was about to leave a paper at his door, the man came running out, took the newspaper from John's hand, slapped him with it and accused John of trying to trick him into having to pay for the paper at the end of the month. John explained that he was trying to get him to subscribe so that he could go on a few more trips. The man looked at John and, without another word, slammed the door.

For most 13-year-old kids, that would have been enough to stay away from the place for good. Not so for John; he took it as a challenge. John went to the man's landlady and found out that the potential client's name was Chauncy Roland and that he was in the Navy. When John saw him several days later, about a block away from where he lived, John said, "Hi, Mr. Roland." Mr. Roland stopped, puzzled as to why this kid, whom he had given a hard time, would recognize him and know his name. John kept it up and every time he saw the gentleman, he would shout, "Hi, Mr. Roland. How are you?" Mr. Roland would just nod his head and keep moving.

It was getting close to Christmas and John was on his usual paper route. He was just passing in front of Mr. Roland's place when the door opened and Mr. Roland stepped outside. He told John to come back once he had finished delivering papers for the day, "'I have a Christmas present for you," he said before disappearing from sight. John was excited, so he rushed back to Mr. Roland's house once he had completed his deliveries. Mr. Roland invited John inside and presented him with two new outfits, including shoes and socks. That alone was a truly wonderful gift, but in addition to the new clothes, there was also a brand new bike with balloon tires!

John had never owned a bike, because his family could not afford one. For a moment, John was speechless, but he knew that he could not accept the wonderful gifts. His father would never allow it. He reluctantly told Mr. Roland that his father would simply not believe that he had been given all these things, but Mr. Roland insisted and told John that if he had any trouble to come back and he would talk with John's father. So, John went home, excited and afraid at the same time, and showed everything to his mother and then to his father who, as predicted, sent John back to return everything.

A short time later, there was a knock on the door. When John's father opened it, he looked into the face of Mr. Roland. They went inside and, over a cup of coffee, Mr. Roland explained to Roy Sr. that he had bought the bicycle because John reminded him of his own son whom he had left back on the East Coast. While the two men talked, Mr. Roland realized that there were ten people living in the two-bedroom home, with two or three people to each bed. A few weeks later, he brought the Olguin family a gas stove and then helped them find a three-bedroom house on Palos Verdes Street. And, yes, he finally did subscribe to the newspaper.

Eventually, in 1936, Mr. Roland left the Navy and moved to Illinois where he became a prison guard. Each year, for a few years thereafter, he would send a package for Christmas filled with gifts for everyone at John's house. The Olguins would respond by posting back thank-you notes. Then suddenly, from one year to the next, it was over. No more messages, no more packages.

John treasured his bicycle and used it to deliver his papers more efficiently. Then one day a car ran him over and John was badly hurt. His bicycle was almost completely destroyed. Somehow, John managed to get home and, because he was so afraid his father would find out and forbid him to continue delivering newspapers, he hid his bloody clothes under the house. John waited for several days and then took his bicycle to a repair shop. It took all of John's perseverance and persuasive powers to convince the man to fix it as best he could. John hid his injuries and pain so well that his mother only found out about the accident when one of the neighbors inquired about John's condition. His mother was a supportive and intuitive woman, so she never told John's father. She knew that her husband would have had no sympathy for John, only physical punishment.

Delivering the newspaper at that time also meant collecting the subscription money from the customers and passing it on to the newspaper, minus the payment for the delivery of course. Like all other paperboys, John had to collect from everyone himself. If a customer did not pay, it came out of his profit. At the time, John had about one hundred customers and most of them were honest people. Occasionally someone would move out and leave him hanging, but that was all part of the game.

It was all worth it to John. So much so that he didn't only work his own route, but he also took on those of other paperboys. He wanted it more than anyone else did, because he wanted to win more trips and see the world. Being No. 1 also had its benefits, such as the perk of a "gold pass" that gave him unfettered access to the five theatres in town: the Cabrillo, the Fox Strand, the Globe, the Barton Hill and the Warner Grand. John would go and watch the shows, even if it was just for ten minutes. He could walk out no matter how good the show was, because he could go to any show, anytime.

John could not have been happier. He loved what he was doing and enjoyed being recognized for his hard work. But these accomplishments quickly became an old hat for John. He loved to challenge himself and had already set his sights on a new prize: student-body president. Like many schools in those days, Dana had an honor society called "Commodores," providing campus leaders with different responsibilities. In addition, the school held elections in which every student got a vote to elect two officers: student-body president and vice-president.

One of John's friends, Bob del Rio, who would later join John as a lifeguard, lived across the alley. The two boys were the same age and walked to school together every day. When they walked up the steep hill from Palos Verdes Street to Dana Junior High School, Bob would put his hand on John's shoulder to make it a bit easier for himself. John remembers always asking Bob to take his hand off his shoulder. Bob would always agree, but his hand would be back on John's shoulder again in no time. John felt as if he was carrying Bob up the hill.

One day, in 1937, John asked Bob if he would like to run for student office. He explained that he had a plan that would make him president and Bob the vice-president. Bob liked the idea, but thought the roles may as well be reversed. It took a few games of coin toss and a bit of persuasion before Bob eventually agreed to John's plan. The plan was based on John's understanding that when students voted for student-body officers, they usually voted for people they knew. The two boys agreed to stand in the center of the school grounds for half an hour before school started each morning, greeting every student that passed by and asking their names. John felt confident that by the end of the semester, he would know everybody in the student body by their first name. If he did not, then surely Bob would.

While there was a sense of professional campaigning surrounding Bob and John, they retained a good portion of juvenile mischief throughout, promising to shave each other's heads should they indeed win. On Election Day, they were both elected! By then, John had met a beautiful young girl and he was afraid that she would not talk to him anymore if he lost all of his hair, so he tried to back out of shaving his head. Bob's head was already shaved, so he was not keen on allowing John to get out of their deal. John's friends jumped him and shaved his head after school. When they returned to school the next day, their principal was anything but happy. John, in his charismatic and charming way, turned it all into a big laugh when he declared during the installation ceremony, "I promised that

if I got elected, I would make a clean shave of the whole thing!"
Needless to say, the young lady kept talking to John.

With the end of John's junior high school years approaching, he had already accomplished so much. Beyond being the best paperboy in town, he had also successfully run for elected office, and was now delivering milk with his older brother Gus who, although still in high school, was one of the milk-truck drivers. John always managed to be more successful than anyone else, quite astonishing for a kid who, just a few years earlier had remained largely silent and was thought to have a learning disability. Despite his heavy schedule, John woke up at 4 a.m. and rarely slept more than six hours. He knew how to pace himself and set priorities.

When John needed something for himself, such as new clothes to wear to his junior high school graduation, he would work even harder. On one such occasion, John needed fifteen dollars and asked his boss at the milk delivery company how much he would be paid if he solicited new customers. The boss promised John five dollars for every customer who would take milk for at least thirty days. With his experience in the newspaper business, John felt confident he could find at least three new customers. He went out and, to everybody's astonishment but his own, he returned with a list of eight new customers.

His boss was so impressed that he asked John to work eight-hour shifts. John's answer was that he did not need more money at the time. He had earned enough for his shoes, a pair of pants and some other items. That's all he wanted. But John would return whenever he needed some more money for himself, make another seventy or eighty dollars on new customer orders, and leave it at that. It drove his boss crazy, but John never worked the eight-hour shifts.

For John the daily grind continued to be difficult: waking up early, doing housework, going to school, working all afternoon, doing homework after dinner and finally going to bed. Almost every day was the same schedule, as everyone had to work to help the family survive. John's father, Roy, was around less and less, and he would eventually leave the family for good in 1937.

Like his older brothers, John juggled several jobs at a time. For a while, he would help to finance his and his family's needs with abalone, especially white abalone. Abalone are edible sea snails whose flesh can be consumed raw or cooked. The inner layer of their shells is composed of highly iridescent mother-of-pearl, whose changeable colors made the shells very desirable to collectors. When John needed a pair of shoes or clothes, he would often paddle out to a reef off Point Fermin Lighthouse, put on his Japanese goggles, dive down and get a few white abalones. John would give the meat to his mother, who turned it into delicious dinners, and he would sell the shells to collectors at the Pacific Shell Club and the Malacological Society for ten cents apiece. It was like a bank. When he needed more money, he would get more shells. He did this for a couple of years before one day he found the bank empty, robbed bare: the abalones were gone. The natural resource that had sustained him had collapsed. Sixty-four years later, the white abalone became the first marine invertebrate to receive full federal protection under the Endangered Species Act.

Fifteen was to become a milestone age in John's life for yet another reason beyond entering high school. From his earliest childhood, John had always loved the beach and the ocean. His father would not let the kids go to the beach, because he wanted them to clean the yard, or work and earn money to support the family. But when it was hot in the summer, John and his brothers would sneak away anytime they could, and go to the beach anyway. When they returned home, their father would touch their heads and, if their hair was still wet, he knew that they had been swimming and were lying about what they had been doing. To avoid their father's discipline, they would sometimes go down to the docks by the E.K. Wood Lumber Company, climb down the ladder until only their heads stuck out, so their hair would remain dry. It felt wonderful and they hung onto the ladder until they got so cold they had to get out. Then, they would crawl back up, dry themselves off and go home.

John had known the lifeguards at Cabrillo Beach since he was 5 years old. They were his heroes: huge, strong men who spent all day surrounded by sand, sea and sun. John was particularly impressed by a Filipino lifeguard named Carlos. He went to see Carlos as often as he could and kept insisting that he was going to be a lifeguard too. Carlos told John that he could not be a lifeguard because he wore glasses. As time proved, his glasses did not stop John from becoming a lifeguard, but they did end up preventing him from joining the Air Force, the Navy and the Marines during World War II.

San Pedro had a swimming pool at the time, known as the Plunge. John and his brothers would go there as often as they could and eventually John attracted the attention of its director, Jack Chaney, who took a liking to John and made him his maintenance man. John would clean and scrub the pool and do anything that Jack asked of him. In return, John could swim for free. Jack loved burritos, so John would often bring food to him at the Plunge. Sometimes Jack would even come to the house to get some fresh, hot burritos prepared by John's mother. John and Jack established a lasting friendship that ended prematurely when Jack died on December 23, 1959, at the age of 51.

For all the years they knew each other, Jack had a profound and lasting impact on John's life. Jack tutored John in his first aid and lifesaving classes, and taught him everything he needed to know to become a lifeguard. Unfortunately, Jack could do nothing about John's poor vision. John was so determined to become a lifeguard that it did not bother him to indulge in a little bit of cheating, or circumventing the system, to succeed. In fact, he would become an expert in getting around obstacles by bending the rules, sometimes all the way to their breaking point. When the time came for his eye test, he was ready: he had memorized the letters on the eye chart - E_D_C_F. With his right eye closed or with his left eye closed, he never missed a letter. Passing the test with flying colors, John later turned his prescription glasses into sunglasses and wore them all the time. Eye exams were required every year, and John made sure he passed every single one.

After acing the eye exam, John turned his attention to the next challenge on his path. All lifeguard candidates also had to pass a mandatory swim test. John was only 15 years old in 1936 when Jack signed him up at City Hall to take the test. The minimum age to be a lifeguard back then was 18, so Jack lied about John's age. They both knew that it would prove to be a physical challenge for John, because he would be competing against 18-year-olds and would have to prove that he possessed the necessary skills, but Jack had no doubts that John would make it.

The entire swim test was very competitive and the candidates were graded on everything, including swimming in the ocean and using the paddleboard. The greatest challenge for John was the rescue challenge, in which a big individual played the role of a drowning and panicked swimmer. Basically, a big guy would jump on top of the candidate and wrap his arms around the lifeguard's neck as though he was going to choke him. The lifeguard candidate had to break the stranglehold correctly and then bring the pretend victim safely back to the edge of the pool. It was tough for a small-framed guy like John, but Jack's superior teaching skills paid off and John passed.

In the water, he was among the best in the class, even though he was competing against members of Fullerton Junior College swim team who were also taking the test. John Olguin, the "human fish," could do anything in the water. It was a slightly different story when it came to the bookwork. John struggled, but in the end, he passed the test. John was now ready to seize the first opportunity to put his newly certified skills to work.

When John took his first steps as a lifeguard in mid-1937, at the age of 16, Cabrillo Beach was a twenty-six-acre aquatics and recreation center serving eight thousand to twenty thousand people per day in the summer season and one thousand to five thousand people daily in the winter. Facilities included a bathhouse, recreational hall, picnic pergolas, a 1,500-car parking lot and a marine museum that was essentially just a seashell collection. Cabrillo Beach also hosted a boathouse, private boating, fishing and refectory concessions. Most importantly, people could swim and bathe in smooth waters on the Inner Beach and enjoy the surf on the Outer Beach.

Cabrillo Beach was the location of many community activities and affairs, including such memorable events as the Spanish Fiesta held on December 1, 1934, to welcome the U.S. Fleet. The program included an Army anti-aircraft demonstration, and a Coast Guard and Fire Department rescue exhibition. The lifeguards also demonstrated their skills and equipment, and then comedy and music performances added to the enjoyment of everyone in attendance. Cabrillo Beach was also the site of the annual Harbor Day celebrations, which often included sailboat and paddleboard races, swimming and diving contests, lifesaving exhibitions, and more. Historical records also show that on September 4, 1938, Cabrillo Beach hosted a large motorcycle rally with 2,500 bikes and an additional 5,000 people crowding the beach.

With boats and swimmers being in close proximity, safety concerns were quickly becoming an issue, as motorboats would occasionally speed carelessly among the swimmers. It is not clear whether or not any ordinances or laws governed the speed of motorboats or similar craft within the waters of L.A. Harbor at the time, or who, if anyone, could possibly have enforced them. However, it appears that the swimmers and boaters coexisted without any major mishaps and lifesaving at the beach was always the job of the lifeguards.

At the time, Cabrillo Beach had such a reputation as a well-managed facility that the Department of Playground and Recreation was asked for advice and guidance by State Recreation Director W. Leo Sanders of the Conservation Department within the State of Indiana's Department of Public Works. Sanders wanted to develop an adequate recreation service in aquatics, particularly swimming, and was especially interested in lifeguard staff and safety protection for any swimmers on the beaches of his lakefront shores. No doubt, the lifeguards contributed to the beach's great reputation; one more reason for John to join their ranks.

John officially became a lifeguard in 1937. He was still

attending junior high school at the time, but during the summer he would work as a lifeguard. He got his first assignment in the summer of 1937 at the Sierra Vista pool in El Sereno near Pasadena. For three weeks, John took the electric railway operated by Pacific Electric, known as "Red Cars," for the twenty-two-mile trip to Los Angeles, continuing on a streetcar for another fifteen miles, and finally connecting to a bus that took him to the swimming pool. The daily journey took about two hours each way and he worked at the pool between 10 a.m. and 5 p.m. Despite the long hours, John was happy and he made twenty-five cents per hour.

At the end of three weeks, his dreams were fulfilled and he was transferred to become a beach lifeguard on Cabrillo Beach. Being a lifeguard at Cabrillo Beach was a great assignment indeed. Regular lifeguards were paid sixty cents per hour for the summer season and usually worked from 9 a.m. to 5 p.m. Lifeguard captains were paid one hundred and eighty-five dollars per month to work steady all year long. John's salary doubled to fifty cents per hour and his travel time was cut to minutes. Once again, John had not only beaten the odds, but had almost changed the game. Nobody questioned his eyesight and nobody checked his age. He was 16 years old and already a beach lifeguard.

To gain experience, John was assigned to different areas between San Pedro and Venice, where the lifeguard headquarters was located at the time. John later admitted that he really needed to hone his skills. At Cabrillo Beach, things were fairly easy with the sandy beach, but in Venice, they had a pier that went all the way out into the surf. If a person was washed under the pier, the lifeguards had to be able to get there and rescue the individual without being thrown against the pilings or cut up by barnacles. John's first few attempts were quite unnerving and remained with him for years. He would always have the utmost respect for his fellow lifeguards who faced pier rescues every day.

In the winter, John's focus was going to school. Come April, though, he would leave school at noon and hitchhike to Los Angeles, where he would work in the Olympic Swim Stadium for a few hours in the afternoon. When more life-guards were needed on Cabrillo Beach in May, he would return to act as one of the twelve to fourteen lifeguards who made sure people were safe. John wore his uniform with pride and quickly became a popular figure on the beach. He was a well-built, good-looking young man, and there was usually some young girl talking to him despite the fact that he was on duty.

At times, John was posted at the foot of the Cabrillo Beach boathouse pier where, in addition to being responsible for the safety and well-being of bathers on both sides of the pier, he had to make sure that no one dove off the end. Authorities did not allow people to walk out on the pier wearing only a bathing suit, because they considered that a sufficient indi-cation that they were interested in jumping off the pier. The restriction served the public because, as the authorities put it, "so many non-thinking youths wanted only to dive off the pier and swim back to the beach." Swimming at the end of the pier did indeed involve some danger, as there were water taxis and fishing boats, plus assorted pleasure crafts operat-ing in the area on hot summer days. There was also the risk of head and neck injuries from diving from the high structure during low tides.

Of course, rules are clearly there to be broken, especial-ly when you are a teenager. Among the rule breakers were John's friends Bud (Earnest) Williams and his brother, Bob.

ABOVE: John Olguin (left), standing in the back Gus and Roy (left to right), their mother Josephine, holding Albert, and Alfonso to the right. 1928. Photo Courtesy John Olguin Private Archive

LEFT: Roy jr., John's father Roy, Albert, two childhood friends, and Gus (from left to right). 1928. Photo Courtesy John Olguin Private Archive

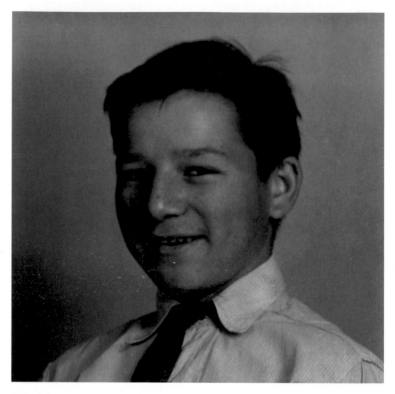

John Olguin at age 13 attending Junior High School. 1934.
Photo Courtesy John Olguin Private Archive

From left to right: John, family friend, Alfonso, Roy, and Gus. 1935.
Photo Courtesy John Olguin Private Archive

ABOVE: *John Olguin's mother Josephine 'Josie' Main Olguin (second from front in center aisle) working at the French Sardine Factory in the 1920s. Photo Courtesy John Olguin Private Archive*

LEFT: *John Olguin as a teenager with the family dog in the mid-1930s. Photo Courtesy John Olguin Private Archive*

John in 1944 as a member of the 1st Cavalry.
Photo Courtesy John Olguin Private Archive

ABOVE: *John's sketch of one of the army camps during WWII. Exact date unknown. Courtesy John Olguin Private Archive*

LEFT: *John's letter to his mother before being shipped out to the South Pacific. Exact date unknown. Photo Courtesy John Olguin Private Archive*

LEFT: *John Olguin showing off his conditioned body. 1944. Photo Courtesy John Olguin Private Archive*

BELOW: *John and his brother Gus meeting each other at the end of WWII in Tokyo. 1945. Photo Courtesy John Olguin Private Archive*

OPPOSITE ABOVE: *Sgt. John Olguin in 1945 in his full army uniform as a member of the 1st Cavalry. Photo Courtesy John Olguin Private Archive*

OPPOSITE BELOW: *John Olguin topside a vessel during WWII. 1944 or 1945. Photo Courtesy John Olguin Private Archive*

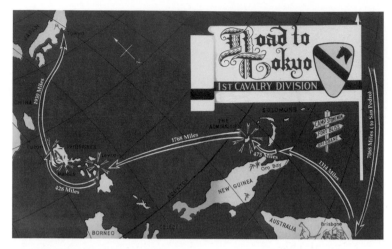

Movement of the 1st Cavalry Division from Australia to Tokyo, Japan. John joined the Division in New Guinea, serving under the legendary General Douglas MacArthur. Based on a map published in The 1st Cavalry Division in World War II. Tokyo. 1947 B.C. Wright.

Jack Chaney and John Olguin lobster fishing at Spanish Breakwater at Cabrillo Beach. 1946 or 1947. Photo Courtesy John Olguin Private Archive

Bud and Bob would crouch around the corner of the building until they saw John was involved in conversation with an attractive girl. Then they would run past him and out onto the pier, ducking and scrambling among properly attired patrons, and dive into the water, swimming hard. Of course, John could not swim after them because he was responsible for the other patrons back at his post. From a relatively safe distance, they would usually give him "the finger" and yell, "This is for you, All-gin!" They always, and to this day, called him "All-gin," a deliberate mispronunciation of his last name. Jumping a bit ahead in John's story, after John returned from World War II, he would be instrumental in launching both Bud's and Bob's lifeguarding careers. Eventually, both Williams brothers would serve under the command of Lifeguard Captain John Olguin.

John loved being a lifeguard, no matter what the weather or the number of people on the beach. For twenty-five years, he would continue to serve most of his time on the beach, watching out for others, keeping them safe, and teaching them to sail, row or kayak. When things were slow and few people were on the beach, John would sometimes become bored. During those times, he would walk over to the Cabrillo Marine Museum at the bathhouse and help for a while, just to stay busy.

John saw opportunities that most others would miss, and he shared his good fortune with others. He loved his hometown and appreciated the importance of living in a community where people cared for one another. While still in Grade 10, he co-founded the Knight Organization at San Pedro High, a group that promoted leadership and excellence. In high school, his charm and perseverance led him to be elected student-body president, just as he had done at Dana

Junior High. He was awarded the American Legion Award and was an honorary member of the Rotary Club. Together with Sylvia Isham, Eva Mary Nurse, and Preston R. Truex, John was elected a member of the Ephebian Society in recognition of his scholarship, leadership and service to the school.

When John graduated from San Pedro High School, in January of 1941, he had a wealth of experience. He had lived through the hardest of times, experiencing hunger and despair, but had never become desperate. When things looked bleak, he would see a bright spot. When others did their best, he would do better. He sought responsibility where others did not. John had already been successful in multiple jobs, including realizing his dream of becoming a lifeguard. For John, that meant saving lives on and off the beach. Securely rooted in the Mexican heritage of his own family, John was a happy young man, content with himself and the world, and ready to live an adventurous and meaningful life.

ADVENTURES OF AN
AMERICAN HERO

*H*aving graduated from San Pedro High School, John was looking forward to spending the rest of his life on the beach as a lifeguard. Then came December 7 and the attack on Pearl Harbor. America was at war.

John, wearing his steel-rimmed glasses, volunteered to join the U.S. Marines, the Coast Guard, the Navy, the Air Force and the Merchant Marine, but was turned down each time because of his poor eyesight. The Army just did not appeal to John, so he decided that if the Army wanted him it had to make the first move. In the meantime, he went down to the shipyards to support the war effort. The Port of Los Angeles played a significant role in World War II, with every company involved in constructing new vessels, converting and repairing older ones and collectively employing more than ninety thousand workers.

Having recently completed high school, with no shipyard work experience, finding a job was not as easy as John had imagined. He eventually found employment with Todd Pacific Shipyards, formerly Los Angeles Shipbuilding and Dry Dock Company, as an office boy running errands for all the shops across the shipyards. Always thinking ahead, John used his time among the various shops to learn the name of each foreman and to also determine which shop was the busiest and could use an extra man. After a couple of months as an office boy, John spoke with the supervisor of the busiest boiler shop and soon became the boilermaker's helper.

Knowing the Army would eventually call, John began to condition himself for the challenges that lay ahead by jogging, doing push-ups, swimming and tackling any workout that would enhance his fitness. John did not really need much conditioning and his record as a swimmer was already legendary. In fact, John and his brothers were gifted swimmers who fared very well at swim meets, both in open water and swimming pools. In high school, John swam eighty-one yards under water in two minutes and one second, shattering the Los Angeles high school record. A year before entering the military, John and his brothers Leonard and Albert swam at the Olympic Stadium in the Aqua Gala. John set a new Pacific Coast record of 285 feet underwater and then Leonard established a new world record with 363 feet. At the end of the meet, their younger brother, Albert, swam 225 feet. It was a family affair that day.

Despite being in great physical shape, John continued his workout regiment until the Army finally drafted him. He entered into active service on May 3, 1943. By that time, his brothers Gus and Alfonso were in the Navy, Roy was in the Coast Guard, and Leonard had joined the Merchant Marine. Their mother, Josephine, remained behind with remaining three children, fearing for not one or two, but for the lives of five of her sons who were serving their country at the same time. Like so many other mothers, she could do nothing but hope that her boys would be safe and return home some day.

John's pre-training conditioning and his Olympic Stadium efforts really paid off once he was working for Uncle Sam. During basic training at Camp Roberts, near San Miguel, California, he finished among the top in his class. Promoted to Corporal and transferred to Fort Ord, near Monterey, California, John served as a swimming instructor for all soldiers passing through. Swim training took place at the pool of Monterey High School. It was John's responsibility to ensure that all soldiers swam well enough to dog paddle across a swimming pool before they were sent overseas. Wanting to be the best soldier that he could be, John applied himself with remarkable enthusiasm, dedication and commitment. Along with swimming instruction, John also practiced at the shooting range and later trained others. He loved his assignment, as for all practical purposes it did not feel much different from being a lifeguard.

John knew that he would eventually ship out just like all the others he had trained. That day came on June 26, 1944, about thirteen months after he was drafted. Ordered to report to Oakland, he boarded a ship filled with thousands of other young men who were also unsure of their future and their destiny. John later remembered the eighteen-day voyage as standing in line a lot: long lines for breakfast and long lines for dinner. While waiting for word on where they were going, John tried to calm himself by reading as many books as he could and looking out at the ocean. It was the beginning of an eighteen-month journey that would cover more than fifteen thousand miles, and take John to New Guinea, the Philippines and Japan.

After a rather uneventful, and at times outright boring, initial voyage, John and his fellow soldiers arrived in Port Moresby, New Guinea, in mid-July. At the time, New

Guinea and Papua were two separate territories that would be combined into Papua New Guinea only after World War II. Once there, John was assigned to the 1st Cavalry Division, 7th Cavalry Regiment.

John quickly found out that his unit had fought in the Battle of the Little Bighorn, in June 1876, under the command of Lieutenant Colonel George Armstrong Custer; a battle also known as Custer's Last Stand. Part of the Sioux War, the battle took place near the Little Bighorn River in what was then the Montana Territory. Crazy Horse and his Indian warriors defeated the 7th Cavalry Regiment, including Custer's battalion of about seven hundred men, and wiped out five entire companies. Custer himself also died on the battlefield. As John would tell the story from what he had heard, the Army, infuriated and humiliated by this dramatic defeat, stripped the 7th Regiment of its vivid red-and-white pennant emblazoned with a racy seven. It was only after 1945, almost seventy years after the events at Little Bighorn, that the pennant was returned to the regiment in recognition of its contributions during World War II.

What John did not know, and could not have even imagined, was that his future wife's grandfather was a member of that same regiment under Custer. Had he not been on leave at the time of the Little Bighorn action, he would have likely perished, never had children and hence John would have never met his wife, Muriel. And so in what seems an amazing and serendipitous twist of fate, John's future wife Muriel's grandfather was among those who lost the pennant and John was one of many who helped win it back. John had no way of knowing at such a young age that playing this notable role in history was just beginning.

By the time John arrived in Port Moresby, the 1st Cavalry

Division had been in New Guinea for about six months. The division had been part of the Admiralty Islands Campaign, which included significant fighting on Los Negros and Manus islands, and had officially ended on May 18, 1944. Port Moresby was a staging area where people and supplies were assembled before combat. John spent his first few weeks there unloading and stockpiling ammunition, fruit, canned beef and other goods arriving from Australia, and loading supplies onto ships that would distribute them where they were needed.

At the same time, the American forces under General Douglas MacArthur, the Supreme Commander of the Southwest Pacific Area, developed plans to return to the Japanese-occupied Philippines. A compelling political dimension existed with the Philippines that did not apply to other Japanese-occupied targets. The Philippines had been of special concern of the United States since 1898, and the political, military and humanitarian responsibilities arising from that relationship could not easily be discarded. In addition, the Japanese assault on the Philippines in 1941 had forced MacArthur to leave the Philippines, and he and others insisted that the United States had a political and moral obligation to liberate the Republic's 17 million citizens from their harsh Japanese occupation as soon as possible.

Once General MacArthur was given permission to recapture the Philippines, his first objective was Leyte, an island situated between Luzon, the largest island in the archipelago and home to the Japanese headquarters, and Mindanao, the second largest and easternmost island. As one of the larger islands of the Philippine archipelago, Leyte stretches across 110 miles from north to south and is about fifty miles across at its widest point. Of the two valleys, the larger Leyte Valley runs from the northern coast to the long eastern shore and was home to most towns and roadways at the time.

Leyte's land surface offered challenges and benefits to both attackers and defenders: the sandy beaches were well suited for landings but the interior of the island was heavily forested and mountainous, providing formidable defensive opportunities for the Japanese. The late-season assault by the American troops risked being hampered by monsoons and other storms. However, MacArthur counted on the support of the population of over nine hundred thousand, many of whom were already supporting the guerrilla struggle against the Japanese. The liberation of the Philippines was about to begin and John would be part of it.

On October 12th, 1944, John Olguin and his fellow soldiers of the 1st Cavalry Division sailed away from their base for the Leyte invasion, code-named Operation King II. On October 20, the invasion force swept the eastern shores of Leyte and the waiting Japanese forces. The first wave of the 1st Cavalry Division landed at White Beach, between the mouth of the Palo River and Tacloban, the provincial capital of Leyte. Troopers from the 5th, 7th, and 12th Cavalry regiments, John among them, quickly spread out across the sands and pushed deeper inland. Before nightfall, General MacArthur would once again set foot on Philippine soil and deliver his famous "I have returned" speech, while standing on the beaches of Leyte. By the end of the next day, the provincial capital of Tacloban was secured. The Americans would continue to fight their way up and through the mountain ranges that separated the Leyte and Ormoc valleys and would reach the west coast of Leyte by the end of December, 1944.

The difficulties John and his comrades had to endure, especially in the mountain ranges, were immense. Rain, fog and mud kept everyone uncomfortable and made moving around incredibly challenging. Patrols and individual units could quickly become cut off and supply lines were often interrupted. At some point in December of 1944, John and his troop found themselves in just such a predicament while they were deep in the mountains chasing the enemy. Donkeys were used to bring in in food and supplies, but when bad weather prevented the delivery of any food for four or five days, John's talent for turning lemons into lemonade proved invaluable. John gathered the extra rations some of the men carried and asked some Filipino soldiers to dig for edible roots and collect banana hearts. He then added the shredded meat from coconuts and water, and boiled the jungle stew in three steel helmets over a fire. It was delicious, rich and fed everyone. When no food reached the men the next day, they prepared another jungle stew before a small Piper Cub aircraft finally dropped food for all to enjoy. They were still alive and it was Christmas. Even in the midst of the most difficult conditions, and with many supplies lost to the enemy, the holiday spirit was in the air.

John not only fought, survived, and helped his fellow soldiers to do the same, but, at his first opportunity, he began to create a personal dictionary of Visayan, one of the local languages. He loved people, so he would approach the locals, try to use the words he knew, and learn a few new ones every time. He did it with no other thought than advancing his own knowledge, but his continuing efforts to improve his local-language skills would not go unnoticed.

Heavy fighting continued on Leyte until the end of December, when the last Japanese holdouts were finally defeated. American casualties from the Leyte campaign exceeded 15,000, with 3,504 killed in action. Japanese troop losses were estimated to have reached close to 50,000. With the fighting on Leyte still raging, the American forces took their next step toward the eventual liberation of Manila, the capital of the Philippines: the invasion of Mindoro.

Mindoro, a rainy, humid, mountainous island to the south of Luzon, held minimal Japanese forces and was closer to the northern island of Luzon than Leyte. Mindoro could also support airfields, which would be needed for the air assault on Luzon. The invasion of Mindoro began on December 15, when clearer weather allowed for a full-power attack against very little resistance. By the end of the day, Army engineers had begun to prepare two airfields to support the invasion of Luzon. By the end of the following day, the island was secured. Soon afterwards, American aircrafts began preemptive strikes on kamikaze airfields and attacks on Japanese shipping lanes.

The subsequent battle for Luzon began on January 9, 1945, when more than seventy allied warships sailed into the Lingayen Gulf on the eastern shore of the island. The 1st Cavalry Division, depleted in strength of both men and material due to the Leyte campaign, landed in the Mabilao area of the Gulf on January 27. Landing on the Lingayen Gulf's sheltered beaches on the northwestern coast placed the troops near the best roads and railways on the island. These roads ran through the plains and south to the capital city of Manila, which was the main objective. After the Lingayen Gulf was secure, recapturing the capital would allow domination over the core of the island and Manila Bay, which would make Japanese defensive operations more difficult.

By January 30, the division had largely moved to its assembly area near Guimba, thirty miles farther inland. The following day, General MacArthur ordered John's 1st Cavalry Division to go on to attack Manila as quickly as possible, free the internees at Santo Tomas, and take the Malacañang Palace and the legislative building. A fast-moving task force – including two motorized cavalry squadrons reinforced with armor, motorized artillery and other support units – was quickly formed. This "flying column" rushed toward Manila, while the rest of the division, including John and the other men of the 7th Cavalry, followed and dealt with any resistance. John and his fellow soldiers of the 7th Regiment were poised to endure weeks more of heavy fighting.

After two days, the task force had dashed its way through one hundred miles of enemy territory and was approaching Manila. Individual units were racing for the honor of reaching the city first. The next day, February 3, parts of the 1st Division rushed into the northern edge of the capital, with only the Tuliahan River separating them from the city itself. Only narrowly avoiding Japanese efforts to destroy the bridges, the way to Manila was clear for the rescue column to enter the city. In less than three hours, the four thousand civilian prisoners in the internment camp at Santo Tomas University had been liberated.

On February 7, 1945, the members of the 1st Cavalry Division flying column were relieved of their positions in the northern part of Manila by the arrival of the 37th Infantry Division. Most units joined the effort to free the southern sections of the city and the surrounding regions, in order to pry the capital away from Japanese control completely. Fighting continued in the streets of Manila for nearly a month, as American troops and their Filipino allies fought to eliminate resistance throughout the capital. In an effort to preserve his force, Imperial Japanese Army General Tomoyuki Yamashita ordered a complete withdrawal of all Japanese troops from Manila. Disobeying his order, about ten thousand fought on, unnecessarily prolonging the fighting and forcing the allies to bomb the city to drive out the remaining Japanese forces. The Japanese troops massacred countless people and, at the end, the death toll stood at more than a hundred thousand.

On March 4, the allied forces liberated Manila. Fighting on Luzon continued, though, with John and the 7th Cavalry Regiment in the midst of it, until all remaining Japanese had been cleared out. In early May, the 7th Cavalry moved to Siniloan, some thirty miles southeast of Manila, where some of the remaining Japanese forces were attempting to reorganize. From there, John and his comrades continued through the rugged jungle environment toward the city of Real on the east coast of Luzon. Often the Jeeps could not navigate the trails, so the troops would be forced to move on by foot. On May 13, the 2nd squadron of the 7th Cavalry reached the shore in the vicinity of Binangonan Point, where they waited for the reinforcements and supplies that were going to be arriving by landing craft from Mauban.

While waiting on the shoreline, the 7th Cavalry sent out patrols toward the city of Real. Fifty years later, John would still remember how he and his brothers-in-arms went up a mountainside on one of these patrols and came into a wooded area that was so dense they could not see ten feet in front of them. While traversing this path, the troops came under enemy fire and were pinned down, not able to continue forward or go back. John, who was now leading the squad, ordered the 155mm Howitzers to shell the enemy position. The problem was that the U.S. and Japanese troops were in such close proximity that John's unit could have easily fallen victim to friendly fire. Essentially, John was asking his comrades to fire on his own position!

John's unit could hear, way behind them, the loud "BOOM" of the artillery and then the shells coming in to drop right near them. Luckily, the risk paid off. They eliminated the enemy and proceeded on toward the next battle. It was on that day, May 18, 1945, that John Olguin earned his Silver Star. To quote Major B.C. Wright, Division Historian for the 1st Cavalry Division:

> *Corporal John M. Olguin of San Pedro, California crawled fifty yards through dense underbrush with both friendly and enemy fire crashing around him to assist two wounded men to safety. He carried one and led the other back to the security of their own lines. His act definitely saved the lives of his two comrades.*

John rarely spoke about the incident and if he did, he always emphasized that he had only done what he was trained to do as a lifeguard: save lives.

The Luzon campaign was officially declared over on June 30, 1945, but the campaign to liberate the southern Philippines would continue into July. MacArthur felt that the shame of the forced American surrender of 1942 could not be redeemed if any Philippine citizens were still at risk. Thus, he remained committed to providing assistance to all of the islands and to protecting the Philippine citizens from possible Japanese retaliation. Of course, continued victories also benefited the planned invasion of Japan, since the Philippine islands' cities, ports and airstrips would prove useful.

By the time the Luzon campaign was over, John had been promoted to Tech Sergeant. He had always maintained his efforts to learn Visayan and, for a brief moment, that skill had him off the front lines and on with the intelligence staff. Unfortunately, John could not type and, thus, could not file any reports, so he was quickly sent back to continue fighting with the infantry. Returning to the front lines did not faze

John. The way he saw it, he was returning to his friends and he was confident his luck would hold. He had already survived the fiercest battles, the long marches through extreme terrain, and had recovered from malaria, which he had contracted during the campaign in New Guinea. He was still young in years, but much older now in experience and wisdom.

With the Philippines liberated, John and his 1st Cavalry Division began preparations for the invasion of the Japanese homeland. John's battalion was practicing island landings: going down with the cargo nets into the landing barges, hitting the beaches, running up five hundred yards and regrouping. Rumors were flying that the war was going to be over soon and the soldiers often talked about that day coming. John told his men that he wanted them to shove him over the top of the rail into the ocean when the anticipated news arrived. He would do a backflip to celebrate!

Then one day, John and the men were sitting on deck talking when the PA voice carried across the deck: *Now Hear This, Now Hear This, The President of the United States has stated that the war is over.* John shouted, "There it is, men! Shove me over the side! That's an order!" Two guys took hold of John's feet, counted to three and threw him way out. John flipped, landing in the water like an Olympic diver. As soon as John hit the water, the first mate jumped in too! Then all of the other soldiers started jumping in, until there were at least three hundred people in the water. Up on the ship, the remaining men grew increasingly worried, putting ladders and cargo nets over the side and starting a chorus of yelling, "Come up quickly, the sharks are coming!" Soon everyone was climbing back up the ship. But no sharks were ever seen that day.

General MacArthur chose the 1st Cavalry Division to move into Tokyo with him as part of the forces that would occupy

Japan. In the early morning hours of September 2, the long line of ships steered into Yokohama Harbor, past the battleship Missouri, where the formal surrender ceremony would take place later that day. Then on September 5, at noon, a reconnaissance party entered Tokyo and became the first official movement of American personnel into the capital of the Japanese Empire. On September 8, the commanding general for the 1st Cavalry Division, along with representatives from each of the troops within the division, set out for Tokyo. The convoy paused at the city limits before the general stepped across the border. The Allied Occupational Army was officially in Tokyo.

John's unit went ashore and set up its tents in a park, nice and neat in a row. John's platoon was then assigned to stand guard at the Bank of Japan and to protect other valuable targets. John, always keen to learn, was already starting to study, both speaking and writing, the Japanese language. Also while in Tokyo, John received a letter from his mother telling him that his brother Gus, who was in the Navy, was also reportedly in Tokyo. Gus received a similar letter, and both boys were instructed to try to find each other. Having not seen each other since 1943, it seemed like an incredible opportunity. Unfortunately, neither of them knew the name of the other's outfit.

Gus made the first move, but when he came ashore, he found himself surrounded by thousands of soldiers. Unimpressed, Gus asked the first soldier he ran into whether he knew his brother John, John Olguin.

"What outfit is he in?" the soldier replied.

"I don't know but he is in the Army," Gus followed up.

"You stay right here," an amazed Gus was told, "your brother will be here in a few minutes; he's delivering chow to all those standing guard." By sheer luck, which some might call fate, Gus had run into a soldier serving in John's unit. Five minutes later, the truck arrived, but John was not on it. He had decided to go back to headquarters, which at the time was at a local university. So, they took Gus on the truck, finished delivering the chow and then drove to headquarters where the two young brothers from San Pedro had an emotional reunion.

John invited his brother for lunch at the Army mess. When Gus took two slices of bread, he was told he could only have one. He asked for two pieces of meat, but could get only one. When the brothers sat down, Gus commented on how the Army was rationing food, while in the Navy they could have whatever they wanted. Gus quickly followed by asking John what foods he missed the most from back home. "Bacon and eggs," John responded. The next day, Gus fulfilled a late-night promise and brought John and his group a whole case of eggs and bacon. With two little gasoline pump stoves, they cooked a feast for everyone. "The smell of bacon and eggs was all over the building and all my men came and lined up. It was so good, it tasted delicious," John remembered.

Before Gus left, he told John that if he came to his ship, he could feast on all of the ice cream he wanted. Tempted, and wanting to see his brother again, John got a pass a couple of days later and made his way to the dock. Unfortunately, John did not know how to find the right ship, as many were anchored in the open sea. Crafty as always, John tapped into his lifeguard rowboating skills, appropriated a rowboat and made his way from ship to ship.

It was dark by the time he found the right one. John tied up the rowboat and went on deck where a large crowd was watching a movie. Standing in front of the screen, John waved his arms until Gus emerged out of the crowd. Soon heading toward the freezer, Gus gave John a soup bowl and then swung open the freezer door to reveal gallons of chocolate, vanilla and strawberry ice cream. As the two caught up, John treated himself until he felt that sharp pain in his throat and head that is familiar to anyone who eats too much ice cream too fast. Shivering, he drank a cup of coffee to warm up, quickly recovered, and then had to leave. It was late, but John rowed back to shore and made his way into Tokyo. When he got back to his unit the next morning, he told the men about how he had eaten more ice cream than ever before in his life. It took only moments before all of the men announced that they, too, wanted to visit John's brother.

John had a special way with people: he was engaging, curious and always wanted to make contact. No matter where or when, John would attempt to speak to the Japanese he came across, always trying to learn a little bit more of the language. He learned simple words, similar to those anyone planning to visit a foreign country would want to learn, including simple phrases: "May I ask you something?" and "Do you speak English?" He kept the notes that he took throughout his time in Japan, which proved invaluable when he returned with his wife many years later.

While many Japanese studied English, they often had difficulties speaking the language due to a lack of practice. John saw this as an opportunity for both him and whomever he approached to practice. Often, after he asked a local a question, he or she would just reply that they did not understand. John would then respond in Japanese, "I don't understand either," and everyone would have a good laugh. Overall, however, many Japanese, especially youngsters, were somewhat scared of Americans. Often, when they saw GIs walking down the street, locals would yell out, "Danger, Danger."

John told stories of how, despite the locals' trepidation, they would often open their doors, hearts and minds once he started speaking to them in Japanese. His experience illustrates so clearly how the language skills of even just one soldier on the street can make a difference.

One of the valuable targets in Tokyo that John and his unit protected was the American Embassy, where General MacArthur had set up his quarters. On the grounds, John found a palatial pool that was empty at the time. He sought out the caretaker, persuaded him to fill it, and then put on a comedy diving show for the troops. It could well be said that John could add, "First to take the plunge in Tokyo," to his list of firsts during World War II.

Eventually, John was ordered to go to headquarters. The Army wanted to know whether or not he would be interested in enlisting for one more year. Thousands of American troops would remain in Japan to help rebuild the country, in much the same way that allied forces were helping to rebuild Germany and the rest of Western Europe. For John, staying in Japan for another year did sound exciting and would provide the opportunity to learn more about the culture and improve his language skills. After careful consideration, though, he knew that he longed to be a lifeguard on Cabrillo Beach again. It was time to return home.

John's long journey back to his hometown of San Pedro began on November 29, 1945. Also on board the ship was John Quefada. The two young men had gone through basic training together, but then had served in different companies of the 1st Cavalry. The voyage took them from Japan through the Aleutian Islands, and then to Seattle. Everyone on board was anxious to get home; nobody wanted any more adventures, just smooth sailing.

Winter storms are common in the North Pacific, though, so the men found themselves in swollen seas with breaking waves. Even though they were supposed to remain below deck, the two friends could not resist and went up on deck. After all, who knew if they would ever have another chance to witness such a spectacle? Instantly, they both found themselves in absolute amazement of what nature was throwing at them: the ship almost disappearing under the huge waves and oceans of water rushing all over the deck. The men stayed on deck until halfway through the night, screaming out of excitement, not fear, as John would always point out.

Once the ship arrived in Seattle, the soldiers disembarked and boarded a troop train. It was December and snowing in Seattle. The train began to move south, destination San Pedro. With momentum building as they drew closer to home, it seemed as though they were nearly home free. Unbelievably, as the train moved into Wilmington, at Wilmington Boulevard and Los Alamitos, someone tried to beat the train and did not make it across in time. That person died at the scene and the train could not move until officials arrived to report the situation and recover the body. One thousand soldiers were stuck on the train. They had not eaten all day and were anxious to get back home to their families. Finally, after several hours, the train resumed its run and stopped at the intersection of 5th and Front streets in San Pedro, and then again at the Ft. MacArthur lower reservation where John was discharged. After an extensive journey, he had made it home. It was December 22, 1945.

Of the five brothers, John was the first one to return, but the others all did make it home in time for Christmas that year. One can only imagine the exuberance and relief that their mother, Josephine, must have felt. Christmas 1945 became the most remarkable and special Christmas for the Olguin family. The boys themselves were so excited that they could not sleep for days. Instead, they settled on the floor of their home and took turns sharing stories with each other, nodding off here and there only to get right back into sharing their adventures. San Pedro had a group of Olguin veterans back in town.

The war was over. The war was won. Soldiers were now veterans, many of them still incredibly young and without families. Many had never even had a real job before they were drafted. Now, a living had to be made. Countless lives were waiting to be lived. These young men courageously resumed their places in hometowns all over the country, while those who had stayed behind welcomed them home with open arms. Millions of women had kept the factories operating and had taken care of their families during those wartime years. They were ready to embrace their husbands, fathers, brothers and sons finally returning from the battlefields. Applying the same perseverance as on the battlefields in Europe and the Pacific, the returning soldiers began to work toward a better for future for themselves, their families, their communities and the entire country.

Like thousands of other young men in 1946, John was looking for work. It was January, so lifeguards were not in high demand. Instead, John tried to get work on the docks, but the competition was stiff. John was still hanging out on the docks when his former lifeguard captain, George Wolf, called to ask him to return to work. While John was very happy to resume working as a lifeguard on Cabrillo Beach, but old-timers took all of the year-round positions so he could only work there during the summertime. Without employment possibilities on Cabrillo Beach until the summer, George offered John a full-time job at the Hansen Dam, about an hour away from

San Pedro in the San Fernando Valley of Los Angeles. Built in 1940, the dam controls floodwaters. John figured that since no one else seemed to want to work there, he would go, gain experience and seniority, and hope to get back to Cabrillo Beach eventually.

The City of Los Angeles provided John with a trailer to live in and put him in charge of the entire lake from 9 a.m. to 5 p.m. each day. The 25-year-old veteran felt like he was going to have a little vacation. Unfortunately, memories from the battlefields came flooding back the first night he stayed in the trailer. After a great day, John retired to his accommodation, read a book for a while and then went to sleep. In the middle of the night, he woke up to a loud "BANG" and saw a bullet hole in the trailer! Another "BANG" and another bullet hole. John rolled out of bed and called the police, explaining that he was the lifeguard on duty and he was being shot at in his residence. The police told him that someone would be right out. Half an hour passed, one hour, two hours, and nobody arrived.

The next day, John went into town and got himself a few tools so that he could dig a foxhole, as he had done countless times while in the Army. From that second night onward, he slept the winter nights away in a sleeping bag in his foxhole under the stars. It was a familiar feeling that provided comfort and a connection to the elements and nature. John's appreciation for sleeping outdoors never subsided. He and his wife, Muriel, would eventually move their own bed onto their porch, sleeping outside under a canopy for most of their sixty-two years of married life. John returned to San Pedro in the spring of 1946, having earned his stripes as the lifeguard at the dam. As he had hoped, he spent the following summer in his hometown as a full-time lifeguard on his beloved Cabrillo Beach.

In the fall of 1946, John felt it was time for a real vacation. He had served his country and reestablished himself as a lifeguard back home, but now he wanted some time to explore and play. Together with his brother Leonard, he hatched a plan to travel to the Virgin Islands, then to Mexico City, over to Acapulco and then catch a boat from there back home to San Pedro. All was on track for the journey until Leonard fell in love and refused to leave San Pedro. John asked his mother if she would join him, but she did not want to go either. In fact, she did not want John to go, as she was afraid that John would get into trouble, get robbed or worse. For a young man who had returned from war, his mother's concerns did not make much sense. John was determined to embark on this new adventure.

Eventually, John went with Phil Marino, whom he had met on Cabrillo Beach during the summer. John packed his one bag with a bathing suit and towel, a shirt and tie, and his beige suit. Then, in November 1946, off they went on a four-month adventure. John and Phil traveled to Mexico City and then to Acapulco, which was a sleepy town at the time. It is not known whether or not Phil went on from there, but John settled in and began teaching Spanish to American tourists and English to Mexican businessmen. He still had ample time to do a lot of skin-diving and learn more about his heritage. John's father had emigrated from Mexico, but he never spoke much about life in his home country. This was John's first opportunity to gain firsthand experience about how people lived, what they did for fun and what they thought about those who had immigrated to America. John did not make much money while there, but he had the time of his life.

While in Mexico, John ran into a movie crew that was shooting *Captain from Castile* with Tyrone Power and Jean

Peters. Howard Hughes was also there at the time, along with Ralph Hempfield and his boat the *Flying Cloud*. Ralph took a liking to John right away and invited him to come along with the crew for a one-day outing to dive for lobsters to prepare lobster cocktail. John assumed that he was invited merely to entertain the film crew, so he asked them to also invite his friend Apolonio Castillo. Apolonio, a member of Mexico's Olympic swim team, was the best lobster diver in the area. His knowledge of the region certainly helped to ensure that they dove over the side of the boat at just the right spot. He and John dove in first and started to throw lobsters up over the side and onto the deck until, within fifteen minutes, they heard the crowd calling, "No more! No more! We can't eat any more than this! It is enough!" The group feasted on fresh lobster cocktail that evening.

Impressed by the show that the two young men had put on for the crew, Ralph Hempfield challenged them to a contest to see who could catch more seafood delicacies, pound for pound and for variety. For the contest, Ralph wanted Apolonio and John to use only spears, while he would use the tools of a sport fisherman. John was eager to play along, but he only had another week or so before he had to begin his journey home. So, Ralph quickly solved that issue by inviting John to travel with him on his boat from Acapulco back to California. They would have the contest along the way.

A week later, John boarded the *Flying Cloud* and began his journey back to San Pedro. They sailed north from Acapulco to Zihuatanejo, about 130 miles up the Pacific coast of Mexico. A very remote town at the time, the only way to get to Zihuatanejo was by boat or mountain trail. When they checked in with the port authorities for the night, the port captain came strutting out of his office wearing a coat with big gold buttons and an admiral hat with the traditional gold braids. He was also barefoot, wearing a pair of old shorts and sporting a big bare belly that protruded through the undone buttons of his official coat. John did not have a camera, but that captain's image burned itself into his memory as one of the most delightful moments of his journey. As they ventured into the town, there were chickens, pigs and sheep running around in the middle of the street. For the first time on his trip, John truly felt as though he were in another country.

They spent one day in Zihuatanejo before traveling up along the coastline, diving in several places and going ashore in others. At one spot, John came across some locals and asked them to go spear-fishing. They went out in a canoe and caught plenty of fish. At the end of the day, John and Ralph compared their catch: John had caught a greater diversity of fish, while Hempfield, who had fished from his boat, had caught more pounds of fish. The contest was a tie. They continued their journey on the *Flying Cloud*, bringing John all the way home in March 1947. John loved every minute of the four months that he had spent in Mexico, the country that his father had left to find a better life in California some thirty years earlier. It felt as if an entire year had passed, not just one winter.

John was happy to be back in his hometown of San Pedro. He was looking forward to lifeguard duty on Cabrillo Beach, a place he had loved since he was a little boy. Unknowingly, John was poised to continue along a path that would take his life in a direction so incredible and unlikely that no one could have imagined. Throughout his journey, two things propelled John forward: his love for people and the place he loved more than any other, San Pedro.

SAN PEDRO

J ohn Olguin's land of enchantment and his life-long home, San Pedro, California, is a working-class town about twenty-five miles south of downtown Los Angeles. Today, San Pedro is home to the largest port complex in America and third largest in the world. Unlike what its founders discovered more than four-hundred years ago, San Pedro today has an ethnic mix of Serbo-Croatians (from the former Yugoslavia), Italians, Mexicans, Greeks, Scandinavians, and African-Americans. It has become a very close-knit community of about one hundred thousand, where there are no secrets and everyone seems to know someone else's business. This atmosphere creates a relatively positive and tight bond that fosters the kind of community involvement and commitment that John Olguin tapped into to create so many of the opportunities that were born of his dreams. John's drive to chart new paths associated with San Pedro, the ocean, the port, and the thrill of exploring the earth had few bounds.

San Pedro has a history that reaches as far back as the mid-16th century. As part of John's deep love for the community's history, he enjoyed the occasions when he was able to dress up as the mariner who discovered San Pedro: Juan Rodriguez Cabrillo. In 1542, Cabrillo, a Portuguese navigator in the service of Spain, set out to chart the coast of California and claim it for the Spanish crown. Commanding two ships and a brigantine – his personal vessel, the *San Salvador*, as well as *La Victoria* and the smaller *San Miguel* – Cabrillo reportedly arrived on September 28 in San Diego Bay, which he called San Miguel. Farther along on his voyage northward, Cabrillo discovered the Channel Islands in October; what we know as Santa Catalina, he named San Salvador, and the island we call San Clemente, he named Victoria.

Cabrillo continued across the channel to the Bay of San Pedro, which he named *Bahia de los Fumos* or *Fuegos* (Bay of Smoke or Fires), because of the many fires that appeared to be burning ashore. The explorer interpreted the fires as evidence of a large population inhabiting the area and decided not to go ashore. Instead, he continued to sail around the peninsula of what is known today as Palos Verdes, anchoring in the Bay of Santa Monica on October 9, 1542. The expedition reached as far north as the San Francisco area before winter storms forced Cabrillo and his men to turn south and seek protection off the Channel Islands.

Cabrillo's life was cut short by an accident in late December. Even though there are conflicting reports as to whether he fell and broke his arm or his shinbone, it appears clear that gangrene set into the wound. Cabrillo is presumed to have died on January 3, 1543. His men, now sailing under the command of Bartolomé Ferrelo, continued the expedition in the spring of 1543 and traveled as far north as the Rogue River area of Oregon. Sadly, they never found the Northwest Passage.

As geographical historian Henry Wagner pointed out in 1941, "the most cruel thing that happened to Cabrillo, however, was that he was deprived of all evidence on the maps of California of his visit to this coast." In 1602, almost sixty years after Cabrillo's death, Spanish explorer Sebastian Vizcaíno explored the same area and endowed the coast with an entirely new set of names, many of which persist to the present day. Like Cabrillo, Vizcaíno saw plenty of smoke on both the mainland and the Channel Islands, but interpreted the fires as navigational aids. When wind and sea conditions prevented Vizcaíno from entering the Bay of Smokes – which he renamed the Bay of San Pedro after Saint Peter, the Bishop of Alexandria – he charted a course toward the fires on Catalina Island and reached safe harbor on its leeward side. If those fires were indeed navigational aids, then perhaps the early inhabitants of the area had set them as invitations to sail into the bay and trade. We will never know for sure, but maybe San Pedro Bay was a thriving trade center and important port already back in the mid-16th century. After Vizcaíno's visit to the area in 1602, it would be another 150 years before the first permanent Spanish settlements were established.

The late 18th century saw the arrival of Spanish missionaries, soldiers and settlers moving north from Mexico. They established the presidio and mission at San Diego in 1769, the San Gabriel mission in 1771, and an increasing number of outposts throughout California. Among the men who sought a new beginning was retired soldier Juan Jose Dominguez, who was granted grazing rights for cattle and sheep on a 75,000-acre property by Pedro Fages, the Governor of Alta California at the time. It was on this land that Dominguez started Rancho San Pedro, one of the first major Ranchos of Spanish California. These ranchos or ranches were created out of large land grants that the Spanish, and later the Mexican government, used to encourage settlement of California. Juan Jose Dominguez's death in 1809 set off the famous dispute between his nephew Cristobal Dominguez and the Sepulveda family, which lingered until 1846 when

Governor Pico confirmed the Sepulvedas' rights to what was then called Rancho de los Palos Verdes and which is now known as Rancho Palos Verdes.

Around the same time, the port of San Pedro was facing difficult times. In the early 19th century, the entire Bay of San Pedro was considered treacherous, especially during the winter months when southeast winds prevailed and a ship anchored too close to land could be blown onto shore. To contend with this issue, cargo was unloaded into smaller boats and rowed ashore, a method known as "lighterage." Despite these challenges, ships continued to sail into the bay because the inhabitants of the Pueblo of Los Angeles, the largest settlement in California, with a population of about 1,000, needed supplies. Once Mexico declared independence from Spain in 1822, the port of San Pedro, like all California ports, officially opened for trade. At that point, it seemed bound to develop into the major port of entry for California.

Then the discovery of gold in California in 1849 threatened to change everything. With the gold came the declaration of statehood in 1850 and the ensuing gold rush. Thousands of people immigrated to San Francisco and the city developed into the port of entry for California, meaning that all imported goods destined for Los Angeles had to be shipped through San Francisco. San Pedro harbor returned to its low-grade pre-1822 status, and routing all goods through San Francisco stifled the economic development of Los Angeles. After petitioning Congress for two years, San Pedro was finally designated a port of entry with its own customs house in 1853. Over the following decades, the importance of San Pedro continued to grow.

In 1851, Phineas Banning, an enterprising man in his early twenties, arrived in San Pedro. It was his entrepreneurial vision that eventually turned San Pedro into a modern, deep-water harbor. In 1858, he built a wharf in the inner bay and transferred his own shipping business to the new location. His port facilities were the first to be sheltered from the elements of the open sea, while at the same time shortening the trip to Los Angeles by six miles compared to the distance from Santa Monica to Los Angeles, the competing possible alternative location for a port at the time. Almost immediately, a new community called New San Pedro developed around his wharf.

When the Civil War broke out in 1861, Banning and his partners donated 60 acres to the government to establish Fort Drum, where thousands of Union troops were stationed. New San Pedro and Banning's business boomed, hauling military supplies and selling provisions to the Army. In 1863, New San Pedro changed its name to Wilmington. A year later, Wilmington was established enough to have its own post office.

Banning was elected to the California State Senate from 1865 to 1868. He played a significant role in bringing the first railroad to the San Pedro Bay area when, in 1866, he sponsored legislation authorizing a bond measure to fund a new railroad connecting the City of Los Angeles with its port. After two more years of wrangling and lobbying, voters finally approved one hundred and fifty thousand dollars in Los Angeles County and seventy-five thousand dollars in Los Angeles City bonds, which were complemented by one hundred and seventy-five thousand dollars in private funds. Work on the twenty-two mile railroad began in the fall of 1868 and was completed within a year. Regular daily service commenced on October 26, 1869, a mere 403 days after the groundbreaking. With the construction of the Los Angeles and San Pedro railroad terminal at Banning's wharf, conditions were set for the harbor developments that followed.

Banning and his partners had developed the inner San Pedro Bay, but the sandbars that ran from Deadman's and Rattlesnake islands to the mainland allowed only vessels with a very shallow draft to enter the sheltered lagoon. To make the lagoon fully accessible, the Army Corps of Engineers constructed the first breakwater in the L.A. harbor between the tip of Rattlesnake and Deadman's islands. This project began in 1871 and took nine years to complete. It also turned out to be more than twice as expensive as originally budgeted, with a cost of four hundred and eighty thousand dollars. In 1899, the construction of a second breakwater, known today as the L.A. breakwater, began and was completed in 1912.

Rattlesnake Island was a sand-dune spit in San Pedro Bay that received its original name, *La Isla de la Culebra da Cascabel* ("Island of the Snake with the Rattle"), from the Spaniards who found thousands of rattlesnakes inhabiting the island, having been washed down from their mountain homes by heavy rains. In 1891, a group of St. Louis capitalists, called the Terminal Company, purchased Rattlesnake Island and changed its name to Terminal Island.

On the ocean side of Terminal Island was Brighton Beach, which was a remarkably beautiful, gently sloped beach. It had a spacious bathhouse built by Fred Burke and the Brighton Beach Hotel, which attracted the wealthy from the Los Angeles area. Brighton Beach was also host to a pavilion for dances, a long wharf called the Pleasure Pier, and the Terminal Tavern, where one could enjoy lunch right at the ocean's edge. Many well-to-do people built summer homes on Brighton Beach, giving them names such as Las Conchas, Saltair and Jib-o-Jib. When construction began on the L.A.

breakwater, a lot of dredged sand was deposited in front of the Brighton Beach homes, pushing the water's edge almost a mile away. The rich began to leave and soon their summer homes became permanent residences for some of the hard-working people of San Pedro, including the Olguin family.

By the end of the 1880s, San Pedro had a population of 1,800 and two trains operated daily to connect the town to Los Angeles. San Pedro had a post office, a telegraph and telephone office, a public school, four meeting halls, two churches – Presbyterian and Episcopal – and seven hotels and boarding houses. The town also had a bank, two commercial buildings, an electrical power plant, a public library, a drug store, two markets, butcher- and barbershops, a hospital, a volunteer fire department, a literary society and a welfare society. By all accounts, it was thriving. San Pedro also had two newspapers, the *Harbor Advocate* and the *San Pedro Times*, which began a long history of newspaper businesses in the community. On March 1, 1888, as the town continued to grow, San Pedro was incorporated as a city under the Municipal Corporation Act of March 13, 1883.

By 1895, businesses were concentrated on Front, Beacon and Sixth streets, and First, Second, Orizaba and Ancon streets cut across the north hill. Homes were scattered, with several residences perched on hills to provide their owners with spectacular views. Sweeping avenues with modern-looking homes were built on the south hill, overlooking Timm's Point. The post office, often considered a good indicator of development in those days, had continued to grow; it now had eighty-five rented boxes and exceeded twenty thousand dollars in money-order transactions. The Postmaster enjoyed a raise in his salary to twelve hundred dollars per year.

More than 450 children attended two schools, which were housed in large, modern buildings on 5th and Center streets and on 15th and Mesa streets. The San Pedro Literary Association managed the library and a public reading room, housed in a brick building at the corner of 7th and Palos Verdes streets. San Pedro had a beautiful park at Point Fermin, including a large pavilion suited for orchestral performances and social gatherings overlooking the ocean and beach. A trolley car connected downtown, Cabrillo Beach and Point Fermin Park, making it easy for people to get around.

Plans for further development continued to roll out. There was certainly no shortage of ambition, but a lack of funding stood between certain plans and their implementation. San Pedro and Wilmington lacked the tax base to guarantee bonds that were needed to fund projects, and Los Angeles could not spend its funds outside its own boundaries. The solution was to turn San Pedro and Wilmington into districts of the larger Los Angeles area. The California Legislature passed the necessary bill in 1909, and voters approved it in the same year. Once the L.A. breakwater was completed in 1912, the harbor became known as the Port of Los Angeles. A year later, it had become the world's leading lumber port, loading or offloading almost one billion board feet. The growth of the port continued to attract people from everywhere and the San Pedro population swelled to about 8,100 in 1913.

Among the newcomers was John Olguin's father, Roy, who was born in Mexico but of Spanish descent since Roy's father had emigrated from Spain. Roy arrived in San Pedro sometime between 1910 and 1912, after walking all the way from Mexico, a journey that took him almost a year to complete. A cook and baker by profession, Roy, like so many others, came to San Pedro in search of a better life. With the economic boom San Pedro was experiencing, he did not have any problem finding a job. Keeping it would prove much more difficult. Even though San Pedro continued to provide opportunities to many, Roy had a difficult time holding a job. He would work for a while, but soon move on to another job. Then he would quit and start all over again.

Roy met his future wife, Josephine Main, around 1915. Josephine was born in Long Beach, California, to Juanita Lopez, who was of Apache descent, and an Irish father, Frank Main. Although Josephine grew up bilingual, culturally she was raised Mexican. Josephine attended St. Anthony's Catholic School in Long Beach, but left after Grade 3 or 4 to work and support her family. No one seems to know exactly how she met Roy, who was working as a cook at the time. They were married in 1917 and most of their nine children were born twelve to thirteen months apart: Roy Jr. (1919), Gus (1920), John (1921), Alfonso (1924), Lucille (1925), Leonard (1926), Albert (1927), and then Esther (1932) and Belia (1933).

Meanwhile, the importance of the port to the entire country continued to grow. To provide protection, an artillery battery was set up at the "Old Government Reservation," adjacent to San Pedro Bay. In 1914, it was named Fort MacArthur, after Lt. General Arthur MacArthur, who was awarded the Medal of Honor for his service during the Civil War. He was also the father of General Douglas MacArthur, who would play an important role in John's life by leading the U.S. forces to victory over the Japanese thirty-one years later. In 1917, the entry of the U.S. into World War I brought countless contracts to the shipyards, where more than twenty thousand people were employed building steel and wooden vessels, mostly for the war effort. Fort MacArthur also became a training center for soldiers shipping out to France.

For additional harbor protection, extra gun emplacements were installed on Deadman's Island.

As the port activities increased so did the rest of the local industries. In 1915, the construction of a warehouse on the municipal pier began. Then, in 1917, a shipyard was established on the channel side of Terminal Island, while the east side saw the construction of a fish harbor, which later on, around the mid-1940s, became formally known as Fish Harbor. Its completion attracted canneries and eventually led the L.A. port to become one of the largest fishing-industry centers in the world, creating thousands of jobs. Among the people who found long-time employment there was John's mother, Josephine, who started to work at the canneries in 1924. After the end of World War I, in 1918, the shipyards continued to be busy and normal maritime activities resumed, which created a healthy and growing economy. With an increase in people coming to work in the yards, the economy began to shift to meet the increase in demand for home construction.

By 1925, San Pedro was still a town of great cultural and economic diversity, but the population had grown to more than thirty thousand. Fruit and vegetable markets scattered from 6th Street, between Mesa and Palos Verdes, to the south, and to the north along Pacific Avenue. LaRue Pharmacy was on North Pacific, as was the Scandinavian Bakery. Car dealers were numerous and San Pedro had its own hospital. Among the many merchants on 6th Street were Perham Jewelry, Newberry's, Woolworth, Haden's Photograph Supplies, Clarks Dollar Store, and a number of clothing stores. Several doctors had their offices there too, often preferring the upstairs rooms of two-story buildings.

San Pedro had five movie theatres built between 1912 and 1932: the first was the Globe, built in 1912 on 6th Street, followed over the years by the Cabrillo on 7th Street, the Strand on Pacific Avenue and 11th Street, and the Barton Hill on Pacific Avenue. The last was the Warner Theatre on 6th Street, which opened in 1931. It was built by the original Warner brothers of movie fame – Jack, Harry, Albert and Sam Warner – who had opened their West Coast movie studios in 1918 after building several theatres in New York, Connecticut and Pennsylvania. In addition to the now-historic San Pedro Warner Grand, they also built historic theatres in midtown L.A. – the best known being the Wiltern Theatre at the corner of Wilshire Boulevard and Western Avenue. Downtown, they built a theatre at 7th and Hill streets in what is now used as a jewelry district mall, and another on Hollywood Boulevard at Cahuenga Street. The Depression of the 1930s forced many businesses into bankruptcy, but a few survived, such as the historic Warner Theatre in San Pedro and William's Book Store on 6th Street. In fact, William's Book Store is the oldest bookstore in the City of L.A.

Until 1920, Beacon Street in San Pedro was the main business street in town: the best banks, the telegraph office, the chamber of commerce, department stores, the best bakeries, ship supply houses and the only bar, the Shanghai Red, owned by a navy man of the same name. Writers liked to describe the bar as *the gutter of blood* in one of the toughest seaport towns in the country. But that was not true. While the bar had its fair share of brawls, Beacon Street was a safe place. On Saturday nights, all of the town's people would come and shop and women could shop independently without being harassed. Often, a bunch of sailors would stand outside, talking ships, bragging about their voyages and so forth. They would fill up the sidewalks until a police officer would say, "Move along fellows, scatter out." And that would be it.

Despite the economic downturn San Pedro experienced in the late 1920s and throughout the 1930s, it seems to have been a remarkable place to live and grow up. San Pedro was a town of great cultural diversity where people of various ethnicities all lived together and yet apart. Yugoslavs and Italians worked mostly as fishermen, while the small Greek population was often involved in the restaurant business. Both the Mexicans and the Japanese worked the boats and in the canneries, at least until the Japanese were removed from the military zone and forced into inland camps following the attacks on Pearl Harbor. As for San Pedro's children, they all went to school together, but would go home to their individual neighborhoods. For instance, Mexicans concentrated below Pacific Avenue in the Barton Hill area. Coming up 15th Street and down 9th Street, you would find Italians and Yugoslavs. When you got up into the hills, you would find the well-to-do, mostly white people.

San Pedro has always had a smalltown feel to it, unlike the rest of Los Angeles. While many places in California were transient, San Pedro was not one of them. Most of the time, people who came to San Pedro really meant to be there, and not just because the freeway ended there. If you ended up in this port community, you were there because you wanted to be and that created a special bond between everyone in town. There has always been a strong sense of commitment among the entire community of San Pedro, to work together for the benefit of everyone, for a greater common good. Of course, San Pedro was not free of ethnic tensions altogether as the city grew, but it seems that the ethnic differences were less serious in San Pedro than in other, even nearby places. And mostly these differences did not threaten the cohesiveness of the overall community.

There has always been great ethnic diversity in San Pedro, which frequently led to some very interesting exchanges and learning experiences between people from different backgrounds. Some of these examples are enlightening and some are cute. Other examples reflect the reality that some cultures were viewed as lacking the ability or capacity to succeed or compete with others who had a different experience or view of the lesser-accepted ethnic residents. People who moved beyond any issues with multiple languages or cultural differences sometimes produced more smiles and chuckles than nasty smirks.

For example, when John was in Grade 3, his principal Mrs. Wikersham, saw him eating beans and a burrito for lunch in the schoolyard. She went up to him and asked him what he had eaten for dinner the previous night and breakfast that morning. John's answer was beans and tortillas. He always had beans and tortillas, or burritos. Mrs. Wikersham took his burrito away and gave him what she considered real food for a kid his age, a peanut butter and jam sandwich. No doubt she had good intentions, but for John sandwiches were gringo food. He would rather have eaten beans three times a day because that was part of the norm in his Mexican culture. To this day, San Pedrans stay closely connected to their ethnic culture and foods, while openly embracing their American roots.

Then there was John's brother Leonard. Like any student in school, he went to see the school counselor one day for guidance. The counselor took a quick look at Leonard and suggested he take six semesters of welding and machine shop because he would make a good laborer. The counselor's advice reflects how school officials generally viewed Mexican-heritage kids, as potential laborers, not as potential business leaders or intellectually capable future success stories. Leonard did not know any better, so he followed the advice. When he finished school, he went to work in the shipyard as a welder.

Over time, it dawned on Leonard that reciting poetry and reading good books was much more satisfying, so he decided that he did not want to be a welder anymore. After he returned from serving in the Merchant Marines in World War II, he went back to high school and then on to college. Eventually, he completed his doctoral studies in Language Arts at the University of Southern California and started his career as a 5th and 6th Grade teacher.

Leonard became well known for his work in bilingual education and was later appointed to the Mexican American Education Research Project for the California Department of Education. In 1970, he was instrumental in putting together the White House Conference on Children and Youth, and, in 1973, he served in a special assistant capacity to the program director of the National Right to Read program. Later, he would head the department of foreign languages at California Polytechnic University in San Luis Obispo and was involved in teacher training at the University of California, Irvine. Leonard also became an accomplished writer and creator of training films.

Little did Leonard know that his work on bridging the cultural divide between whites and Mexicans would bring him back to a place in California where he and John had experienced discrimination in their youth. It was back in 1938 when John was working as a lifeguard and had his first car, a small Austin in which you could move the seats back to have enough room to sleep. One day, the brothers decided to drive up U.S. Highway 1. At around noon, they arrived in King

City in central California. The two young men were hungry and went into a grocery store to buy some bread, mayonnaise, bologna, cheese, lettuce and tomatoes to make some sandwiches. They drove to the edge of town, made their sandwiches, and had just taken their first bites when a police officer drove up. He stopped, took a quick look and immediately asked them to get on their way. John told the officer that he was a lifeguard in San Pedro, but the officer just kept calling them "chili peppers" and telling them that they needed to get moving. John and Leonard packed up and drove for a while before stopping again to continue their lunch, but Leonard was so upset he could not eat a thing.

Decades later, some people in King City still had issues with Mexicans, especially migrant workers. They felt that every time migrants came to town, they would come in gangs; men carrying knives. Not knowing how to handle this, the mayor called the California Department of Education and requested help. His request was passed to the Mexican American Education Research Project. When Leonard learned about King City's problem, he immediately volunteered to go there. Before he went to King City, he called the mayor and asked him to assemble all administrators, city council members and department heads in the largest meeting hall on the first day of his visit. Then, the following day, to invite all the migrant workers.

When Leonard arrived, everyone who had been invited was there, together with merchants and the Chamber of Commerce. The stage was set. The mayor introduced Leonard: "Ladies and gentlemen, I would like you to meet Dr. Leonard Olguin, who is with the Department of Education in Washington, D.C. He is here to talk about the problems we have been having here in our town."

At that moment, Leonard came out wearing a big sombrero and a sarapé: a colorful, long, rectangular textile garment worn by peoples in Mexico and Central and South America for protection against the natural elements. He was barefooted with his pant legs rolled up to his knees. He walked out on the stage singing, "*La cucaracha, la cucaracha.*" Once he finished the song, he said – with a heavy Mexican accent – "I come to speak with you, the Americanos." Then he sang another song while playing the guitar. The crowd looked at each other, likely thinking that this guy was nuts. When he finished the second song, he went back to the mike and said, "And now, Señores and Señoras, if you will wait just a minute, I have to go and take a leak. I will be right back." And off the stage he walked.

Backstage, he quickly put on his shoes, a tie and coat, and returned to the stage. He walked up to the microphone and said, "Ladies and gentlemen, I just gave an example of the Mexican culture. And what is going on in your community is the reason I have my job." He then told them what had happened to him and his brother John, all those years ago. He elaborated on the concept that if their town still had the same issues as back then, it meant that they still did not understand the culture of the Mexican people. He then explained some of the differences that they did not understand or appreciate. He told them, for example, that when an American goes to the bathroom, he goes to the bathroom by himself. When a Mexican goes to the bathroom, he often has his brothers with him to talk to while he is going to the bathroom. He also told them that when an American goes to the store, he jumps in the car by himself and will be back in ten minutes. When a Mexican goes to the store, he takes his kids, his grandkids, and his next-door neighbors... a gang goes to the store! They talk the whole time, because they have a lot to say and never run out of stories.

The next day, Leonard stood in front of the migrant workers and he did it all again, with his pants rolled up and the sarapé – they cheered and clapped and were thrilled that they finally had a man to talk to who was on their level. He spoke to them in Spanish and explained to them the differences in culture. Leonard detailed how the town's people were scared of them and thought they would pull a knife to hold them up or kill them! Leonard hoped that by exposing and emphasizing the differences to these groups wary of each other, both sides would be able to find common ground to better understand and respect each other.

As a young man back in San Pedro, John Olguin also knew that you could meet and grow to appreciate the differences of people from other countries, cultures and even other parts of the USA. Beyond being chock-full of diverse groups of people, San Pedro was also home to wide-open spaces where youngsters could go to play. From swimming down at the beach, to investigating tide pools at Royal Palms, or climbing the cliffs of Portuguese Bend, there was always plenty to do. During the summertime, there were arts and crafts programs at White Point, for those kids who were not having fun sneaking in, or out of, Fort MacArthur. San Pedro was certainly not a boring place. It was a nurturing place, where body, mind and soul could develop and grow, and where children could explore the world around them. It would prove the perfect place for John, who, from a very early age, was determined to make this world his own.

John's sometimes difficult experiences as a young man – and those of his brothers and sisters – along with his fascination with the rich history of San Pedro, served to cement his love of his community and his commitment to making a difference. His time frolicking at the water's edge, his days as a lifeguard, and his uncharted entry into the world of education and what we now know as marine science, has turned San Pedro into a modern-day mecca for all who aspire to understand and experience our oceans and marine life.

John never accepted barriers to his dreams or his passion for the beach, the ocean, and every seashell and creature that came from the water. Mostly self-taught, with no formal education or college degree, John was open to any ideas that could advance his burning desire to make a living at the water's edge. Taking all that he could learn, he would soon begin to share his passions and show people that there was more to this edge of the world called San Pedro than just sand. John Olguin was determined. Under his care, a small museum would succeed and earn its due credit for being an educational anchor to the sea and not just an appendage of Cabrillo Beach.

FATHER OF THE CABRILLO MARINE MUSEUM

*T*he cradle of the Cabrillo Marine Museum lies in Venice, California, about twenty-five miles up the coast from San Pedro. Bob Foster, a lieutenant lifeguard stationed at the headquarters of the Los Angeles County Lifeguard Service in Venice, had begun to display seashells, crabs, seaweed, and other objects the tide brought in, on a table in front of the lifeguard tower in 1934. When the tide brought in a dead pelican, the dead bird was added to the collection. Soon after, a fish specimen in formaldehyde also joined the collection. In the fall of the same year, the collection was moved into the hallway of the Sunset Pier Bathhouse.

Those were the days of red streetcars and bathhouses on the beaches. Families would come down dressed in their Sunday best to promenade the boardwalks and rent bathing suits for a nickel apiece. Ten cents covered the rent for the suit, a towel, soap and a shower. When people began to drive their own vehicles, the need for bathhouses declined, and many turned into white elephants: valuable yet no longer useful, structures of times past.

Once Bob Foster had started exhibiting sea life, it did not take long for a number of kids to start helping him pick up shells, label them, and put them on a card table in the hallway. Soon there was not enough room to accommodate the growing exhibit and, in 1935, the entire collection was moved to the Cabrillo Beach Bathhouse in San Pedro, which at the time was brand new and sitting empty.

With the museum established at Cabrillo Beach, C.P.L. (Captain) Nicholls, supervisor at the time of Aquatics in the City of Los Angeles Department of Playground and Recreation – who would later become John Olguin's mentor – asked the Board of Education for a naturalist to curate the collection. They sent Dr. William L. Lloyd, a retired dentist. Dr. Lloyd and his wife, Edna, had come to San Diego, California, from the Midwest in the 1920s. Reportedly, he lost all of his money while in San Diego during the Great Depression of 1929 and subsequently moved to San Pedro. Like tens of thousands, he was looking for work and had joined as many as three thousand jobseekers who assembled every morning in hopes of finding employment with the City of Los Angeles through the federal government's Works Projects Administration (WPA).

There are no records as to how Dr. Lloyd came to be hired by the Board of Education or why the Board felt he was well suited to assume the position at the new museum on Cabrillo Beach. Maybe they were persuaded by the fact that he was not only a dentist, but also a naturalist. Even though he was a specialist in butterflies, not in marine life, his skill set must have made him a prime candidate for the position. At first, he worked as an employee of the Board of Education, but soon the city gave him a full-time position as playground director to run the museum. It was a position without a budget, meaning that the city would not allocate any substantial funds to support the development of the museum. They provided only pencils, paper and a typewriter. Had it not been for Dr. Lloyd's ingenuity, the museum probably would not have survived, let alone grow into one of the world's best marine education institutions.

While he did have to familiarize himself with new organisms and their life histories, Dr. Lloyd's cataloguing skills quickly provided organization and structure to the collection. He also exhibited a fine talent for improvising and making the most out of very little. He could take a shirt box or shoebox, a bit of wire and glass, paint it all black and fashion himself a nice little display case. Ben Grier, the proprietor of the Cabrillo Beach Café, also saved one-gallon glass mayonnaise and mustard jars to give to Dr. Lloyd, who then used them to preserve fish in formaldehyde. That is how the museum received its early nickname, "the Cabrillo Mayonnaise Jar Museum." Dr. Lloyd also learned how to stuff birds, take apart lobsters and crabs, and reassemble them into displays. Even after more than seventy years, some of these original items continue to be on display.

John first became interested in the museum in 1937, during his first season as a lifeguard on Cabrillo Beach. John was a young, agile lifeguard and when Dr. Lloyd asked for help at the museum, George Wolf, the lifeguard captain at the time, would allow John to go over and help Dr. Lloyd clean the museum cases and label the exhibits. John had trouble meeting Dr. Lloyd's strict hand-lettering requirements. Never shying away from a challenge, though, he purchased himself a Leroy Lettering Kit and proceeded to create exhibit copies. John struggled in the beginning, when many times he would finish exhibit copies only to make a mistake and have to start all over again.

Dr. Lloyd believed that this dedicated 16-year-old had a great interest in the museum, but at first John was just bored during the slow, cold days of late fall and winter. A few years went by and John somehow managed to both fulfill his duties as a lifeguard and continue to work with Dr. Lloyd at the museum. Then the war began. Instead of walking on Cabrillo sand, John fought his way alongside thousands of other soldiers, from the jungles of the Philippines to Tokyo.

After John returned home, he reconnected with Dr. Lloyd in 1946 and started to work at the museum again. By then, Dr. Lloyd had developed the idea of having an aquarium in Los Angeles. He had formed a citizen's committee and had contacted the major aquariums in the country, asking for anything they thought might be helpful in planning an aquarium for Los Angeles: advice, copies of annual reports, building costs, attendance information and programs. But he had made little progress and three years later, on a sunny day, Dr. Lloyd came to the lifeguard station on Cabrillo Beach, walked up to John, gave him the museum keys and said: "Today is my 70th birthday. You are now the director of the museum. You know more than anybody else, and you can open and close it until they hire a director in a couple of weeks." John had responsibilities as the lifeguard captain and did not know anything about running a museum, but he was happy to open and close the doors everyday for a few weeks.

Dr. Lloyd did stay around for several years selling seashells and mentoring John on how to operate a museum, but he deferred all responsibility to John, whose role as a lifeguard captain was still his primary responsibility. Yet, from that day in 1949, when Dr. Lloyd unexpectedly handed him the keys, John became the de facto acting director of the Cabrillo Marine Museum. He essentially remained at the helm of the museum for over thirty-eight years, until he retired himself in 1987. Who would have thought that a lifeguard with no formal training would develop the exhibits in the Cabrillo Beach Bathhouse into one of the most recognized, state-of-the-art, research and education facilities in the country? Anyone who knew John Olguin, that's who!

For the first 15 years, from 1949 through 1963, John was in charge of both the lifeguards and the museum on Cabrillo Beach. He had two supervisors: Myron Cox and C.P.L. Nicholls. Myron Cox was the chief lifeguard in charge of all the beaches, but he felt that John was already busy enough and wanted nothing to do with the museum. After all, John was not only the lifeguard captain on the beach, but he had also begun teaching junior and senior life-saving classes and instructing people in canoeing and rowing. Also, Cox was very much aware that John's work at the museum put additional demands on his fellow lifeguards, something John would only come to realize many years later. Cox made it very clear to John that his primary responsibilities were the duties of a lifeguard captain and if someone drowned on his watch, he would have no choice but to let John go. John clearly understood the point. Then there was C.P.L. Nicholls, who was Cox's boss and who headed the Aquatic Department. He encouraged John to do both jobs and promised to cover for him. He thought John was doing a wonderful job.

John understood the issues at stake and decided to take some precautionary measures to make it easier to do both jobs. Ever the ingenious, practical man, John started with his uniform. At the time, all lifeguards wore their bathing suits under their trousers. When somebody needed help in the water, the lifeguard would strip down and spring into action.

Since John was now also working in the museum, he felt that he should wear a coat and tie. However, he also needed to be ready at a moment's notice to run into the water if someone was in trouble, so he wore his thick fabric bathing suit underneath. At times, it was so hot that John was afraid he would pass out. So his wife, Muriel, took the lifeguard emblem off his bathing suit and put it on his undershorts. She sewed on a fly and then dyed the shorts red. Now he could wear his uniform, a coat, and a tie while giving talks without passing out. When there was an emergency, he could quickly throw off his suit and be on the beach scene.

When Dr. Lloyd retired, the museum had the largest public display of California seashells on the Pacific Coast, a nice collection of stuffed shorebirds and a plaster cast of a leatherback turtle. A new, fiberglass cast of the same specimen is still on exhibit today. At the time, John knew very little, if anything, about the job but approached it with the adage, "you either accept the challenge or you don't." It would have been easy for him to say that he didn't know anything about plankton and get someone else to help. Instead, John educated himself and then turned around and taught whatever he had learned to anyone who would listen.

John began to read and memorize the labels of all the displays and to read up on seashells, seabirds and other specimen exhibited at the museum. John would get up at three o'clock in the morning and study marine life. Whatever he learned, he would use that week in his talks. At the same time, he focused a lot of his attention on the visitors to the museum. Dr. Lloyd had focused on making displays and cataloguing everything, while engaging very little with any visitors. He had an especially hard time dealing with children. Not so for John! He loved people and he loved children even more.

The Cabrillo Bathhouse (in the background), home to the Cabrillo Marine Museum from 1935 through 1981. Late 1930s. Photo Courtesy Cabrillo Marine Museum/Cabrillo Marine Aquarium

D. William Lloyd (left), the first Director of the Cabrillo Marine Museum. He served from 1935 through 1949. Photo Courtesy Cabrillo Marine Museum/Cabrillo Marine Aquarium

The first floor of the Cabrillo Marine Museum in the bathhouse displayed sea life, including seashells, representing the origin of the museum. Photo Courtesy Cabrillo Marine Museum/Cabrillo Marine Aquarium

The second floor of the bathhouse was used as a maritime exhibit hall from 1951 through 1981 when the items were moved to the new Los Angeles Maritime Museum on Harbor Boulevard in San Pedro. Photo Courtesy Cabrillo Marine Museum/Cabrillo Marine Aquarium

John teaching children about fish using a number of specimens mounted on the wall on the first floor of the museum. 1950s. Photo Courtesy Cabrillo Marine Museum/ Cabrillo Marine Aquarium

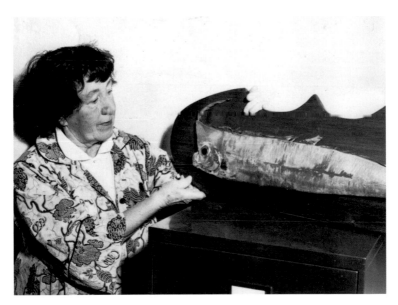

Beatrice Hess, who prepared many of the marine life specimens exhibited at the museum. 1950s. Photo Courtesy Cabrillo Marine Museum/Cabrillo Marine Aquarium

Tours of the Cabrillo Marine Museum were so popular that the bathhouse could not handle the crowds. And so in the 1960s John began to host some tours outdoors. Photo Courtesy Cabrillo Marine Museum/Cabrillo Marine Aquarium

John shares one of his many lessons with a group of children in front of the cast of the 1100-pound leatherback turtle caught in 1938. Photo Courtesy Cabrillo Marine Museum/Cabrillo Marine Aquarium

John Olguin and his long-time right-hand Marji Frank. 1980s. Photo Courtesy Cabrillo Marine Museum/Cabrillo Marine Aquarium

World-renowned architect Frank Gehry's design of the new Cabrillo Marine Museum. Photo Courtesy Cabrillo Marine Museum/Cabrillo Marine Aquarium

John Olguin and Susanne Lawrenz-Miller, co-directors, in front of the completed new Cabrillo Marine Museum. 1981. Photo Courtesy Cabrillo Marine Museum/ Cabrillo Marine Aquarium

John Olguin (right) and Los Angeles Mayor Tom Bradley (left) at the ribbon-cutting ceremony of the new building. 1981. Photo Courtesy Cabrillo Marine Museum/Cabrillo Marine Aquarium

Lifeguard Captain John Olguin (standing far right) with his crew and supervisor Myron Cox (standing left). Photo Courtesy John Olguin Private Archive

Lifeguards posing with their beach dory in 1952. From left to right, Leonard Olguin, Albert Olguin, Donald Raskoff, Bill Arendain, Dave Taylor, Donald Landwher, Frank Obuljen, Donald Krebs, Ronnie McKinon, and Chauncy Hubbard; kneeling in front is Capt. John Olguin. Photo Courtesy John Olguin Private Archives

Capt. John Olguin in 1960. Photo Courtesy Cabrillo Marine Museum/Cabrillo Marine Aquarium

He would talk to everyone who found their way to the museum and would answer any questions as best he could.

In those days, the beach was the destination of most people, including groups of schoolchildren, and many did not even know the museum existed. However, once there, they seldom forgot. Some teachers began to bring their students to the museum and John would give tours and share what he knew. Because of John's multiple responsibilities, he would often give tours to larger groups that included children of various ages. Quickly though, he realized that he had to approach 1st graders differently than 4th or 6th graders, so he began to schedule tours so he could do a better job educating all ages appropriately.

The number of artifacts donated to the museum continued to grow, including many maritime artifacts. Up until that point, the second floor of the bathhouse was used for meetings and exercise classes. One class, called "Slim and Trim," was composed of a dozen women using ropes to jump and skip on the wooden floor all at the same time. It resonated like a big drum: BOOM, BOOM, BOOM. The reverberations could be felt throughout the entire building. People exercising would often make such a racket that the schoolchildren could not hear John talk. Eventually, John asked them what it would take to have them move. Their greatest concern was how they would relocate their piano to wherever they moved, so John offered to move the piano to their new home at Anderson Memorial Playground on the corner of 9th and Mesa streets.

When the second floor became available, in 1951, John obtained permission to use it for maritime exhibits. To bolster the fledgling maritime collection, John wanted to add a few anchors. He quickly found that he needed to know more about maritime artifacts and history, so he began studying as much as he could. Once he felt he had learned enough about anchors and other maritime pieces, he began to teach others with the same enthusiasm as when he spoke about marine life.

In an effort to enlarge the maritime collection, John would go around town giving talks about the story of the museum. The 30-Year Club, founded in 1937, was the only organization concerned with historic preservation until the San Pedro Historical Society came into being in 1974. Two of its most prominent members, Clyde "Lucky" Foote and Bill Olesen, solicited most of the ship models and nautical instruments for the museum. One time, John was giving a talk at the club and at the end Clyde Foote interrupted to point out a factual mistake in his presentation. John was flustered on the inside, but he did not miss a beat. He announced that he was a young man and was allowed up to two mistakes per day, and that was only his first. John was skillful at acknowledging his shortcomings while still maintaining his credibility with his audience.

In the late 1950s, the Cabrillo Marine Museum had several ship models on display. At least two of them received public mention in the *Los Angeles Times* and the *San Pedro News-Pilot*. One of the models was the *Tradition*, a replica of a brig with that name, which some claimed to be the biggest little ship. The model had been built by Capt. Cedric W. Windas, a retired mariner who devoted seven years to building it using only hand tools. It was 12 feet 6 inches long, 3 feet 6 inches deep, and 14 feet high. The *Tradition* was the only model in the museum that allowed for demonstrations of working running gear and yardarms. Another model was the *Cutty Sark,* built by Wayne Shirer, a former sea captain who had spent three thousand hours building the replica. Both models are still displayed prominently at the Los Angeles Maritime Museum in San Pedro, at the foot of 6th Street on the waterfront.

By 1953, John had been quite successful with the museum. Some fifty children and a few adults would visit the museum every day and John had adjusted well to his double-duty as a lifeguard and the director of the museum. By this point, the second floor was beginning to burst at the seams and it was becoming clear that they would soon have to find a new home for all the maritime artifacts. John had also found a volunteer, Betty Valahov, who would come to the beach almost daily to help John with the children and answer the phone. Betty and John worked together for almost thirteen years; she only stopped after more volunteers had come to John's aid.

The City of Los Angeles, however, decided it was time for a professional to take the reign and hired Lloyd Mason Smith. John was not thrilled about giving up the work at the museum, but, on the other hand, he had never been paid for that part of his job. After Smith started, John was left with less responsibility and the same salary, about eight thousand dollars per year. He could now sit back a bit to relax and enjoy life.

Smith asked John to show him around, so John gave him a tour and walked him through the entire building, upstairs and downstairs. When they had finished, Smith asked John who was answering the phones and who would talk to the children. John said that he would. Smith realized that this was a one-man show and that it required a lot of work. John had managed to recruit a group of volunteers to help him out, but then that was John's specialty: working with people. John's volunteers were not thrilled that Smith was taking over, so John knew Smith would likely have to find his own way.

With that, John gave Smith the keys and the responsibility for the museum changed hands for the first time in almost fifteen years.

With fewer responsibilities resting on his shoulders, John and his wife, Muriel, felt it was a good time to fulfill their long-time dream and travel to Europe. Lifeguards were allowed to accumulate vacation days and, over a period of several years, John had accumulated about two and a half months of time off. Now he and Muriel could go for a two-month paid vacation. They went to England, rented a car, visited museums and historical locations, including Stonehenge, and then continued on to France, Italy, Spain, Holland, Germany and Switzerland. Eventually, they returned to England and made it back home to San Pedro. It was not their last trip overseas; they later returned to Europe and visited Japan, Africa, South and Central America, the Fiji Islands, as well as many places across the U.S. and Canada.

When they arrived home from their European holiday, John found Smith was gone, the museum abandoned and high school kids wandering around without instruction or supervision. John was not surprised. He had realized from the very beginning that Smith was unhappy at the museum, but he could not say nor do anything about it. Soon after, his supervisor, C.P.L. Nicholls, called and asked John to meet him for lunch. Nicholls didn't waste any time in telling John that the city wanted him back at the museum job. Even though John was thrilled, he realized that he was, for the first time, in a position to list some of his long-time grievances. He had hopes that he could resolve some of them before he would return to the museum. John did not get any money for working at the museum, and because there was no operating budget, he could not buy anything. If he wanted to move a piece of furniture, he needed someone to sign off on it. There was a ten-dollar petty cash account, but even back then that was not a lot of money. In John's view, "unfunded" was not the way to build and develop a successful museum.

The City of Los Angeles supported the museum, but if John asked for five thousand dollars to purchase a piece of equipment, he was told there was no money. Whatever he asked for, the answer was always the same - no. If they wanted him back on the job, John explained, they would have to allow him to develop the museum and make mistakes along the way. At the same time, he said he was not asking for a blank check and he promised to seek official approval for his plans. Nicholls agreed and John was reappointed as the director of the Cabrillo Marine Museum. Unfortunately, as he would soon find out, not too much would change for a while. However, the City of Los Angeles did hire Mable Dixon in 1954 to answer the phone, clean the museum and do whatever else John needed.

John became an expert in circumventing the city's processes and procedures, and a skillful fundraiser as well. If he needed anything, he would just go out and find a way to get it. Forget the bureaucracy, the paperwork and all that. John always found a better way to get things done. He also intensified his efforts to become more proficient and learn new things. Back in the early days, John would sometimes accompany Dr. Lloyd to the Los Angeles County Museum of Natural History to discuss exhibits with Dr. Howard Hill, who was the curator of marine biology. It was during those trips and meetings that John made valuable connections he could rely on if he had specific questions.

At the museum, the number of exhibits steadily increased and, while it had started out with a seashell collection, the museum had received a lot of other items and artifacts from around the world. Perhaps more importantly, John was developing the museum from an exhibit space into an educational, hands-on experience for people of all ages. Children now started to come to the museum by the busloads. His work was first widely recognized in 1957, when the National Museum Association named the Cabrillo Marine Museum the "Top Small Museum in the USA." John was elated. He did not rest on his accomplishments, however; instead, he challenged himself to rethink the larger strategy of the museum.

In 1959, more than 500,000 people from fifteen states and three foreign countries visited the museum, and more than 40,000 students participated in tours of the facility. At a time when most museums around the world were still focusing on their exhibits and providing very little interpretation, John shifted the focus from exhibits to the education of people, especially children, by talking and interacting with them. He felt that communication was more important than anything else. John realized that he would need a number of volunteers to work by his side greeting and teaching the hundreds of people who would come to the museum every day. He needed people who liked to be with children and were interested in conducting the tour and beach-walk programs he had developed. So John reached out to his community, posting messages in supermarkets, stores, gas stations and any other places he could think of, hoping someone would respond.

Making the visit to the museum a great experience also meant changing things around, to make it more inviting. The museum was still in the bathhouse, which had not been designed to house exhibits or accommodate tours. The layout was not ideal either. When guests walked through the door, the museum was hidden behind a lobby, which included the office. Sometime in the early 1960s, John wanted to tear out the middle of the wall, open it up, and create one great big beautiful hall. Back then, John was still seeking the approval of his supervisors for any changes, but they routinely denied his requests. After a couple of weeks of thinking over his plans, John decided that the worst thing that could happen is that he would be fired. Even if that happened, he would still have his lifeguard job. Plus, he was still not being paid for the museum job anyway.

One evening, John and a couple of his friends took the renovations into their own hands. They went to the bathhouse, knocked the entire wall out like mad men and trucked everything to the dump. Then they put up showcases and made a nice large entrance hall from where you could see the length of the displays. A couple of months later when John's supervisor visited, he sensed something was different, but he could not put his finger on it. John only admitted that he had rearranged things a little bit. His supervisor liked it and commended John for his good work. John had won this battle; he took a risk and it worked. John realized that circumventing the system by not asking but just doing would benefit the museum. It would become a trademark of his leadership and management style: if it is good for the museum, let's do it.

Next John felt the museum needed a front-door display. In his mind, it should be a huge fish, like a black sea bass. John called his buddy, John Fitch of the California Department of Fish and Game, and about a week later a 300-pound specimen was waiting to be picked up. That was the thing with John, he connected with people and nurtured relationships, so his network seemed to have no boundaries. Fitch suggested John have a fish fry after he made the cast for the model, and that is just what he did. After he made the cast, he invited the community down and everyone ate as much delicious fish as they wanted. The next day, John found out that the cast had fallen apart. He felt terrible. He called Fitch, told him what had happened and a week later another 300-pound black sea bass was on its way to the museum. This time, Beatrice Hess, a taxidermist working with John at the museum, insisted that they wait on the fish fry until the cast had completely set, dried and was found to be strong and usable.

Ms. Hess had worked with Dr. Lloyd in the early days of the museum and became a full-time employee in the early 1950s. She appeared to resent the fact that John was just a lifeguard and not a museum professional, so the two had their fair share of disagreements. She had received art training in what was then Czechoslovakia and quickly learned to cast fish, assemble crustaceans and paint them all so they looked realistic.

Among the many things Ms. Hess had worked on was a fish made of plaster that hung on the wall close to the back door. It was very artful and beautiful. One day, the door slammed so hard that the whole thing came down and broke into pieces. John knew that she would be terribly unhappy about this, so he quickly locked the doors and painstakingly put the pieces back together. He finished it with some paint and hung it back on the wall. She never realized what had happened until someone told her the whole story. She went to John demanding to see her work and, even though she could not point out where it had broken, she argued that she should have been the one to repair it. John quickly figured out not to argue with the nice, older woman, but he did make sure his supervisors knew about the situation so they could back him up when she went to them to complain. He did, however, always respect her work and acknowledge her contributions to the museum and the community.

In case of the black sea bass, the second cast worked out perfectly and so did the second community fish fry. After the black sea bass model was complete, it was mounted inside the front doors of the museum. John soon found that young visitors were frightened by the sheer size of the fish with its gaping mouth, so he moved it to the back of the museum where it eventually broke apart.

With all the progress John was making, college kids started to come to the Cabrillo Marine Museum too. It took John a bit longer to get as comfortable around them as he was with everyone else. The main reason was that John had never attended college himself; he had taught himself everything he knew. Yet here he was, about to meet kids who were studying the very same subject. At the beginning, John put in extra hours to be even more prepared to tour the students, make his presentation and be able to answer any questions they had.

In 1961, the American Nature Study Society had a convention in Los Angeles and contacted John for a special tour of the Cabrillo Beach Museum, including a talk on grunion, the little, silver-colored fish that spawn on the beaches along the Southern California coast. Naturally, John agreed and began to spend time studying so he would lead a good tour. When the group showed up, John was the only one around without a PhD. There were experts from big eastern universities like Harvard and Yale and John was a little bit worried that he might not be up to par with such well-educated people. Then again, they would probably know nothing about grunion. So, he gave them a tour of the museum, made his presentation and showed them the grunion movie. Dr. Lloyd, who had come with the group, shook his head in amazement at how much John had learned in such a short time.

In 1963, John became the official director of the Cabrillo

Marine Museum and retired from lifeguard duty. He would no longer have to worry about anything but the museum. Despite all of his success, John always felt that he needed to work harder and do more. In part, this was due to his insecurity about having had no formal museum training. He wanted to ensure that whatever he did reflected well on the museum. Clearly, his self-esteem was vulnerable, especially when dealing with adults. Working with children was a different matter. John knew that attending college to earn a degree was out of the question, as there were already not enough hours in the day for John to do all the things he wanted to do. He did, however, persuade his wife, Muriel, who already felt that he spent more time with everybody else than with his own family, to let him take classes from time to time, one day per week at Harbor Junior College, Long Beach State College and UCLA.

Beyond the odd classes he took, John tackled his lack of formal education in various other ways. He would seek the advice of people he knew, including his schoolmate Henry Niska, who had spent about a year redesigning the museum's exhibit cases. In order to find out what other museums were doing, John subscribed to a number of magazines, including the *Museum Curator* and the *Museum News*. In one of those periodicals, John read an article about Bob Wade, of the Los Angeles County Museum of Natural History, who had won an award for his coordination of the California Hall exhibit that highlighted the natural history of California. John was eager to meet with Bob and asked his wife's first cousin, Harlin Athon, who was the head of the Photography Department at the L.A. County Museum, for an introduction.

John had connections and was happy to use them to cultivate new relationships with people in all sorts of places and positions. Networking was as natural to John as swimming or rowing. With the help of Harlin, John invited Bob Wade to a lunch in San Pedro in 1971 and told him about the museum and the upcoming renovations to the ground floor. John said he would be honored if Bob would take a look and share some thoughts. After lunch, John brought Bob to the Cabrillo Marine Museum and asked, "What would you do here if you had all the money in the world?" John and Bob walked through the museum with John taking notes on what Bob suggested: replacing the mismatching floor tiles; bringing sky, water and sand colors into the museum; and putting up signs where people can see them easily. John took everything to heart and got to work.

When Bob returned one year later, he was amazed. No one had ever followed his directions so exactly. For John, though, that was not even a question. After all, he felt he was just a lifeguard and certainly did not know more than a professional, award-winning curator. It was not that John felt too inadequate to come up with the right answers himself, but he was always looking to others in an effort to learn, to hone his skills and for some reassurance. Fortunately, for everyone, his ego never stood in the way when it came to improving the museum and the visitor experience, although dealing with supervisors may have been a different story. Bob, delighted by so much confidence in his advice, became John's best spokesperson. He told everyone to help John if they could, and he gave John some display cases and a few other items for the museum.

John knew very well that there was a mile of difference between reading about something and experiencing it or seeing it with your own eyes. He made a point of visiting other institutions during his travels, including the Steinhart

Museum in San Francisco and the Vancouver Aquarium in Canada. Each visit would inspire him and he would bring new ideas back to make the exhibits at Cabrillo Marine Museum shine.

John's visits occasionally led to humorous moments, like the day he visited an aquarium in Hermosa Beach where they had an exhibit of a live electric eel. This exhibit really impressed John because it had a wire that came out of the tank and used the electricity generated by the eel to light a small lightbulb. The staff told John that these eels did not live more than about two years. Despite the short life expectancy, the staff had still gone through the trouble of naming this particular eel Eli. After a couple of years, John received a message from a staff member at the aquarium telling him that Eli had passed away. John called back to say how sorry he was that Eli had passed and asked where he could send a card with his condolences. With a laugh in her voice, the staff member reminded John that Eli was one of their eels and that he could come by to pick it up and turn it into an exhibit. After a good laugh, John thanked her for the new specimen for his museum.

With all the input from outside professionals and the support of his growing league of volunteers, John was constantly working on things to improve the museum. John and his volunteers put up more and more lights until one day the entire electric panel blew out. He called the electrician, who turned out to be on vacation and would only return to work in two weeks. Instead of waiting, John called his supervisor and asked him for help. He needed the power turned back on because there were a thousand children coming every day. His supervisor, Nicholls, told John to close the museum, cancel all tours, lock the door and come back in two weeks. John would not take that for an answer. After all, people had everything planned: the teachers, the buses, and the whole enchilada. Of course, John also appreciated his supervisor's orders not to let anyone into the museum while it was without lights, as somebody might get hurt and sue.

Challenges like this were John's strong suit. He thrived under such pressure. He gathered his volunteers, who had taught children outside of the museum before, and told them that for the next two weeks they would have to work with the kids only outside. John gave them a quick training tour of how to do it: pick up shells and talk about what they were, how they function, how they protect themselves and so on. When the schoolchildren arrived, the volunteers would explain that there were two museums, one inside the bathhouse and one outside, on the beach. It was a great success and the volunteers loved it so much that they voted to continue the outside museum even after all problems in the bathhouse were fixed and the lights were turned back on. John agreed. He always listened to suggestions from his volunteers and pursued their ideas with the same excitement as he would his own.

John was always facing new challenges at the museum. Back in 1938, the Japanese fishing boat *IZU* had caught a leatherback turtle. Dr. Lloyd had put the 1,100-pound turtle in the weight room of the bathhouse and then made a cast of it, from which two models were made. One model was used at the San Francisco World's Fair in 1939 and the other stayed at the museum. Often museum visitors would sit on the turtle to have their picture taken. John Olguin did not like the way people were using the model. So, in 1971, when he found pieces of timber that had washed ashore after falling off a ship, he built a stand to mount the turtle at an angle, to make it look like it was diving. When he asked the city for some plate glass to surround the model, he was told, once again, that there was no funding. John was disappointed, but not surprised. If the city did not want to help, he would help himself.

John was especially creative when it came to meeting the financial needs of the museum. Often asked to visit groups and talk about the museum, John was occasionally offered an honorarium for his services. The problem was that, as a city employee, he could not accept payment. Furthermore, any money donated to the museum would go to the city, with no guarantees that it would benefit the museum. So, when the local Rotarians asked John to talk about grunion, he asked that, in lieu of cash, they pay for the glass he needed for the turtle exhibit. They eagerly agreed and paid the San Pedro Glass Company for both the glass and its installation.

In other cases, John would accept cash given to him by volunteers and he would put the cash in an envelope or a shoebox. Each payment, or donation, was properly noted and Helen Andersen, the retired accounting manager of the *San Pedro News-Pilot,* would keep records of those monies. John knew that this was not the way to run a museum, so in 1982, he contacted his friends Leonard Bennet, of the Security First National Bank, and Gilbert Drumond, a CPA, and together they created the John Olguin Trust Fund. Finally, John had a structure in place that allowed his friends and supporters to donate money directly to the museum and permit John to spend those monies on his own without having to ask his supervisors.

Not everyone appreciated the trust fund concept. One unknown individual complained to the city that John was acting against the city policy that said that all monies made by city employees were to go to the city. John's general manager, William Fredrickson, requested an audit of the financial records. The auditor, Jerry Lee, came to the museum, but could not find anything wrong with the financial records. John was in the clear, so he enjoyed his newfound freedom by using his new funding source to make necessary improvements and help the museum. When a pump on the seawater life-support system failed and the city wanted to close the museum down because there was no money to keep the aquariums running, John used twelve hundred dollars from the trust fund and sent his chief aquarist, Bob Johnson, to buy a new one. After an entire night of hard work, everything was running again the next morning.

When John wanted the museum to participate in the Christmas parade, and the City of Los Angeles denied his request for funding, he went ahead and sponsored the museum's participation with seven hundred dollars from the trust fund. For one event, John and his volunteers created a float shaped like a bunch of fish and a whale that was a hundred feet long. Unfortunately for John and his volunteers, they were walking behind an elephant who did what elephants do. Volunteers marching inside the massive whale float were unable to see the street in front of them. Not surprisingly, a lot of yelling and swearing could be heard over the Christmas music as the human feet of the whale walked through the elephant dung.

John was a hands-on leader and involved himself in all aspects of running the museum. At one point, he wanted to have a book about gray whales that he could refer to and sell. He liked the children's books authored by June Burns. She lived in Southern California, so John contacted her. Burns agreed to write the book and have some of the proceeds go to the Cabrillo Marine Museum. John bought the books wholesale and sold thousands of them, investing the money raised in the trust fund for the museum. That is the way John operated: if it is good for the museum, let's do it!

Volunteers were a crucial element in everything John did. In 1971, a dynamic new volunteer, Marji Frank, arrived at the museum; she would play an essential role in its success. Marji lived in Rolling Hills Estates with her husband, John. Her six children were grown and she needed some outlet besides playing bridge, so she decided to help John with his spring program. Little did she know, they would work together well past John's retirement in 1987. Marji did not know much about the ocean, but John was quick to reassure her that he would teach her what she needed to know. John took her out on the beach, gave the grunion talk twice and then said, "Now you do it," and he walked away. Luckily, Marji was a quick study. Soon she would be at the museum three times a week to give school tours in the morning, and eventually would stay almost all day helping where she could.

In the fall of 1971, Marji volunteered every day and quickly became John's right hand. After three years of full-time volunteering, she took the part-time position of volunteer coordinator in 1974, which she would hold until her retirement in 1993. Over the years, Marji helped John stay organized and relieved him from most of the administrative and organizational duties associated with the operation of a busy museum that had few staff. The time Marji spent at the Cabrillo Marine Museum was as important to her as her tireless work was to the museum. Marji was a shy, introverted woman, but with John giving her more and more responsibility, she developed great people skills and was loved by everyone. Chip Matheson, who volunteered as a youngster at the Cabrillo Marine Aquarium and eventually became a well-known underwater photographer and cinematographer, remembered Marji as a very busy woman who was the most diplomatic person in the world. Marji treated everyone with respect and care.

Eventually Marji moved with John and the rest of the staff from the bathhouse to the new museum facilities. When John retired, Marji became the right-hand person for his successor, Larry Fukuhara. She continued to be an important staff member until her retirement. On Marji's last day, June 21, 1993, Larry declared it *Marji Day*. Shortly after her retirement, the Cabrillo Marine Aquarium Volunteers Steering Committee instituted a special Marji Frank Award. It is given annually to the volunteer who exemplifies Marji's dedication to the organization by showing that he or she: "cares about the Museum and all people participating in its affairs; is ready to help anyone to the best of his/her ability; does more than his/her share; treats everyone with respect; and maintains a cheerful attitude."

By the early 1970s, the collection at the Cabrillo Marine Museum comprised more than fifteen thousand local and foreign seashells and more than 100 varieties of Southern California fish. With the exception of Monterey, the local tide pools contained the best collection in number and variety of sea animals of any area from Mexico to the Canadian border. The quality of sea life was so unusual at the Cabrillo Marine Museum, and provided such a rare educational opportunity, that the American Association of Museums recognized the museum as one of the top ten programs in the United States.

Clearly, the museum was outgrowing the old bathhouse. It was equally obvious that the huge numbers of visitors, more than 140,000 schoolchildren each year alone, who came to tour the two-story building and the "living, growing" outdoor museum, put a lot of strain on the structure and organization. A new facility was needed and everyone knew it. The City of

Los Angeles Department of Recreation and Parks stepped up and initiated the planning process for a new museum building and exhibit space.

When John heard that the city was moving ahead with plans for a new facility, he was full of excitement and eager to contribute to its design and layout. He was shocked when Bill Lusby, the architect the city had hired, was not interested in John's input at all. The architect planned to design and construct the museum and, once completed, would hand over the key to the city to open it up. He did not even want to meet with John, who was stunned by Lusby's actions. John had developed so many ideas from working in the museum all these years and he wanted to develop a gray whale display and much more, but nobody wanted to listen. Eventually, he got to see the design; it showed a circular building with no windows, right on the beach. To John, a building on the beach without windows was just crazy. Fortunately, for all parties, these plans never went anywhere.

At the same time, the city decided to hire Dr. Richard Josslin as the new director of the museum in 1973. They argued that John was not really qualified to run a museum and, since they were about to develop a new facility, they should bring in a true professional. John did not understand. He knew he did not have any expertise or background in building a museum, but he was convinced that he could do it nevertheless. John was especially incensed because he and Bill Samaras had been working with California State Assemblyman Vincent Thomas to secure funding for a new building ever since a whale fossil had been found in 1971. By the late 1970s, their collaboration eventually would provide the L.A. Department of Recreation and Parks with the $3-million needed to build the new facility.

John had made the museum the success that it was. Over the years, thousands of letters praising the museum and his programs at Cabrillo Beach had validated his work. The facts were all on John's side. With news of the new director, John was disappointed and, for a moment, he contemplated retiring from the museum altogether. But then he accepted the actions of the city as just another challenge he would have to overcome.

John was instructed to work with the new boss and he was ready for it. However, cooperation and collaboration did not appear to be on Josslin's mind. First, he moved John out of his office and into a smaller one, then into a restroom. In 1974, Josslin hired Dr. Susanne Lawrenz-Miller. Susanne's job was to design the exhibits for the planned new museum, help teach marine biology to the docents (the volunteers who led guided tours through the museum) and develop research programs. Together, they began to retrain his volunteers. John could not believe it. He felt strongly that teaching the volunteers a college course was the wrong way to prepare them for tours. They cannot communicate that information to two-year-old or six-year-old children. After all, there were hundreds of preschoolers coming to the museum every week. But Josslin and Miller did not see this as a problem, as they wanted to discontinue all preschool programs anyway.

That is where John drew the line and said, "Wait a minute." He believed that the most formative years of a person's life are the first five years. Josslin's response was that there was nothing to indicate that the program was successful and worthwhile. John did not need paperwork and files, the schools brought their students to the museum because they had heard how wonderful the programs were. He never had to advertise them. But if it was papers that were needed, he could produce those too. He telephoned one of the teachers at Dahlquist Pre-School and told her that he needed letters from preschool teachers testifying that the program they had attended was valuable. Within a week, he had dozens of letters, which he took to Josslin. The preschool programs continued.

Next, Josslin decided to handle all the publicity related to the Cabrillo Whalewatch program. John was forced to hand over all the documentation and information. He reminded Josslin to send out the usual advertisements to the newspapers in time for the start of the volunteer naturalist-training season in October. A week went by and, when John checked, nothing had been sent out. Another week went by and again, nothing was sent out. Finally, three days before the start of the Whalewatch season, John confronted Josslin about the fact that there had been nothing about being a volunteer for the Cabrillo Whalewatch program in the papers. Josslin reportedly told John that he simply did not have the time to deal with it, but would attend their first meeting of the year. He added, "And by the way, if there is nobody there, we'll just cancel the program."

John was beside himself. He saw this as another attempt to get him out of the museum. He later recounted the moment as one where he had to calm himself down and remind himself to use his head: "The Good Lord gave me a good head; I had better use it!" He could not call all the individuals who had volunteered in previous years, because their phone numbers were in the museum files, and the files were with Josslin. Soon thereafter, John found all his files in the trashcan on the beach. He recovered them and gave them to his friend Lois Larue for temporary safekeeping.

Without the files at the time, John decided to call Vivian Landy, a teacher at Long Beach City College, and explain the situation to her. Then he called up Ruth Lebow at Pierce College and explained his predicament. Now he could only wait and hope. On the night of the meeting, Landy's entire class showed up, along with Lebow's class. They had driven fifty miles to get to the museum. When Josslin stepped into the room, about 150 people were sitting on the floor listening to John speak about whales and the upcoming whale watching season. John had won a battle, but the fight was not over. The heroes were Lillian Landy and Ruth Lebow, because without them the Cabrillo Whalewatch program might well have ended right then and there.

Josslin kept writing memos, directing and micromanaging John's work, which John found demoralizing. The straw that broke the camel's back was a memo to John forbidding him to speak to groups. John's friends from all over town stood up and petitioned the city to get Dr. Josslin removed. Eventually, the case went before the Department of Recreation and Parks Commission. Dr. Lawrenz-Miller sent a letter to the Commission explaining her assessment of the John and Josslin situation. It was obvious to her that John was a highly creative and charismatic person who had built outstanding educational and conservation programs that were unusually effective in reaching people of all ages and backgrounds. It made no sense to curtail John's activities. At the same time, she worried that the new museum project would collapse if Josslin were removed.

The volunteers wanted John to testify at the meeting, but John felt he could not speak against his supervisor. So, John's friends and volunteers did all the talking. Shortly after the meeting, Josslin was fired. The Commission decided that John and Susanne could handle all the programs and deal with the expansion. And so, as of 1976, John became program director and, together with exhibit director Dr. Susanne Lawrenz-Miller, co-director of the museum. John was satisfied and committed himself to working with Dr. Lawrenz-Miller so everyone would be proud of their future facility and accomplishments.

At first, John felt that Dr. Lawrenz-Miller did not entirely believe that he was knowledgeable. One day, John mentioned in a lecture that sea urchins could drill into rocks and even solid steel. Afterwards, Dr. Lawrenz-Miller challenged John on the accuracy of his statements. John's response was that he would never intentionally disseminate false information and that he was sure he had read it somewhere. She wanted to see it, so John went to the library, but he could not find it there. He called the California Department of Fish and Game and they could not find it either. Then he called Dr. Rim Fay, a marine biologist, and asked him whether he knew whether anything was written about the sea urchins' unusual abilities. He could not confirm it either.

John felt like he was in hot water over this sea urchin affair. Luckily, one of his volunteers came to his rescue with Sam Hinton's 1972 book, *Seashore Life of Southern California*. There it was, in the book Dr. Lawrenz-Miller had bought for all the volunteers to read, nonetheless. Urchins were reported to drill holes in the steel casings of concrete pilings. John Olguin was proven right. A very relieved John went to Dr. Lawrenz-Miller's office, opened the book and pointed out the passage; case closed. With the leadership positions clearly defined, the volunteers started a development branch for fundraising and public membership called Cabrillo Marine Museum Volunteers.

As for Dr. Josslin, he moved to Seattle, Washington, after being fired. Many years later, he would pay John an impromptu visit. The two men spent the day together, went to the beach and talked. They bridged what had once separated them and John had no hard feelings. By then, John was retired and everything had worked out well. Not only was he quite happy, but his name was also on the building!

While the first attempt to plan and build a new museum had failed, the need for a new facility had not changed, but any new facility would require staff and a budget. In 1978, the City of Los Angeles hired architect Frank Gehry to design the new museum. Gehry would later achieve world acclaim with his breathtaking design of the Guggenheim Museum in Spain, the Disney Concert Hall in Los Angeles and many other projects. Gehry had an entirely different approach than the first architect Bill Lusby. Once contracted by the City of Los Angeles, he called John to make an appointment to meet him at the museum and get John's input. John was delighted and suggested he come any day between 10 a.m. and 1 p.m. to see the museum in full swing with a thousand children visiting. He believed that Gehry should see how the museum really operated.

When Frank Gehry came to see the museum, the tide was out. Countless children were in the tide pools, discussing all the animals in little groups. Then the museum opened up and the kids went through the front door, walked through the exhibits, and then upstairs to see the exhibits on the second floor. Once through the museum, the kids came out the backdoor onto the beach where John and his volunteers had put up tables with material about whales, grunion and more. It was a beautiful day with no wind, relatively flat seas and it was not too hot. Some days on Cabrillo Beach, gray whales can be seen as close as half a mile away on their migration to Baja, California. The day Gehry visited the museum was one of those days. There were hundreds of children on the beach and three boats filled with people off the beach. They could hear the "ooohs" and "aaahs" every time a whale surfaced.

John didn't know what day Frank Gehry would visit, as he had left it open. That day, John was talking to a group of children when he saw a group of people with cameras and notebooks taking pictures of him and the kids. Thinking it was another audit by the Board of Education, he introduced himself and asked if he could help with anything. It turned out to be Frank Gehry and his team. He had been observing the activities that morning and told John that he would design the new museum to fit the programs John had developed. Gehry also worked with Dr. Susanne Lawrenz-Miller, with whom he had visited numerous marine museums and laboratories gathering ideas. One such visit at the Steinhart Aquarium in San Francisco led to the open-tank design, which exposes the pipes and valves and shows visitors how the systems work. It would be Gehry's second building in the L.A. area; the first one was at UCLA.

On October 21, 1981, the "New" Cabrillo Marine Museum had its grand opening in the striking contemporary structure. Described by some as a "basketball court with hormone problems," many others consider it to be one of the finest museums, designed for people rather than exhibits. The museum that started with a few seashells displayed on a table on the beach now resided in a $3-million facility with 500 volunteers, 20 staff members and 275,000 visitors annually. In the same year, the museum won a Special Merit Award from the California Coastal Commission for "embodying the importance of educating the public on the marine environment and for its thoughtful design and arrangements of exhibits." Later in 1995, Gehry was the recipient of the John M. Olguin

Marine Environment Award, honoring his contributions to the overall success of the museum.

With the new museum came new staff and a new budget. Dr. Susanne Lawrenz-Miller headed the administration, worked on the finances, the paperwork and the personnel. While the old museum had operated on an annual budget of $40,000 in its final years, the new museum required $276,000 to operate. John was amazed and could clearly recall the old days when he would struggle to get a hundred dollars from the city. Now he would not have to worry, Dr. Lawrenz-Miller would. John could focus on the programs, deal with the children, the volunteers, and, if he needed anything, he could order it. If he got what he had ordered, great; if not, that was perfectly okay too. He would then buy it with money from the John Olguin Trust Fund.

After the museum moved to its new facilities, the 1932 Mediterranean-style historic bathhouse underwent a $3.5-million restoration and was returned to its former glory. Painted in colors from the 1930s, it now meets current standards for building codes, fire safety and the Americans with Disabilities Act. The building was rededicated on October 2, 2002, on the 70th anniversary of its original opening. Since then, it has been used as a film set for a number of movies, including the 1997 Paramount picture *Face-Off*, starring John Travolta and Nicholas Cage.

Throughout the six years following the 1981 relocation of the museum to its new building, new exhibits opened and unique programs emerged regularly, which were met with great enthusiasm. John even found the time to collaborate with Tom Porterhouse to produce *John Olguin's Guide to Whalewatching*, which featured gray whales, dolphins, sea lions, elephant seals, harbor seals and his long-time friends and supporters, Bill Samaras and Diane McIntyre. In 1987, Marineland of the Pacific, the largest oceanarium in the world when it opened in 1954, closed its doors and left the Cabrillo Marine Museum as the only public aquarium in the greater Los Angeles area. That same year, Dr. Susanne Lawrenz-Miller was appointed museum director when John retired and became director emeritus. Without a doubt, the dreams of John Olguin will forever be housed in the Cabrillo Marine Aquarium.

THE RINGMASTER

John always had a passion for sharing what he knew with others. He had a special gift with people, especially children, whom he always treated with great love and respect. As such, it is fitting that a five-year-old girl would help launch John's career as one of the most wonderful, engaging and entertaining educators of all times. It all began one day in 1949. John was working as a lifeguard on the beach when the little girl came up to him with a cup and what she called a "pollywog" inside. Not being a marine biologist, or even a trained naturalist, John did not know quite what to make of it, but he had a natural curiosity and desire to learn something new whenever the opportunity presented itself. He went to work and quickly discovered that it was a grunion hatchling.

Grunion – Spanish for "grunter" – are little silver-colored fish with the scientific name *Leuresthes sardina*. They are members of the New World Silversides family *Atheriniopsidae*, along with the jacksmelt and topsmelt. Grunion spawn in only two areas in the world: in the northern Gulf of California and along the Pacific Coast from north of California's Point Conception to about Punta Abreojos in Baja California. Grunion live close to shore in water no deeper than sixty feet. Every year between March and August, grunion leave the water at night to spawn on the beach. On four consecutive nights, starting after full and new moons, spawning begins following high tide and continues for several hours.

As a wave breaks on the beach, grunion swim with the wave as far up the slope as possible to ensure both incubation and the safe return of the hatchlings to the sea with the following high tide. The female wiggles her body and excavates into the semi-fluid sand with her tail. She twists her body and digs until she is half-buried in the sand, with her head sticking up. She then deposits her eggs in a clutch about two inches below the surface of the sand. Males curve around each female and release milt (sperm). The milt flows down the female's body until it reaches and fertilizes the eggs. As many as eight males may fertilize the eggs laid by one female. After spawning, the males immediately retreat toward the water while the female twists free and returns with the next wave. The entire event is called the "Grunion Dance." The eggs remain buried in the sand throughout incubation, approximately two weeks. The larvae hatch when the eggs are reached by subsequent high tides.

The natural history of grunion had been described in a paper published in 1927 by Dr. Frances Clark, but John knew nothing about it until he began searching for information about grunion in the library of the Department of Fish and Game. Once he had read Dr. Clark's work, John decided to try to hatch out some grunion. He dug up grunion eggs and put them in a bucket in the storeroom of the museum to see what would happen. They all died. Obviously, that did not work and it would take John several more failed attempts before he finally figured that for the eggs to hatch they had to be kept in damp sand and in a cool place. John was thrilled and realized that hatching out grunion eggs was something nobody else was doing, an opportunity he could not pass up. He began to have everyone who visited the museum hatch out a few grunion in a jar. Soon he would hatch out grunion two nights a week.

At this point in his career, John was still putting in eight hours on the beach and often stayed late to work at the museum. But he loved it. Introducing people to marine life was important to him and, above all, he could share what he had learned with others. Less than a year after the little five-year-old had shown John her first grunion hatchling, John took a group of college kids from Compton Junior College out to the beach for the grunion run. In 1951, the museum offered its first regularly scheduled grunion-run program from March through July. By then, John had figured out the key elements of grunion reproductive biology.

The program included a film of the grunion spawning, which the visitors would later see firsthand on the beach. Then John would distribute small jars containing sand and grunion eggs, which had been gathered from the beach earlier and stored. They would add saltwater, agitate the jar and pinhead-size grunion would pop from their eggs like popcorn. In the early 1960s, John began to line the high-water mark on the beach with candles and beautifully colored flags of sea creatures that his wife Muriel had made, then he would take children, families, tourists and locals to the beach to witness the grunion run.

Several hundred people would attend the spring programs, but in the summer the crowd could easily swell to two thousand per night. On a few occasions, there were between five thousand and ten thousand people on the beach. They would surround John, listen, and watch John perform the "Grunion Dance." John believed that physical participation was essential, so he would start by saying, "Put your hands over your head, dance like a little grunion, dig into the sand, lay your eggs, now wriggle up, wriggle up, go back, go back, go back to the sea. Everyone. Do it! Do it!" These words would become a trademark of John's educational style.

In 1954, shortly after John started to take people out to see grunion, he found out there was there was a short movie on grunion available from the Moody Institute of Science entitled *Fish Out of Water*. However, it was not for sale and John had to go to the public library in Los Angeles to rent it. The next challenge was to find a projector. The museum did not have one, even though John had put in requests annually to the City of Los Angeles for one. All his requests had been turned down, city staff were seemingly indifferent to the San Pedro jewel that was in the making. On the other hand, people in San Pedro supported John in any way they could. A local store, A-1 Photo, or one of the local schools, would loan John a projector, but it was a hassle to pull it all together nevertheless.

This was almost 30 years before the John Olguin Trust Funds was established, so John was still in the game of creative financing for the museum projects. John began talking with some friends about raising the money he needed to purchase a projector for the museum. Eventually two of them, Diana McIntyre and Beverly Whitmore, members of the Sierra Club, started having spaghetti dinner fundraisers for the museum. They would invite their friends over for dinner, charge them a couple of bucks, save the money and eventually give it to John for buying the projector. When a new film came out in 1964 from Academy Films entitled *Fish, Moon and Tides: The Grunion Story*, the museum bought a copy and has been using it ever since. This was just the beginning of what would become a very successful fundraising strategy grounded in the local community, where social responsibility and mutual support appeared to naturally work hand-in-hand to demonstrate that great things can be accomplished five and ten dollars at a time.

In the late 1960s, the people running *National Geographic* decided to do a story on the grunion run. John had been running his grunion program for almost two decades and a UCLA scientist, Boyd Walker, had been studying grunion as the topic of his dissertation. Walker had volunteers on the beaches provide him with data on the grunion runs they were observing along the Southern California coastline from San Diego to Santa Barbara. The team of reporters and photographers sent to California by *National Geographic* was blissfully unaware of either man and went to Malibu instead, where they spent a few weeks trying to catch a glimpse of grunion. Eventually they explained what they were trying to do to the lifeguards. The lifeguards, who knew John but had never heard of Boyd Walker, told them to go to San Pedro and the Cabrillo Marine Museum.

When they called John to ask when the grunion would run, John told them to be at Cabrillo Beach the following Tuesday night at 10:30 p.m. and promised there would be grunion on the beach. They started laughing, but having had no success in Malibu, they agreed to be there Tuesday evening anyway. When Tuesday night came around, the *National Geographic* team and John were standing on Cabrillo Beach. It was 10:30 p.m. Within a couple of minutes, the first grunion showed up, then the next one. They just kept coming. Soon the entire beach was covered with grunion! They started taking photographs and asked John if he could find around a hundred people to include in the shot. John happily obliged. He made a few phone calls and within half an hour, more than a hundred people arrived on the scene.

The team came back the next night for another shoot and John once again made sure that there were about a hundred people around. This time it was a bit more difficult. After all, you can't get the same hundred people two nights in a row and expect them to stay until 1 a.m. John asked some members of his church, the Boy Scouts and others to join them on the beach. They came back a third night and returned one more time about two weeks later. By then, John and his friends were exhausted. The project turned out to be long nights and a lot of work for John, who always had to be back at his post the next morning. It reportedly took 1,500 photos to get the images needed for the *National Geographic* story, which was published in the May 1969 issue.

John had become so enthralled with this little fish that he would ask every visitor to the museum if they wanted to hatch grunion. Once they had, John would return the hatchlings to the sea where they became part of a new generation. One day, it must have been in the mid-1960s, a Japanese gentleman visited the museum, but when John asked him if he had a minute to hatch grunion he realized that his visitor did not speak English. So, John repeated his question in Japanese. The man replied that he would love to, and once he had hatched a few, he was so interested that he asked John to show him where he got the eggs. John took him out to the beach behind the museum, and together they dug up some grunion eggs. John explained to him that he could keep the eggs for up to six weeks, and gave him some to take back to Japan.

As it turned out, the visitor was Dr. Yata Hameda, the director of the Yokosuka Aquarium in Japan at the time. The two men stayed in touch and John would send him more grunion eggs from time to time. Then John received a letter from the office of the Emperor of Japan asking if he could send more grunion eggs. John found out that Dr. Yata Hameda had shared the grunion-hatching experience with Emperor Hirohito, who was a marine biologist and reportedly very interested and thrilled to learn about grunion. John was delighted to comply with the request and was later told that the Emperor had raised many of the grunion that he hatched.

After many batches of grunion over a three-year period, Dr. Hameda asked John if there was anything he could do in return. John did not have to think long. He had wanted to create an exhibit with the smallest crab – the pea crab, which is found in the gaper clam at Cabrillo Beach – placed next to the largest crab – the Japanese spider crab – for some time.

John asked, if it was not too much trouble, to please send him a specimen of a Japanese spider crab. About a year later, John got a call from the docks at the L.A. Harbor telling him that there was a crate from Japan with his name on it. John brought the crate back to the museum and when he opened it, he found a beautiful Japanese spider crab specimen.

John turned the Japanese spider crab into an exhibit, which proved to be very popular with visitors. In those days, the museum was still in the old bathhouse. If one entered through the front door of the museum and walked straight through to the back, there was a long, skinny room, where the Japanese spider crab stood in the left corner. It towered 6 feet tall, with its legs hanging down to touch the ground, and the pea crab was right next to it. It was a wonderful exhibit, but eventually the specimen broke apart and quietly disappeared.

Over the years, John collaborated with Professor Jules Crane from Cerritos College in Norwalk on several research projects investigating grunion behavior. They discovered that the male behavior of curling around female grunion when releasing their sperm, could be duplicated if they replaced the female grunion with a wiggling stick. Crane published the results in a paper entitled "The response of male grunion to a wiggling stick." John and Jules also found out that grunion were schooling in huge numbers while waiting to come ashore.

The single act of a curious toddler asking a lifeguard about a tiny little creature she had found had a most amazing outcome, including the discovery of new knowledge about the world in which we live. John's grunion program was among the most successful education programs ever. By the time he retired in 1987, he had introduced more than two million people, mostly children, to grunion. For many of those who met John at one of the nightly grunion events or who hatched some grunion in a jar at the museum, it created lasting memories that they would carry on into their lives and, in some cases, to faraway places around the world.

When John and Muriel travelled to the Fiji Islands, they took a plane from Los Angeles to the main island where they changed to a small plane that would fly them to one of the smaller outer islands. Once there, it took them another eighty-five mile bus ride and a short distance on an ox cart to finally reach their destination: a truly isolated resort. The very first person they met looked at them and said, "Aren't you the guy from California who raises them guppies?" Indeed, as it turned out, she had come to the museum in Grade 4 and had hatched out some grunion in a jar with John.

On another vacation, John and Muriel travelled to Kenya, by train. Sitting across the aisle, four women in their fifties or sixties were having dinner when the one closest to the window leaned over the sandwich and fruit in her friend's lap and asked, "Are you still giving grunion eggs to teachers?" John was amazed, but quickly said, "You bet I am," wondering how she knew. She, too, had been at the Cabrillo Marine Museum hatching out grunion with John. At the end of her story, she added, "It is the closest thing I ever saw to a miracle!"

The grunion program was a fantastic success that inspired John to take on another challenge: tide pools. The tide pools were a favorite of many people who visited the museum, as everyone could get a close look at local marine life. However, people were taking so many animals out of the tide pools, that John began to fear that soon there would be no life left. John felt that it was like people were eating the museum's displays! He felt the tide pools needed protection, so he asked his supervisors at the Department of Recreation and Parks to give him permission to apply to the State of California to create a Cabrillo Marine Museum Marine Life Refuge. After his request was denied for the fifth straight year, he finally went to question his supervisors. They explained to him that they felt he did not have the time to handle another project and, besides, they did not see much program value in just taking a few hundred kids out to see tide pools. John knew that he had to change his approach. The next time he gave a speech to the Sierra Club, he told them that he needed people to help him run his tide pool program, take children out, keep track of how many attended, and so on.

Right away, three women responded: Diana McIntyre, Beverly Whitmore and Barbara Reznick. He used other speaking engagements to solicit additional volunteers and ended up with a group of ten women whom he put through a training course teaching them how to operate the overall program: how to identify tide pool animals, the basics of natural history, and how to interact with the public, especially with children. In the beginning, they would offer tide pool walks at night using flashlights, but after many people slipped and cut themselves on the barnacles and rocks, tide pool walks were offered only during daylight hours. John and his volunteers kept track of everything. Every time a group went to the tide pool, they marked it in the calendar. When they advertised in the schools and got bookings, they marked it down. They took photographs and, at the end of the year, it turned out they had taken thirty thousand children to the tide pools.

When John sent in his sixth request to the Department of Recreation and Parks, he finally got the response he had been waiting for. In 1968, his supervisors sent him to Sacramento and John went before Republican California State Senator H.L. "Bill" Richardson, who chaired the Senate's Natural Resources Committee. Coincidentally, Corona del Mar had already submitted a proposal seeking protection for tide pools in their city. John attached his request to the Corona del Mar proposal and both achieved designation as a State Marine Life Refuge in 1969, with the Point Fermin Marine Life Refuge extending from Cabrillo Beach to the Point Fermin Lighthouse. Except for fishing, the removal of any species was now prohibited.

The inauguration ceremony for the refuge took place in December 1969 at the museum. The ribbon was a piece of seaweed and they used a sawfish bill to cut it. And with that, the Point Fermin Marine Life Refuge was open to the public. The Army band played, there was a parade around the bathhouse, including colorful banners made by Muriel, and then William Fredrickson, General Manager of Recreation and Parks and State Senator Richardson addressed the crowd from a man-made crowsnest. The Reverend Richard Rubottom did the invocation, which read:

Dear God, we thank you for creating this world with all its beauty.

Thank you for the sound of the surf, the cry of the gulls, the smell of the ocean air; the feel of the rocks, the touch of the sand, the sight of the cliff, beach, wave and sky.

Mostly, thank you for these tide pools … these little schools of sea life where we may stoop and learn.

And thank you for the hearts and hands, which brought about this day. Because they care, we will share the marvels of this place.

Help us always to wonder, but not to waste; to study, but not to spoil; to dedicate, but not destroy.

John asked for signs to be installed to inform the public of the new designation, but was told that there was no money for that. He ordered twelve metal signs from the city's sign shop and mounted them on poles. Unfortunately, the signs were stolen within a few days, poles and all. John actively sought a remedy. First, he took a telephone pole and installed it about eight feet into the ground. Now he had only to replace the sign itself. John had 365 signs silkscreened with the help of his wife Muriel. He then began to put some signs high up on the telephone poles with a stapler. He would check the signs every day, replacing any stolen in the night. One day John noticed that someone had started a fire at the base of the telephone pole, trying to burn it down. John figured it would take many nights in a row before the telephone pole would burn down. Eventually, the signs stayed up for longer and longer periods.

Today, the grunion and tide pool programs at the Cabrillo Marine Aquarium are among the most successful educational programs ever conceived in the United States. John, who developed the programs in collaboration with his volunteers, made sure that they were informative but also fun, exciting and inspiring. For John, teaching was always about learning and then sharing the knowledge with others so everyone would benefit, which made John possibly one of the greatest educators of all time. He always had a unique way with people, especially children, and the rare talent of teaching others and always encouraging them to find their own ways of captivating the minds of their respective audience.

Volunteers were an essential part of John's grand plan. Helen Andersen was among those volunteers who developed a life-long relationship with the museum. Like John, Andersen was born and raised in San Pedro. She went to White Point Elementary, then attended Dana Junior High and San Pedro High, from which she graduated in 1973. Helen's first memory of John dates back to when she was a Girl Scout, perhaps 8 years old. She knew him, as many kids did, because they would see John every single day, wearing a suit, a white shirt and a tie, riding his bicycle to work. It did not have any gears and no one but John knew whether or not the brakes were working. Always with his brown-paper-bag lunch in one hand on the handlebars, John would ride down the hill to work at the museum. All the kids walking up the hill to attend elementary school would see him, and he would wave and say, "Hello," or "Good morning, kids!"

Andersen often visited the museum because she enjoyed being there. One summer her sister worked at Sam's Café, a one-room snack bar attached to the bathhouse. Helen would go with her sister and hang out around the museum. Helen's favorite place was the ichthyology hall, in a dark corner called the "Sea Cave." After she graduated from junior high school in 1970, Andersen started volunteering and working at the museum. It was the first time that John had received some money from the city to hire kids during the summer. It was fairly easy to find boys to participate in the program, but with girls it was a little bit more difficult. John asked Andersen's mother, who was a Girl Scout leader and neighborhood chairman, for help. She gladly agreed and compiled a list of possible candidates for the summer jobs at the museum, which included her daughter of course.

Once the selection process was complete, everyone had to go to downtown Los Angeles, twenty-five miles away, and fill out an application to be hired by the city. It was an interesting experience for these youngsters, because it was probably the only time they would be confronted with the wild years of the McCarthy era. As Helen remembered it, as part of their applications, they had to sign a sworn statement that they never had been, were not then, and would never be, a communist.

The city had approved ten positions of forty hours per week, but John, always having his own ideas, wanted twenty kids working twenty hours per week. The city agreed and in this first year of the program, John made things up as he went. For nine months of the year, John and a small staff, plus the volunteers, did the work at the museum. During the summer, high school students would replace the adult volunteers, all of these young people coming from the museum's training program. The high school students worked their twenty hours per week and usually volunteered many more hours as well. Despite the fact that they were being paid, they were still essentially considered – and usually called – volunteers.

The volunteers gave tours at the museum in the bathhouse, but to accommodate the many visitors coming to the museum, John devised "stations" on topics like tide pools, whales and grunion. The stations system worked like a well-oiled machine. On any given day, there were at least several hundred children coming through the museum. Two stations were in different places in the tide pools and one was on the beach where somebody was sitting with a box full of skeletons of different animals, shells or crabs – marine relics. A number of volunteers, including Andersen, loved to be at the whale watching station. They would be on the beach with a portable microphone and loudspeaker, which they used to talk about whales and to imitate their sounds. And when they saw a whale swim by, they would talk about what they saw and share it with everyone.

As they went from one station to the next, the volunteers would demonstrate, explain and try to engage everyone. There was always more to talk about than time to talk about it. John would keep the children moving along so they were able to see every station in time. Each station had a flag so, once the signal was sounded, the volunteers would send their groups on their way: "Go to the red flag over there." Some of the children had never seen anything like this. The system worked so smoothly that it never felt chaotic or confusing. Occasionally there were children who were hesitant at first, but after a while they would usually become engaged and think it was great.

Most of the student summer staff worked forty hours per week, but were only paid for twenty hours. The hourly wage was decent, though, as minimum wage was $1.65 per hour and they were paid $1.89 per hour. John was very much aware that the students were putting in a lot more time than they were paid for. In fact, a lot of them would even come down on the weekends when they were not being paid at all. Most just enjoyed being there and John always managed to organize special events to thank everyone. He took them to the

San Diego Zoo, Sea World and lectures at the Palos Verdes or Santa Monica Library. John would either load everyone onto the back of his pickup truck or arrange for a bus. They all had a great time and nobody ever got hurt. It was a very stimulating environment for the students and volunteers

Helen worked with John on the very first Whale Fiesta in 1972 and was among the individuals who traveled down to Scammon's Lagoon to observe gray whales. She saved all of her money from working in the summer and worked another job at the theatre too. For a youngster who was making less than two dollars per hour, the cost of four hundred dollars was a lot of money. Still, she managed to save enough. Before she left, her parents bought her some film and Andersen went on the fun-filled and exciting trip.

Helen spent all of her summers at the museum until she graduated from high school. Then life brought new challenges and opportunities, so she could no longer volunteer. After John retired in 1987, Helen helped John with record-keeping and accounting. She would make sure that he was reimbursed for expenses and that any remaining money went to the particular cause he was promoting. If John received money for giving lectures, Helen made sure those funds were directed to his chosen charitable organizations. John was not good at record-keeping, so Helen's work was critical in making sure that if the IRS ever did knock on John's door, appropriate records would be available.

John would always say, "Once a lifeguard, always a lifeguard." Many volunteers had a similar motto: "Once a volunteer, always a volunteer." That was certainly true for Andersen. Unlike the others, she would jokingly say that she was not one of John's volunteers, but one of his victims. Then they would laugh together.

While John always said that working with students and volunteers was among the best experiences in his life, there were situations where fun and joy turned into the worst forms of anxiety. When John was with students, he would talk about many things, including his rowing adventures. On one of these occasions, some high school volunteers asked if they could try rowing for themselves. John could not get his hands on enough rowboats, but promised to meet whomever was interested on the beach on a Saturday, his day off, and show them how to paddle a canoe.

About twenty-four students showed up that Saturday. After John demonstrated how to paddle and maneuver the canoe, he teamed them up two at a time and asked them to paddle out to the quarter-mile buoy, then turn around and come back. Everyone had one turn. John insisted they put on the life preservers, but the youngsters gave him a hard time. In the middle of the struggle to get them to comply with his basic safety instructions, John was called to the phone at the museum. He knew that he should not leave his class alone, but the lifeguards were on duty. The sea was also calm, so John felt it was safe to quickly go and answer the phone. What happened next would haunt John for a very long time.

When he came back, everybody was gone. John collected the canoes and the other gear and put it back. At about six o'clock that night, John received a phone call from a concerned mother, telling him that her son, Junior, a boy in his teens, had not come home from the canoe class that morning. They asked John if he knew where Junior was. John responded, "I did not see him. He did not come to the class. But let me make a few phone calls and I'll call you back." John went back to the beach to see if there were any clothes, but found nothing. He started to make phone calls and soon learned that Junior had indeed come to the beach just when John had left to take the phone call. Junior got into a canoe and the last time any of the other kids had seen him was when he was swimming out in the ocean beside a canoe. John had told the entire group not to swim because it is very hard to stay close to the canoe, but Junior had not been there for the instructions.

John was getting nervous. He did not think Junior had drowned because there were no clothes on the beach waiting for their rightful owner to return. But then again, he could not be sure. John found himself in the one situation that he had always tried to guard against since he started working as a lifeguard on Cabrillo Beach. He called Junior's mother back to tell her what he knew; both thought Junior would come home later that night.

The next morning Junior's mother came to the museum. Her son still had not returned. Together they looked all over but could not find any clues. The canoe had been put back on the beach. It did not make sense. If Junior dove off the canoe to take a swim, how did the canoe get back on the beach? There were many questions but no answers. John was both worried and not worried: worried since Junior was still missing, but not worried since there was no evidence of trouble. He felt physically sick when he thought about Junior. No matter how much good you do with children, if one drowns everything you have done in your whole life goes down the drain. Some people may think you can carry on, but John felt differently. He was responsible for those lives; if he lost one, then everything he had done would be nullified.

An entire week passed and on the following Monday, late in the afternoon, Junior walked into the museum. At first, John was not sure whether he should slug him or hug him.

He asked Junior to sit down and tell him what had happened and where he had been. As it turned out, Junior had been late for the canoe class because he did not have any money and had had to walk. Once he got to the beach, all the kids were leaving and John was on the phone, so Junior appropriated a canoe, paddled out, jumped into the water to swim and then brought the canoe back to the beach. With nobody there, he walked up the hill to catch a bus home. He tried to bum a dime for the bus ride, but when he couldn't, he decided to hitchhike back home. Finally, a truck stopped and Junior told the driver that he lived at the other end of town in Barton Hill. The driver's response was that he was going to Oregon and he asked if Junior wanted to come along. And so he did. He did not call his mother because she would not have liked his ambitious plan. Once in Oregon, Junior almost immediately started to hitchhike back to San Pedro, which took him all week. He did not even think of calling home.

John could not believe his ears: an entire week of agony because Junior had gone on an impromptu road trip! Although John was relieved that Junior was alive and well, he did not want to see the young man ever again. John relearned the importance of priorities: you do not leave children or young people alone, ever. This is more important than taking a phone call or anything else. With no lives lost, John continued to teach youngsters how to canoe and they continued to give him a hard time about putting on life preservers.

Despite some anxiety-filled events, John spoke most often of the times that were memorable for their joy or wonder. On one occasion, for instance, John was teaching canoeing when a woman approached him and asked if she and her son could take a paddle. John's impulse was to say, "Lady, would you get lost? I am having trouble with the high school kids." Instead, he told her that he was rather busy, but if she wanted to wait around until he was finished with the students, he would be glad to let her take a ride, as long as they both put on life preservers. That was John, always ready to help someone. After the high school kids had left, John called the woman and the little 12-year-old boy over. They put on their life preservers and got into the canoe. John instructed them to go out to the buoy, stay around it so he could see them, and then come back. They went out for about half an hour and then came back to the beach. Upon their return, the young boy had a huge grin that never left his face. After thanking John, they went on their way.

Two weeks later, John got a letter from the head of Indian Affairs in Arizona, who also happened to be a psychologist treating that same 12-year-old boy. The letter detailed how the boy had never spoken a word in his life: not to his mother, not to his father, not to anybody. The psychologist had convinced the child's parents to take the boy to California, to Disneyland, in the hope that he would begin to speak. They took him to Disneyland and on all its wonderful rides, but nothing fazed him and he never said anything. Sorry, Mickey! Then they went to Catalina Island on the glass-bottom boat tour, and to another amusement park, but nothing made him speak. His parents began to think that nothing would work.

Then, on the last day of their trip, they came to Cabrillo Beach. When they saw the canoes on the beach, they told the boy that John was an Indian and that the canoes were Indian canoes. They continued to explain to the boy that his ancestors had crafted the canoes and used them long before white men ever got to America. Once actually paddling in the canoe, the boy became so excited that he uttered his first words. And he kept talking long after they had left the beach.

The letter came with a silver Indian lapel pin for John, as a token of gratitude for the one person who had made a difference in the life of that little boy. For John, this was literally one of those "chicken soup for the soul" stories.

TRAILBLAZER

*A*mong the many roles that John Olguin played throughout his life, the significance of his contributions to the environmental movement in general, and ecotourism in particular, are often overlooked. John was so far ahead of his time, decades before the words "environmental" and "ecotourism" ever appeared in Webster's Dictionary, that his pioneering contributions must not be ignored. John's love for people in general, the beauty of the world around him, nature, and, perhaps mostly, the ocean and its inhabitants, is what combined to stir his soul and generate a passion that few people ever find in their lives. He didn't just glom onto a popular social or political movement, he *was* the movement. John did not go out and focus on seeking credit of his actions for personal gain, he worked hard just to make sure his sphere of influence and his little world were a better place to live and learn. No matter where John worked or spent his time, and no matter where his curiosity carried him, he made sure he took care of his surroundings and left them better than he found them.

With the Cabrillo Whalewatch program, John gave life to an entirely new industry based on the most benign utilization of natural resources: watching whales. Yet, more than that, the new industry was about learning how whales play an important role in our ecosystem and how they are threatened worldwide.

John remembered seeing whales back in 1938 when he and his friends would play volleyball on Cabrillo Beach. Whale sightings along the shore were frequently reported in local newspapers and date back as far as 1892. Unlike today, whales were not a topic studied in school in the 1930s and 1940s, and there were no grassroots movements aiming to "save" the whales. Quite the opposite! Whaling had been part of San Pedro's history for a very long time. Historical records show that a whaling station operated on Deadman's Island in the 1860s and that twenty-five whales were taken in the 1862 season. It is unclear when the whaling station was established and how many whaleboats might have operated out of San Pedro, however, the California Whaling Company was still operating on Terminal Island in 1937. The company had a boat that would sail north to the Farallon Islands off San Francisco and south to Mexico. It would bring dead whales back to San Pedro for processing.

The company was owned and operated by Edward Perry, who also happened to be a lifeguard known to get up at three o'clock every morning and row five miles to stay in shape. When Captain Perry needed deckhands, he would go to *Shanghai Red's,* a famous bar on Beacon Street in San Pedro and pay the bartender to slip a "mickey," a drug, into a man's drink. Then he would carry the semi-conscious "volunteer" to his boat. The next day the man would wake up as a whaler, shanghaied into service. Eventually, the gray whale was afforded international and federal protection through the International Whaling Commission, the Endangered Species Conservation Act of 1969 and the Marine Mammal Protection Act of 1972. Whaling in the United States officially ended on January 1, 1972.

John Olguin (kneeling and dressed in black), his wife Muriel (kneeling and dressed in white) and Muriel's father Clarence Groat (standing on the far right wearing a hat) during the first night of the grunion phenomenon that John started by inviting the public to watch the grunion run on Cabrillo Beach. 1950. Photo Courtesy Cabrillo Marine Museum/Cabrillo Marine Aquarium

John Olguin was an expert at drawing crowds to the beach for his tales about the ocean and its creatures. Here, he is showing a movie about the life history of the unusual grunion fish. Large groups of people sat on carpet spread over the sidewalk of the Cabrillo Marine Museum to watch the film on a white sheet hanging above the entrance. After seeing the movie and braving the cold and damp weather, people walked around the bathhouse to witness the grunion run on outer Cabrillo Beach. Photo Courtesy Cabrillo Marine Museum/Cabrillo Marine Aquarium

John Olguin holding a jar hatching grunions. Photo Courtesy Cabrillo Marine Museum/Cabrillo Marine Aquarium

John Olguin teaching a group of children at the newly created Point Fermin Marine Life Refuge Photo Courtesy Cabrillo Marine Museum/ Cabrillo Marine Aquarium

The 1976 Cabrillo Whalewatch Class. Relaxing in the foreground, John Olguin left, Bill Samaras, right) Photo Courtesy Alisa Schulman-Janiger Private Archive

In 1978 John took his first group to Baja California to see gray whales in their wintering grounds. Photo Courtesy B. Brunnick Private Archives

John Olguin petting a gray whale in Baja California, Mexico.
Photo Courtesy John Olguin Private Archive

Whale Fiesta 1977. Photo Courtesy Cabrillo Marine Museum/Cabrillo Marine Aquarium

John Olguin engaging a group of children and adults in one of his famous "Do it! Do it!" experiences. Photo Courtesy Cabrillo Marine Museum/Cabrillo Marine Aquarium. Late 1970s.

The Whale Fiesta ended with a feast of whale-looking watermelons for everyone.
Photo Courtesy Cabrillo Marine Museum/Cabrillo Marine Aquarium

The Whale Fiesta of 1987, like many of the celebrations, drew children and adults alike to play in the sand and help create life-size versions of whales. Photo Courtesy Alisa Schulman-Janiger Private Archive

Bill Samaras, John Heyning and Dave Janiger (left to right) after a first inspection of the stranded blue whale. 1980. Photo Courtesy Alisa Schulman-Janiger Private Archive

Blue whale stranded on Cabrillo Beach in 1980.
Photo Courtesy Harzen/Brunnick Private Archive

Gray whale fossil dig at the base of the 110 freeway in San Pedro. The fossil was unearthed by Bill Samaras and his students as an outdoor classroom school project. 1971. Photo by Harold Ericsson

Gray whale fossil. One can clearly discern the large skull (foreground), the ribs and vertebrae. 1971. Photo by Harold Ericsson

Back in the 1930s, however, people did not know much about whales and John was no exception. In fact, he later admitted he was not even interested in reading about them. All that began to change in the early 1960s. John had noticed that whenever people saw gray whales passing by, they would stop what they were doing, point their arms, hands and fingers in whichever direction they saw these giants of the sea, and watch them for as long as they were visible from the beach. People were seemingly mesmerized by the small glimpses they had of the magnificent mammals.

John began to alert visitors to the museum whenever whales passed by Cabrillo Beach. Because he spent so much time inside the museum, John enlisted the help of the other lifeguards to alert him at the museum whenever they saw a whale. He, or one of his volunteers, would blow a horn and everyone would know a whale was passing by. If any children were in the museum at the time, John would take them upstairs, wave to the lifeguard so he would point to the last place the whale had come up, and then would point it out to the kids. The children got very excited every time they were able to see a whale in front of Cabrillo Beach. John knew they would be even more excited if they could get closer to a whale, which would mean taking them out to sea in a boat.

It is not quite clear when the whale watching industry started, but records indicate that the first boat to take people out to see whales up close sailed out of Belmont Shore in Long Beach in 1928; these excursions were called "whale hunts." In the early 1930s, Dr. Theodore Walker followed suit and took groups out a few times a year. It took thirty years before whale watching began to develop into what is today – a multi-billion-dollar industry.

In the early 1960s, whale watching boats would leave from Norm's Landing, now called Ports O' Call Village. Mac McClintock, who ran the Pierpoint Landing in Long Beach, hired Jim Roudy to captain his boat, the *Liberty*, and take people out to see whales. The trips ran on a set schedule and were advertised to the public. Over the years, they grew increasingly popular and, by 1968, John realized that whale watching could become a great teaching tool for the museum. While John had not gone out to watch whales with Jim Roudy, one of his young volunteers named Robert Brownell had. Brownell would become the first whale watcher of the museum, and became the naturalist aboard the *Liberty*. He would later pursue a career in marine mammalogy, receive his PhD, and become the marine mammal division chief at the Southwest Fisheries Science Center in June 1993.

Around this time, John came across an article in the *Los Angeles Times* about Phil Grignon, a high school teacher at Dana Point who had taught a biology class about whales. He had then gone to the Rotary and the Lions Club and asked their members to sponsor his kids to go whale watching on the *Fury II* for one dollar each. Everyone thought it was a great idea, and so did John when he read about it. He asked one of his volunteers to go to Dana Point and find out how Grignon had put it together. Phil's insights and experience proved very helpful to John's whale watching program.

John knew very little about whales back then, but once something caught John's interest, lack of knowledge was not an obstacle. On the contrary, it motivated John to find out everything he could, memorize it and then share it with everyone. John quickly learned that every fall gray whales migrate from cold Arctic waters to the warm and shallow lagoons of Baja California, Mexico. There, the females give birth to their young and mate. Once the calves have grown strong enough for the long return journey north, small groups of whales begin to leave the lagoons. On their journey, they come close to the coastline of Southern California and can easily be spotted.

Together with his fellow lifeguards, John began to pay more attention to detail when they saw whales swimming by. They soon realized that the whales would come close to shore until they reached a particular red buoy right off the point and then they would angle out. As it turned out, the whales moved from point to point on their way south to Mexico and then back to the Arctic; on both passages, they came very close to Dana Point. For John, there was no question, there was no better place than right there in San Pedro for whale watching. He wanted children to go out, see whales close up and learn about them as well.

Bill Samaras, John's close friend who taught at Carson High School, decided to do a test run and took his marine biology class on a whale watching trip. His students paid for part of the cost, then ditched school and were very happy to be on the high seas. John and Bill were glad to have the kids so excited, because the captains had serious reservations about taking out children and it sure wouldn't have been fun if students had gotten seasick!

John knew that he had to figure out how to raise the money himself if his brand of educational whale watching was going to succeed, so he developed the idea of taking children out to watch whales and then using the revenues for a high school whale-naturalist program. First, he needed to convince his supervisor, Bill Frederickson, at the Department of Recreation and Parks. John told Bill about how excited all the children were when they had the chance to see a whale in front of Cabrillo Beach. "Wouldn't it be wonderful if they could be next to a whale instead of seeing them a mile or two away," he asked. Without any hesitation, John declared that he wanted to take children out onto the open waters.

Not surprisingly, Frederickson was less enthusiastic about the whole idea. He immediately thought of liability issues and the possibility of needing to get the approval of the Board of Education. John was prepared for these administrative arguments, though. He countered that all boats had insurance up to $8-million, and since the Board of Education did not object to using the boat to go to Catalina Island, there was no need to get them involved. John kept pressing, pointing out that he wanted to use the revenues from whale watching for his volunteers. After all, he did not have any funds to work with since the museum did not even have a budget at the time. Frederickson acknowledged these facts, but also pointed out that all monies raised during working hours would have to be turned over to general funds. There was no guarantee that John or the volunteers would see any of the money. John was disappointed one more time, but disappointment had always been a motivating force for him. If the city would not help him, he would find another way.

It took John the remainder of the winter of 1968 and the following summer to develop an alternative strategy. As part of his new plan, John decided to join the American Cetacean Society (ACS) and become its president so that he could organize some whale watching trips through an organization other than the museum. In 1967, Bemi DeBus had started ACS together with Clark Cameron to stop whaling. By 1969, ACS still held its meetings at the Santa Monica Yacht Club and the club's members would often go out to look for whales on weekends. In order to initiate the process of getting the museum's high school student volunteers involved with whales, John took about forty of them to one of the organization's Sunday meetings. The students ended up surrounded by adults who were drinking cocktails, so John suggested that they move the meeting to the Santa Monica Library, which they did. However, now the problem was that they had to leave when the library closed at 9 p.m., whether they had finished their meeting or not. Upon John's suggestion, ACS moved its headquarters to San Pedro, where they could meet at the museum for as long as they wanted. John now had his alternative strategy right in his own backyard.

Yet before John could launch the whale watching program, there was still more work to be done. John did not know anything about children on boats. As always, if he did not know something, he knew someone who did. John went to Gene Gregson, the owner of the San Pedro Sportfishing. He had been on the *Liberty II* and was interested in participating in the whale watching program. John was proposing sending one- to two-hundred schoolchildren out on his boats as long as he did not charge more than one dollar per student. Gene could keep ninety cents of every dollar, and John would get a dime. Gregson was not enthusiastic, as one dollar per child did not seem enough to make a living. Then again, the boat was just sitting around during the winter months. Finally, Gregson agreed. They were about to learn how to handle kids on the boat: how to ensure the kids wouldn't run around, climb on anything or throw up into the wind.

The first children boarded one of their boats in 1969. That first year was full of excitement because everything was new and they saw whales every time they went out. All around the boat, they would see whales surfacing to breathe, breaching, raising their heads above the water as if they were scanning their surroundings, and diving. An almost indescribable joy and enthusiasm abounded with each new occurrence. Seeing dolphins while searching for whales was also thrilling. They quickly learned that if they could see a group of birds circling above the water, they would often find dolphins nearby. Birds often take advantage of the dolphins feeding beneath them, on squid, for instance. Of course, it is much easier to spot birds two miles away in the sky than a small dorsal fin at the surface of a moving ocean.

A year after their first trip, John's new whale fans were going out for the entire season of January through March. It was a steep learning curve for everyone. By 1971, nearly all major problems were solved and the program was about to expand with lightening speed. What had seemed impossible just a couple of years earlier was about to happen. As it would turn out, the Cabrillo Whalewatch program (Whalewatch) would become one of the most successful educational programs of any museum in the country, reaching more than one million people and turning a great number of youngsters into world-renowned scientists.

From the moment that John began to fill Gene Gregson's *Liberty II* regularly, more and more captains from Catalina Terminal and 22nd Street Landing wanted to get involved with the Whalewatch program. John's rules were very simple. He would work with anyone as long as they would give 10 per cent of the proceeds to the museum, were available seven days per week, and would allow John's whale naturalists to go along. John never signed any contracts, because for him, a handshake was good enough. Most captains kept their word, but a few did not. John had experienced the same issues as a newspaper-delivery boy; he knew that it was just part of doing business.

John worked with still others along the coast to set up whale watching trips from their local marinas and landings, such as in Long Beach, Redondo Beach and Oceanside. These trips were organized through the museum, but the profits were shared with ACS, with the exception of any trips organized from San Pedro, whose profits went to the museum and the City of Los Angeles as required. With John at the helm of ACS as president, he was able to organize the trips as joint ventures; some of the funds could thus be redirected through the ACS to benefit the students.

With so much going on, John needed help. He found it in Charlene Arnold, a city employee who worked at the museum twenty hours per week. The problem was that John needed someone five days per week during whale watching season, which back then ran from January through April. They created a new arrangement where John would let her take the summer off so she could work forty hours per week when John needed her most. Of course, both John and Charlene knew this was not sanctioned by the City, but they were both happy with the arrangement. John was always prepared to bend the rules if he felt it would benefit the museum.

With more boats getting involved, John knew he had to produce naturalists who could go on the boats and educate the whale watchers. It was the birth of his famous Tuesday-night Whalewatch classes. Classes would start in October and last from 7 p.m. to 10 p.m. In the first year, about eighty high school students attended. In the following years, up to two-hundred students would gather once a week to learn how to communicate with different age groups and the basics about whales, dolphins and the oceans. By the end of the year, everyone was ready to hit the decks of the whale watching fleet. Within the next few years, the volume of people, the intensity of the training and the level of enthusiasm grew tenfold. At one point, applicants even had to be turned away from the program, because it was impossible to accommodate everyone interested in becoming a volunteer.

Until 1972, Whalewatch trips started the first week of January because John wanted to make sure that there were whales around. He did not want anyone to go home disappointed. In order to increase the chances of finding the whales in the vast ocean, even close to shore, John asked his brother-in-law, Dr. Richard Smith, an orthopedic surgeon who owned an airplane, to take his son John out to find whales. They did not have a walkie-talkie or a two-way radio, so Richard would fly out in search of whales and everyone on the boat would look for his airplane. Once Richard found one or more whales, he would circle above them until the boat got there.

The programs continued to develop and expand. One day, John got a phone call from some people visiting from Iowa who wanted to go out and see some whales. It was only December, so John told them they did not do any Whalewatch trips at that time of year because most gray whales pass by later. John figured that he had better do some homework and start looking for solid information on earlier whale movements. John then discovered that gray whales could be seen passing by as early as October. First, perhaps just one a day; a few weeks later maybe two; and then the numbers climbed to about eight whales per day. John concluded that there likely would be sufficient numbers in late December, so from 1973 onward the Whalewatch season kicked off on December 26 and lasted until April. That same year, John told the Board of Education that the museum was offering educational whale watching experiences. If a school sent at least one hundred children to participate, the museum and ACS would send a college student to the school to show movies and slides, and share educational material prior to the trip.

The museum's Whalewatch program was such a great success that more and more captains, and eventually Catalina Cruises, wanted to get into the game. The challenge was that many captains had no training and did not know much, if anything, about whales and their behaviors. John felt it was important to advertise to everyone that the naturalists from the museum were properly trained and worked together with the captains. Starting in 1973, every boat going out under the museum's charter with one of its volunteers aboard flew a yellow flag. Eventually, Catalina Cruises would turn into a long-time partner, providing the first trip of the season free of charge and giving John a discount every time he wanted to charter a boat. John Olguin was the ultimate wheeler and dealer when it came to his passion for the ocean, the whales, the kids, the grunion – and, well, you name it.

The second challenge with which John had to contend was the sad fact that many of the captains did not want to share the profits with competing boats working with the same program. Everyone wanted to have a monopoly. John had to explain to them repeatedly that the sole purpose of the museum's Whalewatch program was to take children out to see whales and to educate them and the public. If they made money in the process, great, but the program was not there to support boat owners or captains. Boat captains can be a tough crowd, though, so it did not take long before reports started to surface complaining about bad behavior, such as one boat crossing in front of another to get into a better position to see the whales.

To make matters even more complicated, the volunteers who represented the museum aboard these vessels were at risk of being dragged into these conflicts. John realized that if they did not police themselves, the Fish and Game Commission and the National Marine Fisheries Service (NMFS) might come down on everyone with rules and regulations that nobody wanted. So, he intensified his efforts to educate the different captains. If he received a complaint, he immediately followed up and discussed it with the involved captains or boat owners.

It only took a few years before Jim Lecky, head of the National Marine Fisheries Service (NMFS), told John that it was time to develop some guidelines for whalewatching and asked him to prepare a draft version. NMFS would review and approve the guidelines, and then print and distribute the flyers. John did not hesitate. In his eyes, it was an opportunity to educate more people. Once the guidelines were written and approved, John's idea was to visit every landing, yacht club and marina with his volunteers for an entire whale migration season and talk to every boat owner or captain who would listen. Jim Lecky loved John's idea.

John and his buddy Bill Samaras began to develop the first whale watching guidelines. With nothing for comparison, they just asked themselves what was sensible. For instance, they thought that it seemed sensible to stay one thousand feet above a whale if you were in an airplane, and one hundred yards away if you were in a boat. If a whale came toward the boat, it seemed sensible that the motor be shut off until the whale had passed. It was okay to get behind a whale, but not to directly approach a whale.

After reviewing every scenario and drafting all potential guidelines, John and Bill asked other folks from the museum, the board of directors of ACS, and anyone else they thought was knowledgeable, to review their draft. After making some modifications, they delivered the document to Jim Lecky. NMFS printed thousands of copies and, as promised, John and his army of volunteers distributed them to all of the yacht clubs, landings, sport-fishing operators, whalewatching boats, and even to individuals who were launching their boats. Many of those first whale watching guidelines are still in place today.

A couple of years into his Whalewatch program, John took a hundred Girl Scouts out on a trip. The leaders had made up patches that read "Whale Watch," and the girls sold them for fifty-five cents. Once all the Girl Scouts had one, they started to sell them to the public. John loved it. The Girl Scouts had paid fifty-five cents and sold them to the girls for fifty-five cents. At the end of that trip, they had a couple hundred left and John bought them for fifty-five cents each. Then he turned around and sold them for one dollar apiece. John soon asked Muriel to design a patch for Cabrillo Whalewatch and, starting in the mid-1970s, a new patch was issued every year. They always sold a fair amount, as the naturalists were eager to put them on their red jackets that identified them as members of John's Whalewatch program. Undoubtedly, a few of the naturalists must have the complete collection, which continues to expand year after year.

John paid for the first run, which cost him around two thousand dollars. Then he saved the money he was paid for talks and lectures to recover his original investment. Some of the money made through the sale of the patches was used to sponsor volunteers of the museum to join Bemi DeBus, who was taking a group to Hawaii to see Humpback whales. The money would pay for the airfare, and De Bus had generously agreed to take the volunteers out on her boat at no cost. Who were going to be the lucky volunteers? John and his team decided that whoever had served the most hours as a naturalist on the Whalewatch boats would be the winner. Over the years, a number of young people earned themselves the trip of a lifetime.

The Cabrillo Whalewatch program quickly earned a reputation across the country and around the world for contributing significantly to greater awareness of marine mammals and the oceans. At the same time, the sport-fishing boats that would often sit idle in the winter slow season, were being used and generating income. John continued to help others set up whale watching businesses in Marina del Ray, Oxnard and Oceanside. He also went as far north as Santa Barbara to speak about the Whalewatch program, inspiring many people to follow his example. Sister programs soon emerged along the East Coast of the U.S. as well.

While the Whalewatch program did not suffer any major problems, it had its scary moments. The program was well underway when John learned from some teachers that it was against the law to charge a child one dollar to go whale watching. However, they told him that children could form a nature club, chip in some money, and then designate the money to go whale watching. John did not lose a minute to pass along that information to all teachers, and nature clubs sprung up like weeds. John insisted that if there were children who could not afford the dollar, he would help them. His mission was to make sure that all children could go out and see whales.

What concerned John much more than administrative shortcomings was the safety of everyone aboard the Whalewatch boats. He knew very well that if anybody drowned or was hurt, it would be devastating and lead to the program closing. To maintain an active presence and watchful eye, John often went to the landings to make sure everything was safe. Of course, even with the best efforts, accidents did happen. Fortunately, nobody participating in the Whalewatch program was ever injured.

Others were not so lucky. Perhaps the most serious whale watching incident occurred in February 1983 in Morro Bay, which is a few hundred miles north of San Pedro. Against the advice of the harbor patrol, one of the whale watching boat operators was taking a group of students out through the rather narrow opening of Morro Bay Harbor when a big wave flipped the boat over and everyone fell into the water. Luckily, they were picked up right away and nobody drowned. The only casualty was the captain, who died after two months in the hospital. This incident was all over the news, so John received phone calls from concerned parents asking him whether it was safe for their children to participate in the Whalewatch program. Inevitably, some cancelled their reservations. John and his team had a lot of talking to do, describing the differences between the narrow entrance of Morro Bay, which is posted as "dangerous," and the wide ocean access of San Pedro. Luckily, after discussions with many parents, he did not have to cancel even one of the boat trips.

John's Whalewatch program was, and continues to be, the most successful whale watching program of all time. Starting out with two thousand participants in 1972, more than eighty thousand people went on Whalewatch trips in 1982. By the early 1990s, one million people had participated in the program.

With the Whalewatch program running like clockwork, John and his volunteers were looking for a new adventure. John always engaged with everyone who attended the classes or volunteered at the museum, and he encouraged them to share their ideas. In 1977, everyone wanted to go to Mexico to see the gray whales in their mating grounds – the lagoons of Baja California. John thought that this was not a bad idea, so he called and invited some of the old-timers to come along. When John asked who wanted to go, eighty-two people responded. At first, John thought that maybe twenty-five would actually make it, as students might have problems getting out of school and others would have parents, husbands, wives or partners who would not want them to go.

But in the end, eighty-two whale-crazy souls departed San Pedro for the gray whale nurseries in Mexico in early 1978. John divided them into groups – vegetarians, unmarried folks, senior citizens and so on – and he put one person in charge of each group. Each group left on its own and, when they arrived in Guerrero Negro, they swapped stories about their adventures along the way. Once there, John needed to find a place that could feed such a large group. Nothing was organized. They went to three restaurants, with John asking at each one how much they would charge per person for 82 people to eat dinner. One can only imagine what the owners must have thought when they saw that many people walking up to their establishments. The first said, $7 per person, so John took the group to the next restaurant until eventually everyone paid $4 for an all-you-can-eat dinner.

Everyone saw whales in Guerrero Negro and then they went to Scammon's Lagoon and saw even more whales. It was an amazing adventure and a unique experience for everyone. Connie Chung, a reporter at the time for Los Angeles' CBS Channel 2, who had met John on the Goodyear Blimp ride that John organized every year, heard that John and the group were off to Mexico to see whales, so she and her photographer flew down. The reports she filed were on the air in Los Angeles while the group was still in Mexico and were an instant sensation on local TV stations. Nobody had seen anything like it. Despite the popularity of the whale watching trips, most people at that point were still largely unaware that these gentle giants migrated along the California coast. John had a natural talent in front of the camera and Chung's reports elevated his adventurous nature and bolstered the visibility of both the Whalewatch program and the museum.

One day while in Mexico, the group ran into a tugboat skipper from San Pedro. Of course, he and John knew each other; it would have been hard back then to find someone who did not know John or know of him. When he learned what John and his volunteers were doing, he arranged for all of them to board the tug and took them out to the opening of the lagoon. On the way there, they passed a red buoy where they spotted a twenty-five-foot-long gray whale entangled in the rope below the buoy. Trying to help the animal, a few people – including Bob Talbot (long before he became a world-famous photographer and filmmaker) – dove into the water and tried to cut the line. The whale began to hit the water with his fluke, which was very dangerous, as had it hit any of John's volunteers it would have easily killed them. John wanted to get out of there, but his young students wanted to finish the job. When the boat closed in to pick up the volunteers, the whale took off. They watched him go, pulling the fifty-five-gallon drum buoy behind him until the drum disappeared. Soon the drum popped up and the whale swam away. Everybody cheered and, aside from John, nobody seemed to have been scared.

For several years, John continued to take groups of students and adults to Mexico. Two of his staff would also go, at no cost to them. It was important to John to include them and provide the opportunity to gain experience. The trips even raised some funds for the museum. Not much, but back then every penny counted.

John would be the first to admit that the great success of the Whalewatch program rested on the enthusiastic support of the teachers and the community of San Pedro. John never took anything for granted, so he was constantly looking for ways to give back. If giving back could be done through an event filled with fun and action, so much the better. For years, Dana Point had a Whale Fiesta in February, a combination of a festival and whale watching, with vendors and boat captains turning a decent profit. For John, it was not about the money, though. He wanted to come together and celebrate the successful whale watching seasons.

John copied the Dana Point idea and created a local San Pedro Whale Fiesta, which gave everyone involved a chance to get together and look back on what they had accomplished. The first San Pedro Whale Fiesta took place in June 1972 at Royal Palms and was organized by the Cabrillo Marine Museum and the American Cetacean Society. Royal Palms was a very nice park, just around the corner from Point Fermin in San Pedro, down by White's Point. It was right next to a cliff and had picnic tables, a fireplace and a dance floor – all surrounded by palm trees. The vista was incredible. Attendees ate, danced, made whales out of clay and painted them, and much more. As with almost everything that John touched, the event was an incredible success, drawing thousands of participants.

Oliver Andrews, an art teacher at UCLA and enthusiastic member of the ACS, had the idea to make a helium-filled mylar (plastic sheeting) whale for the 1972 Whale Fiesta. It was meant to rise above the cliffs so people would know where to go – a classic case of spot advertising. Unfortunately, the helium whale leaked and only part of the head remained inflated, which worked just as well. The first couple of Whale Fiestas were a lot of fun, but very different from the ones today. They used to be huge events that lasted all day long with bands playing and a whale-spotting contest.

One particularly special feature was one of John's creations called "whale dynamics." With his unique enthusiasm, John would recruit six hundred to one thousand people to "bring a whale alive." Anyone who was over 6 feet tall played the part of the whale's blow, which is what one can see when whales exhale at the surface; they would crouch down and stand up and say "blow." Anyone with a red jacket was the heart; they had to pump up and down, imitating the heart rhythmic *pump-pump, pump-pump*. If there were any preschool children, they made a little circle, with a teacher in charge, and made up the eye of the whale: blinking by moving back and forth. Those from the 1st and 2nd grades were the plankton. The rest of the people would stand hand-in-hand representing the outline of the whale's body. They would open the whale's mouth by walking, then the kids would run in or out and the whale's mouth would close. The role of 'digestion' was played by the 4th graders; they had to run in circles inside the whale's stomach. And, of course, the whale had to be kept healthy, so the 6th graders would help by "going to the bathroom" – running out of the whale's rear-end to the nearest tree. And so it went. John Olguin knew this looked and sounded a little bizarre, but it worked. Sometimes natural things in the real world can seem a bit odd.

Once everyone was in position and knew what to do, John would yell, "Let the whale's heart beat!" The red jackets would start with *pump-pump, pump-pump*. "Let the whale blow! Do it! Do it!" And those people would start blowing. "Let the whale swim!" The people in the back, playing the part of the whale's flukes, would take fifteen steps front and back, to make the whale swim. "Let the whale's eye blink!" The preschool children would start with an open eye, and then run back and forth to the middle to blink the eye. "Let the whale eat!" The mouth would open up by the people taking ten steps in one direction, and the children would run in and run out. The outline making up the whale's skin had to wiggle back and forth. The movements of up to a thousand people were perfectly synchronized. It was a very fun activity to participate in! The interactive demonstration even turned up on national television. There was absolutely no limit to John's creativity, and its success.

During the third year of the Whale Fiesta at Royal Palms, a rock on top of the cliff gave way and tumbled down the hundred-foot cliff, landing with a big thump and a lot of dust. On the way down, it hit a table that was full of enchiladas. The enchiladas flew through the air and splattered on everyone. When the dust cleared, two people lay unconscious on the ground but quickly recovered. Nobody was seriously injured, but John decided that this site was just too dangerous, so the Whale Fiesta moved to Cabrillo Beach.

The beach offered new opportunities for the annual event. John had a novel idea, but first he wanted to test it out. He took all the junior high school volunteers to the beach and built a whale out of sand, just to see if they could do it. One of these youngsters was Bob Bonde, one of the many kids who would embark on a very successful scientific career studying marine mammals. He currently heads the Sirenia Project of the U.S. Geological Survey in Gainesville, Florida, studying manatees. Another person involved in the event was Bob Talbot, a young aspiring photographer at the time, who took photographs out of a helicopter of everything that was happening below. The sand whale turned out so well that the *Los Angeles Times* published an article on it. Every year since, a whale is carved out of sand at the Whale Fiesta on Cabrillo Beach and another "comes alive." Today the Whale Fiesta takes place on the inside beach, just across from the new Cabrillo Marine Aquarium. With lots of activities, crafts and food, it continues to be a great community affair.

At the end of each whale watching season, John and Muriel would also throw a huge potluck party at their home for friends and all of the volunteers. It was not unusual to have a belly dancer performing and more than one hundred people in attendance, contributing a smorgasbord of food to create the best potluck dinners ever. John and Muriel would clear all of the furniture out of their living room and play great music. Often the dancing would last into the wee hours, stopped only by the – nearly annual – visit from resigned police officers who would ask them to "keep it down, please." For many of the volunteers, this was THE party of the year. No one wanted to miss it.

When John retired in 1987, he turned the Whalewatch program over to Larry Fukuhara, who took over John's responsibilities as program director. Larry, a former judo black-belt champion and instructor who grew up in Long Beach, first came to the museum in 1981 as a volunteer. He participated in every single volunteer program and, six months later, started to work at the museum twenty hours per week. He was as enthusiastic about everything the museum did as John was. The Junior Docent Summer Program continued to blossom under Larry's guidance and, by 1989, between forty and fifty junior volunteers were giving tours to hundreds of visitors per day.

The docent program was another one of John's innovative ideas. He wanted to give the junior high and high school students training so they could work as docents (tour guides) during the year. Eventually, the program was held during the summer when the adult docents took vacations and the students were available. Still going strong today, the program is now organized so that junior high students are tour guides in July and senior high students lead the tours in August. More than twenty years after taking the helm, Larry continues his incredibly successful work as the program director and he seems to have no plans of leaving. When asked about his future, he laughed and said, "John always used to tell me he'll make a beach bum out of me. I think I'll stay here for a while."

Of the many people who helped John turn the Whalewatch program into a success, Rivian Lande and Bill Samaras stand above all others. Rivian was a biology teacher at Long Beach City College and was among the first to bring her entire class to the evening Whalewatch program. She also recorded information about the program, such as how many children attended, and published it annually. Lande was one of the staunchest supporters of Whalewatch and, as we have already learned, played a critical role saving it.

Bill Samaras was also a teacher. He and John had become very close friends, both known all over town as the whale experts. They not only worked together on whale watching activities, but they also dissected dead whales on the beach and dug out a now-famous gray whale fossil, which all served to increase the public's interest in the museum. Like John, Bill was a San Pedro native. Born in 1932 at the old San Pedro Community Hospital, he then spent four years of his early childhood in Astoria, Oregon, before returning to San Pedro.

Both his parents were from Greece. His father had arrived in San Pedro in 1917, and his mother, a mail-order bride, in 1929. When they returned to San Pedro from Oregon, Bill's father became one of the original longshoremen for the Port of Los Angeles. Samaras found out only much, much later that his father was also one of the biggest bootleggers on the Columbia River.

Samaras himself, known as "the mad Greek," would often race down Pacific Avenue to Cabrillo Beach going 80 miles per hour on his motorcycle. The beach was one of his favorite places to hang out, especially when ditching school, a habit at which he excelled. When the surf came up, Bill and his friends would bodysurf using old mattress covers, which they would wet and fill with air to use them sort of like modern boogie boards. The group would often wander over to the museum and hang out for a while after surfing. Fascinated by the museum exhibits, Bill would look at the fish to see if he could recognize them.

When Bill lived on Bandini Street in San Pedro, there was a major gully behind the house, which was part of the Monterey shell formation. He would often go out for hours, digging and following the fossil beds he found. He did not know what he was looking for, but he was intrigued. Bill always had a very inquisitive mind, but he had never thought about becoming a teacher or scientist. He graduated from high school as a machine shop major when he was 17 years old. Within a year, he was in a Marine Corps boot camp in San Diego; America was fighting the Korean War. After he was discharged, he was not quite sure what to do. He worked as a mechanic for a while, as a longshoreman, and then for the Department of Water and Power. One day, when he was pulling wires on the top of a pole, it occurred to him that this was not what he wanted to do for the rest of his life. He took the next day off, went to Long Beach City College and signed up for classes.

After his first semester, Bill transferred to Harbor College in Wilmington from which he received an Associate of Arts degree. From there, he went to California State Long Beach, to earn his bachelor's degree. He really wanted to become an astronomer, but after a couple of algebra classes, he realized that astronomy was not just looking through an eyepiece and viewing the wonders of the celestial universe. A lot of math was required, and Bill knew he was not a skilled mathematician. Instead, he chose to work toward a social science major and a science minor, studying history, geography and anthropology.

Samaras graduated from California State Long Beach in 1959 and began his teaching career two years later in South Central Los Angeles. He transferred to Carson High School in 1964, teaching history at first. Interested in geology and other sciences, he soon created a marine biology class for the senior high schools in the Los Angeles Unified School District, which he would teach for twenty-seven years at Carson High School. He also founded the Ecology Club, an open forum for discussing environmental education subjects, such as the need to recycle, how to "kill your television," and clean-burning fuels for motorbikes.

Bill remembers John as the lifeguard captain and director of the museum. Despite various encounters over the years, including both men being active members of the Polar Bears Club, they really did not get to know each other as close friends and colleagues until Samaras started teaching marine biology, physical earth sciences and geology at Carson High School. In the 1960s, Bill began to help John with the grunion runs at night and soon began to do his own research on grunion. He spent many nights on the beach with his students, taking samples and recording grunion lengths, weights and sex. He even attempted to tag them, but that did not work out. Failure, as Samaras would explain to his students, was part of the scientific method. Each new challenge meant that they should take a step back, be observant and develop a new approach.

After a rainy day in 1971, Paul Kirkland, a student at Harbor College, was looking for shark-teeth fossils at the cliff face when he noticed a piece of fossilized bone sticking out of the sand. He started digging around so that more of it stuck out. Not knowing what it was, the young man was careful not to break off the bone. Instead, he went to the museum and told John about it. John called Bill and they met at the site less than an hour later. They started digging, exposing more and more bone until Samaras knew they had something important. He was not sure what it was, though, as he had never seen a whale fossil before.

John and Bill decided to contact the Los Angeles County Museum of Natural History. Dr. Shelton P. Applegate, an associate of the L.A. County Museum, and Ed Mitchell, one of the early pioneers of marine mammal research, who was visiting at the time from Canada, both came down to San Pedro and identified the specimen as a gray whale fossil.

Samaras turned the excavation site into an outdoor classroom. He brought some couches to the dig site so everyone could sit down and rest once in a while. Tony Perkov, the owner of Antes Restaurant in San Pedro, would often bring Yugoslavian food out for everyone. Even though the students were not supposed to drink, he would also bring wine. For fourteen days and nights, they worked, lived and laughed together. It was an incredible community event!

Samaras had been ditching school a lot, even before the fossil was discovered. His students also missed quite a bit of school during the excavation time. It was never officially registered, but Bill had a mutual understanding with the other teachers because they benefited as well. The students would write reports on their work and present them as papers for the English department. In math classes, students applied their newfound interest in whales by weighing the mass of whale blubber and measuring its thickness. In the history department, students learned about the old whalers and that San Pedro had a whaling station until the 1960s. The students were obviously motivated. Bill was just the teacher they needed: he was curious and wanted to know the same things that they wanted to know. What they were doing was real life, not just theory.

Samaras missed even more school days than usual while working on the fossil. With the media obsessed with the story, often interviewing him and running it almost every day in the newspapers and on television, more and more people came to know about the excavation. Bill knew he was in trouble and he needed someone to bail him out. While the excavation of the gray whale fossil was still underway, Bill went to California State Assemblyman Vincent Thomas, who happened to live just two blocks up the street from him. He explained how important the find was and made his case that it would be great if the fossil could be exhibited in a new museum. Assemblyman Thomas also seemed to be the right person to ask for help regarding his absences from teaching and he did not disappoint. He called the school superintendent and thus ensured the success of the excavation. Years later, he would also play a critical role in securing the funds for the new museum building.

Bill always used the museum facilities and programs as an extension of his classroom. Many of his students spent much of their spare time on Cabrillo Beach, investigating aspects of the life cycle of gray whales, such as their migration and respiratory cycles. When he first started going out whale watching, Bill recognized that there was a pattern to how the gray whales swam and surfaced to breathe. He realized that to understand the migration of gray whales, one had to do a census. Therefore, in the mid-1970s, Bill started the local gray whale census. As part of this effort, he took two of his students, Jim Beard and Dennis Chandler, to Santa Catalina Island in his old boat. He obtained all the permits for them to stay near the west end and dropped them off with a tent and all the food and supplies they would need for the next two weeks.

Weathering rain and fog, the students climbed up the hill every day to count whales. They spotted as many as forty-one whales a day from Santa Catalina Island, with nearly all passing on the side of the island not visible from the mainland. Those observing the whale migration from the mainland counted twenty-one or fewer on those same days. Their observations led to the discovery that on the southbound leg of the migration, most of the gray whales would stay on the backside of Catalina Island. Returning from the Baja California lagoons on the northbound leg, more gray whales passed closer to shore. It was basic field science back then, as books about these details would only be written later. These were exciting and adventurous times for these budding science pioneers. The two brave young scientists ended up having to stay a little bit longer because bad weather delayed the trip to pick them up. By the time Bill and his crew reached them, the rats had eaten everything!

For many of the high school students, the necropsy of dead whales, dolphins and sea lions provided unique opportunities to learn about the biology and life history of the mammals. They were prepared and well equipped to, at a moment's notice, respond to any stranding and provide assistance to the local agency in their efforts to rid the beach or shoreline of a smelly ocean creature mess. The students brought great energy to the task, which was needed for this less-than-desirable job that adults were reluctant to perform. Students were just happy to have the experience. They had a lot of fun and didn't mind the mess. As they say, one person's garbage is another person's treasure.

John and Bill became so well known that whenever anyone found anything that looked like it could be of interest to the museum, they would call John, who was considered the ocean-oriented expert on whatever. He knew all of the old fishermen in town. If they found something in their nets, they would bring it down to the museum. One day John received a phone call that a whale was floating out by the Los Angeles Lighthouse. As it turned out, a ship coming up the coast from Ensenada, at a speed of twenty-two knots, had hit something that became wedged on its bulbous bow. They only realized that it was a whale when the boat slowed down to enter the harbor and the animal slipped off the bow and floated to the surface. John called Bill, who immediately bailed out of school and they rode out in Bill's skiff to investigate.

When they arrived, they found a very large whale floating upside down. It appeared to be either a blue whale or a fin whale. To verify the species, they needed to see the whale's baleen. Baleen is made of the protein keratin, the same material that makes up hair and nails. Instead of teeth, almost all large whales have baleen plates, with baleen hair attached, hanging from their upper jaws. The baleen allows water to pass through, but holds back any food items. Depending on the species, these plates can be 1.5 to 11 feet long. Bill put on his bathing suit and slid into the water. He swam toward the whale and dove into its open mouth, which, as he later remarked, felt like swimming into a garage. It was amazing! When he saw that the baleen was all black, he knew that it was a blue whale, all fifty-eight feet of it! That whale was roughly ten feet longer than the average size of a school bus. It was an incredible moment in the lives of both Bill and John.

John and Bill requested that the officials close the beach and then they began the slow process of towing the heavy whale onto the beach, using cables, trucks and even a tank. With this being the first blue whale they would dissect, John and Bill decided to turn it into a student project. A lot of the blubber was towed offshore, but some was taken to a meat-processing plant where they disposed of dead animals such as cattle and chicken. The rest of the blue whale went into the storage facility of the Natural History Museum of Los Angeles County.

All of the local television channels aired the story. It was a sensational event. Bill and John considered the huge media attention a wonderful way to get people interested in the Cabrillo Marine Museum as a place to learn more about marine life. However, the media extravaganza also made it a little bit more difficult to keep people away from the site. Of course, for dedicated marine-life lovers like John and Bill, that was a small price to pay. They loved every minute of it.

GODFATHER TO
A GENERATION

$\mathcal{E}$very year, tens of thousands of children and countless other groups came to the museum to explore tide pools, see grunion late at night on the beach or go see whales. Over the span of John's career, a few million people participated in these programs, most of them encountering John at one time or another. When they did meet John, it often had a lasting impact on their lives, their careers, and sometimes both. For the volunteers and staff who worked with John, this was an even more poignant truth.

Taking care of thousands of visitors required a small army of indispensable volunteers, and it was John's responsibility to teach and prepare them. In the past, local high school students would hang out at Cabrillo Beach all the time, but as the years passed by an increasing number of them had cars and would drive to other beaches. Junior high school students would still hang out at Cabrillo Beach, though, and they would often come to the museum to volunteer. Generally, however, they would not study, take notes, or do their homework to prepare for their volunteer work.

Not knowing how to motivate these youngsters, John turned to Carol Eiser, one of the teachers at Dana Junior High School in San Pedro. John explained that he would give the students all the material they needed to study, so they could volunteer and share what they had learned with those visiting the museum. However, they just did not seem interested. Together, John and Carol developed the idea of presenting the information verbally and then asking the students to immediately report what they had just learned. In addition, John would challenge the students to tell him what they wanted to do and then do it. It was the birth of one of the museum's most successful programs, which would soon have its own signature slogan and trademark: "Do it! Do it!"

As planned, John asked the students to list the five museum-related things they wanted to do more than anything else in the world. Their top wishes were to: (1) meet famous marine explorer Jacques Cousteau; (2) visit the Channel Islands; (3) go to Sea World and the San Diego Zoo; (4) visit Catalina Island; and (5) learn how to canoe. John then told them that they would not have to do any more bookwork. Instead, he would present the information and they would recite it back to him in their own words. They broke into little groups, studied a topic, talked about it and then one of them would present the topic to the entire group. Every Monday, he would take the students on a road trip, visiting some of the places on their wish list. To this day, volunteers go to Catalina and to Sea World or the Los Angeles Zoo once a year. John was again following through on his life-long mission to help his young museum constituency – the curious, the future marine scientists, and the new converts to the magic of the ocean – achieve their seemingly impossible dreams.

John took this same approach with the high school kids he recruited each summer for the Whalewatch program. Starting in October, about 150 teens from various schools in the area – and some all the way from the San Fernando Valley, fifty miles away – would gather on Tuesday nights at the museum. When the museum was in the old bathhouse, they would sit between the display cases, an atmosphere that is sadly missing from the auditorium of the new building. Soon John would appear and it would take newcomers only moments to realize that John was special, charismatic and animated. He was always very excited about what he was saying.

John's way of speaking was a ride for his audience; he would touch on any subject, end up somewhere else and then come back to where he started. Most of these students had never experienced someone like John, but everyone enjoyed the wild learning journey. If one of John's scheduled speakers did not – or could not – show up, John would just go up to the stage and blow his audience's socks off for the next couple of hours. The topic did not matter: whale biology, mythology, Native American or Inuit artwork or rowing. John was a walking, talking encyclopedia of life, nature, and education.

John loved to share his adventures and challenge his audience to learn new things. The ever-growing cadre of fascinated students was captivated by John, who often was larger than life as he exploded with that special energy he had for the museum and its collection of exhibits. It did not matter whether he had visual aids or not, the excitement kept everyone on the edge of their seats the whole time. He educated everyone enthusiastically, without being boring. John would speak about everything from life to parents, love, air, earth, water, people, religion, dignity, pride and learning. He made everyone feel as though they were the only people on the planet to be given the key to unlock the secrets of life. He was pure, but genuine, MAGIC!

Enthralled by John's talks, many people would inevitably

sign up to volunteer. School children would come to the museum by the busload, and the volunteers would be waiting for them at different stations to talk about the many aspects of ocean life. The volunteers would learn how to pitch what they were saying to different groups. John wanted them to get all students to participate, so he taught them to teach by mimicking the actions of ocean animals. John would say, "Put your hands like this, swim through the water like a whale, put your hands like that and swim through the water like a jelly-fish." He would always end with "Do it! Do it!" to encourage participation. Of course, many volunteers were shy and hesitant, but eventually John's enthusiasm and persistence would win them over and they would join John's league of animated interpreters and educators. "Stand on your head like a barnacle and use your feet to put food in your mouth. Do it! Do it!" It may have sounded silly to some, but John's sincerity was palpable.

Over the years, John worked with thousands of student volunteers, perhaps tens of thousands. For many, their years at the museum would have a significant influence on their entire lives and, in many cases, on their future careers. Some acquired and honed their communication and people skills, while others learned some of life's important lessons. Some would even find love and meet their future spouses. One of John's greatest legacies is that he created and nurtured an entire generation of world-class researchers, scientists and artists.

John planted seeds, listened and encouraged, provided support, and mentored. Everything started with an idea and no dream was impossible. John taught individuals how to find success and achieve whatever they put their minds to. The Whalewatch classes, in particular, were the breeding ground and cradle for young people with great aspirations, drive and perseverance. Among the countless careers whose cradles lay with John and the museum are those of Ted Cranford, Barbara Brunnick, Robin Makowski, Alisa Schuman-Janiger and Bob Talbot.

Ted Cranford was attending Long Beach City College in the mid-1970s and – according to his own recollection – was floundering around. He was a strong student, had a good memory and enjoyed learning different things. However, he did not really know which career to choose. He took many different classes, including law enforcement, cultural cooking, politics, psychology and a marine biology class taught by Rivian Lande, a John Olguin aficionado and a committed Cabrillo Marine Museum recruiter for his programs. Lande gave her students a research project and suggested various ideas, including: going out in the bay with different substrates (surfaces a plant or animal lives on) to see what grows on them; towing a plankton net and identifying how many types of critters could be found; collecting different types of algae; and conducting a survey of an intertidal reef. A few weeks later, she would ask her students to write down their project on a piece of paper. Ted, being the mischievous wise guy he was, wrote he wanted to do his project on something bigger than a breadbox. Having read his note, Rivian suggested Ted sign up for the summer Whalewatch program at the museum. Soon he would be bitten by the John Olguin curiosity bug, which would change his life forever.

Once there, Cranford could not get enough of the marine environment experience and he ended up volunteering for five years. During that time, he continued his studies at Long Beach City College, working hard to complete his undergraduate work so that he could attend university and focus on taking classes for his major. He paid his own way by working in the oil fields, but despite being busy, he continued to volunteer at the museum. Ted began to read books about marine mammals, the first of which was *Man and Dolphin* by John C. Lilly. He would later remember how he was sitting in his small apartment in Long Beach thinking about all that Lilly had written about the brain and its complexity, the sensory system, and how much sensory input dolphins have in their skin. Dolphins, he thought, could be sort of a counterpart to humans, but in the ocean. They are in a different place, they do different things, but obviously the complexity of their brains is comparable to our own. He was hooked!

Cranford soon came across the name Ken Norris and began to read his work and that of the other pioneers in marine mammal research. Before long, Ted decided that he wanted to study with Ken Norris. Most people thought that Ted was nuts. Even his family told him that it was impossible, and that he would never be successful or make a living. Many budding marine biologists wanted to study with Ken Norris at his lab at the University of California Santa Cruz (UC Santa Cruz), as he had a reputation that reached around the world. Norris was a great observer and teacher. He also had a talent for drawing a dolphin using just seven strokes; It looked great, just like a dolphin swimming in the water.

Despite all the naysayers, Ted remained determined. He had already learned one very important lesson from John: nearly anything is possible as long as you really want it. Ted learned that no idea was too crazy for John, who would sometimes come to the Tuesday meetings and say, "Alright, what should we do? Let's have some ideas." It did not matter how crazy the ideas were, because John could make them happen. If you wanted to make a life-sized blue whale out of sand on the beach – five hundred shovels and one thousand people, and if you wanted to feed everybody who came out to help, six hundred watermelons, John would show his troops how to get it done. You could have Los Angeles television weatherman Dr. George Fishbeck from KABC Channel 7 down on the beach, or the news helicopter and blimp flying overhead. Nothing was impossible. If you could conceive it, it could be done. One of John's greatest qualities was that he was positive about everything and, over time, that quality embedded itself in Ted's psyche too.

With John's encouragement, Ted wrote a letter to Ken Norris and drove up to Santa Cruz to meet him. Cranford succeeded in going to UC Santa Cruz to finish his undergraduate work. He was fanatical about Ken Norris' marine mammal class, recording the entire class and then transcribing it. His five years in the Whalewatch program had clearly made a huge difference. Ted was known for his pointed and perceptive questions, which must have helped him to achieve the highest grade of all students in the class.

A couple of years later, Ted managed to pass through the very competitive selection and enroll in Ken's very popular Natural History Field Quarter class. More than fifty students applied and, after an extensive process that included individual interviews, only about twenty students made the cut. Those students boarded a bus and drove around California for a couple of months studying the natural history of different natural reserve systems. During that trip, when Ted talked with Ken about doing research at some point, his response was, "Let's do it." He sounded just like John Olguin. Ted was confident that his time floundering had not been for naught, as it was the space he had needed to find his way to this moment.

In 1987, Cranford completed his master's thesis as Norris' student. It was the first time anyone had made a CT scan of a dolphin's head. Ted had reached his goal. He knew that John had played a critical role in his success, by instilling in him the message that you can do anything if you put your mind to it, so he dedicated his master's thesis to John Olguin. Ted went on to generate head CT scans for many more species, including a huge sperm whale. He obtained his PhD from UC Santa Cruz in 1992, while still working with Ken Norris. Ted joined the faculty at San Diego State University in 1997, where he continues his investigations into the functional morphology of marine mammals.

Today, Cranford and his colleagues are using information from CT scans to build computer models of whale heads. These models allow Cranford's research team to simulate how disturbances or perturbations are propagated through a whale's head, and more specifically how sound exits and enters the heads of the whales. These models have led to several discoveries about hearing and sound production in toothed whales. Like John Olguin, Ted looked at every obstacle as a step on the road to success. One of the hurdles he needed to overcome was how to make a CT scan of a large whale head. He solved that problem by using a CT scanner that was built to scan solid-fuel rocket motors; so there is a bit of rocket science in what he does.

As the lab manager at Ken Norris' facility at the University of Santa Cruz during his graduate school years, Cranford met another graduate of the John Olguin Whalewatch classes. They had never met back in San Pedro, but clearly belonged to the same fraternity. Barbara Joan Brunnick was her name, and she too would become an exceptional marine mammal scientist. Brunnick had grown up in Toluca Lake,

California, the youngest of five children. Her father, John Ryan, had died when she was only 5 years old, leaving her mother, Evelyn, with two teenage boys, two pre-teen girls and Barbara. They were a middle-class family, which meant living in a modest home, sending the children to good schools and having enough money for a few days of vacation per year.

When Brunnick was about 8 years old, she was treated to a boat trip on the Pacific Ocean. She remembers little about the day, except that she was caught playing with an older boy's snorkeling gear and he had pitched her into the sea for her naughtiness. As she watched the boat sail away, adults waving frantically from the stern, it happened: a sleek grey body swam past her at great speed. She felt the water move as it glided by her. A dolphin, agitated, was swimming fast in tight circles around her, blowing bubbles and whistling. Occasionally, the dolphin would stop swimming and they would make eye contact. Barbara was so excited she did not realize the trouble she was in or that her mother was frantic to see a creature circling her youngest. However, the dolphin did make it easier for the captain to keep his eye on her and come to her rescue.

A chance encounter, but it would change everything. Brunnick was in love, the kind that lasts forever. She needed to know more about dolphins. Unfortunately, in the mid-1960s, there were very few places to learn more about marine mammals, let alone a wayward dolphin. Even so, Barbara made several trips to Marineland of the Pacific, and delighted in convincing the staff to let her feed the pilot whale on occasion. She watched for dolphins and whales from the beach during family outings and wrote about them every chance she could in school.

In 1975, Brunnick decided to skip most of her senior year at Our Lady of Corvallis High School in Studio City, California, to attend Pierce Community College instead. Within a few weeks of starting classes, she heard about the American Cetacean Society and jumped at the first opportunity to attend one of its meetings. It was there that Barbara heard firsthand reports about whale and dolphin research and the advances in this new science. It was also at that meeting that she first met John, who spoke about the Whalewatch classes at the Cabrillo Marine Museum in San Pedro on Tuesday nights.

Barbara had some history with San Pedro. Her grandmother, Ethel, had lived in San Pedro for many years and Barbara had visited her there during her childhood. She had only good memories. It was a fifty-mile drive from the San Fernando Valley to San Pedro, but, fortunately, Barbara had both a car and the determination. Wasting no time, she got behind the wheel the following Tuesday and drove over the hill, through downtown Los Angeles, to the harbor town of San Pedro. It was quite a trip for the shy girl, but the rewards promised to be immense.

When she arrived at the museum for the very first time, which in late 1975 was still in the old bathhouse, she was directed upstairs where the class was just getting started. She walked through the museum, past displays of seashells and model boats, to find about twenty-five people, mostly sitting on the floor around a makeshift stage. Barbara moved all the way to the back where she sat down in front of a maritime display case. Then John arrived, introduced himself and gave a short lecture about gray whales. John pointed at someone sitting right in front of Barbara and said, "You – get up! Okay, we are all 3rd graders. Tell us about gray whales." Barbara's heart sank and she slid farther under the display case. She could not get up and do that! She worried about the possibility of John calling on her and focused her attention on the display case next to her, which held several sextants and compasses. There, in that case, a small plaque read, "Donated by Mrs. W. A. Brunnick." Her grandmother! Barbara was puzzled, but felt a connection. That display was her shield until she was ready to walk up to the front and accept John's challenge.

Barbara attended several classes that season, but when the classes ended, she still did not know anyone at the museum except for John's right hand, Marji, who always greeted her with a smile and asked about the long drive. Barbara was keen to find out how the Brunnick name had ended up in the museum, so she went to see her grandmother Ethel. Barbara quickly discovered that her paternal grandfather, Walter Allen, had been a sea captain of some note and he held a license for every Pacific Coast bay, inlet, gulf and stream. He was at sea most of his adult life, leaving his wife and children in San Pedro for months on end. He died at the end of World War II, long before Barbara had been born. Barbara's mother, Evelyn, did not talk about Walter, and Barbara's father had died when she was only 5 years old, but her grandmother had kept an amazing scrapbook that included newspaper clippings and photos explaining how the Brunnick name had become part of the Cabrillo Marine Museum history.

As it turned out, Barbara's father, John Ryan, had been born at the Point Fermin Lighthouse, where Barbara's grandmother stayed with the Engles family while her husband was at sea. Barbara also learned how her grandfather and his crew had captured and transported the first elephant seal in captivity to the San Diego Zoo in 1923. Barbara had discovered a marine mammal connection in her family's history! Several years after finding the photos of that expedition in her grandmother's scrapbook, Barbara would participate in an elephant seal research program in Año Nuevo, California. It seemed that San Pedro, the ocean, and even marine mammals were in her blood.

After a one-year scholarship to the United States International University in France, Brunnick returned to California in 1977 and continued her studies at Pierce Community College. Her oceanography professor, Ruth Lebow, another John Olguin aficionado and a committed Cabrillo Marine Museum recruiter for John's programs, offered extra credit to anyone willing to drive to San Pedro and attend the Whalewatch class at the museum. Barbara immediately volunteered to drive as many as could fit in her car. Later that year, Barbara signed up for the expedition to Scammon's Lagoon, in Baja California. John looked at her as she signed her name and asked if she had ever been to the Whalewatch class before. He could not specifically remember ever having seen her, but he had a great memory and prided himself on knowing everyone by name. With a smile, Barbara responded that she had been there many times. Minutes later, after the class had started, John looked at her and said, "You – get up! Okay, we are all Rotarians. Tell us about gray whales! Do it! Do it!" This time, she was ready.

Brunnick's world during those years revolved around whales, dolphins and the Cabrillo Marine Museum. Although she continued to live in the valley, 50 miles away, she very rarely missed a meeting. She even served on the board of ACS for a while as the speaker coordinator. Volunteering for more and more Whalewatch trips, Barbara became very dedicated. In 1982 alone, she gave a record eighty-five lectures. Barbara met Bob Talbot, Tony Bernot and Chip Matheson in the Whalewatch classes. Together, they would go to Vancouver Island in 1979, where they successfully photographed and filmed orcas in the wild and recorded their sounds.

Bob Talbot was in school with Tony Bernot in 1977 when they first learned about the Whalewatch classes in San Pedro. Talbot and Bernot were 19 years old at the time and already had a few years of joint adventures behind them. They had started diving together when they were about 13 years old and Bernot's parents had a little inflatable boat the boys would use to go out looking for whales and dolphins. When they heard about Whalewatch classes, Bob and Tony were living about a thirty-mile drive away from San Pedro, but that did not deter them. Bob was already in hot pursuit of his dream to become a photographer, so the Whalewatch classes were a great way to meet like-minded people and learn more about the animals. This was an opportunity not to be missed. They went to the Whalewatch classes at the Cabrillo Marine Museum as often as they could, captivated by John Olguin and Bill Samaras speaking about whales and sharing their personal stories. John and Bill's exuberance, affection, support and love for everyone seemed almost unreal.

John quickly realized that Bob was pursuing a career as a photographer and filmmaker. When the Whale Fiesta came around, he asked Bob to go up in a helicopter to take some photos of the giant sand sculpture of the gray whale they had made on the beach. Somehow, Peter Gibson, who was working on a book about California beaches, heard about it and asked Bob if he could use some photographs for his book. Bob was excited that someone was interested in his work and went up to Malibu to meet with him. When the two met, Bob casually mentioned that he, Tony and Chip Matheson, whom they had met in a Whalewatch class, were planning to go up north to try to film wild orcas later that year. They really had no idea where they were going and what they would do when they got there, but they were confident, as 19-year-olds are, that they would figure it out once there. As it turned out, Gibson had just done a story about one of the Indian tribes and had met and worked with Mark Overland, who had worked a lot with orcas. Gibson suggested Talbot give him a call because maybe he could help.

A few months later, in the summer of 1977 – two years before the trip with Barbara – Bob, Tony and Chip packed for their big adventure. They had Bob's little Mazda, and Tony's small truck pulling a small inflatable boat on a trailer. They had not arranged anything, so it would be a great adventure no matter what. When they arrived in Tacoma, Washington, Bob called Mark Overland from a payphone at the side of the road. Overland, who was 23 at the time, was very nice and, without knowing any of our three young adventures, invited them to his parent's house, where he was living. Mark helped them find their way to a tree house on northern Vancouver Island, in Johnston Strait, British Columbia, that belonged to Paul Spong, a well-known researcher. That is how they began a number of trips to the northwest coast to film orcas in the wild. The photographs and footage they produced on these trips would be the genesis of Talbot's career.

In 1979, Barbara joined Bob and his friends. On that trip, she made some of the first sound recordings of wild orcas. It was a watershed year. In fact, they had one defining day that would make all the difference. Bob, Tony, Chip and

Barbara had set up camp on Vancouver Island. They were out on the water and had swum out to a little patch of kelp to wait for orcas to come by. A mother with a calf swam by and Bob hit the record button and filmed them making a few passes. Then another orca came by, started circling Bob in the water, and did not let him get back to the boat for about ten minutes. Bob was a bit nervous, but also very excited. He managed to get some great footage on 16mm film. When it was over, exuberance filled the boat. What a great day! Forgotten were the hardships of being an explorer in the wild: the cold nights, limited food choices, mosquito bites and mice.

On their way back to camp later that afternoon, they encountered another group of orcas moving down the strait. The wind had died completely and the light was gorgeous, so they decided to turn around and follow the whales for a while. Barbara was driving the boat. She was able to maneuver it into a perfect position so Bob could snap a few photographs of orcas with their blows beautifully lit. It was an amazing sight. Everyone took photographs. Soon afterward, Bob and Barbara began to sell framed photos at local art shows, but eventually the incredible photographs would be the basis for Bob's line of posters, which sold millions all around the world in the 1980s and 1990s.

The film footage Bob shot that day also launched his motion-picture career. A year or two later, he got a call from Jacques Cousteau's team. They were looking for some killer whale sounds for a TV production. Over the phone, Bob played some of the sounds Barbara had recorded for him and told the team that he could come by and drop off the recordings. Realizing that this could be a big break for him, he did not forget to mention that he also had some great footage if they wanted to take a look. They had already cut the film, but told him to bring the footage along anyway.

A week after he had delivered the sound and film footage, Bob received another phone call. Jacques Cousteau wanted to include Bob's footage in his film. Even more amazing, Cousteau wanted to meet Talbot and invited him to join him and his crew of the *Calypso* (his famous research vessel) on an upcoming trip to the Amazon. Somehow that did not work out, but a few years later Talbot did work with Cousteau filming orcas in the same area where he had gone before with Bernot, Matheson and Brunnick.

Talbot, Bernot, Matheson and Brunnick had reached a first milestone in their careers within a few years of meeting John Olguin. They knew that without John and the Whalewatch classes at the museum, things might never have unfolded the way they did. John was always there to help if they needed something. If something was broken and needed to be repaired, or if they needed a piece of equipment, either John would help them directly or someone he knew would help out. For these young explorers and the friends they made in Whalewatch class, their common experience would form a lasting connection.

John and Barbara developed an ever-closer relationship. John was the perfect audience for Barbara to vent her desire to be involved with marine mammals and she loved to listen to his stories. Every Tuesday night, once the museum was locked up tight, John and Barbara would rush to the Olguin home to make popcorn and coffee for the gatherings Muriel held with fellow artists. John also began to invite Barbara to join him and the scheduled speaker for dinner before ACS meetings. Most importantly, John made her believe that she had the right stuff to "Do it" too!

No doubt, Brunnick loved what she was doing. Life was great. Then an old problem reemerged with such vigor that it would put her life on hold for several years. Barbara had been born with a deformed vertebra. After years of trying to manage the pain with medication, she eventually required spinal surgery. Undergoing five surgeries, she spent the better part of five years in a body cast. Her vivid memories of whales and dolphins, along with John's encouragement that she could eventually resurrect her marine mammal career, helped her get through each day. During those long years of surgeries and recoveries, Barbara made the decision to get a science degree and become a bona fide whale scientist. With John's support, she was accepted into the University of California Santa Cruz in 1989 and became a student of Ken Norris. Norris soon hired her to work in his lab, where she worked with John Olguin protégés Ted Cranford and Randy Wells. The three of them all developed highly successful careers studying whales and dolphins.

After completing her studies at Santa Cruz, Brunnick left California for Florida in 1993 to study Atlantic spotted dolphins in the Bahamas. She discovered many secrets of their social organization, which earned her a doctoral degree in 2000. Today, she serves as the research program director of the Taras Oceanographic Foundation, managing a dolphin-population study in Palm Beach, Florida. She has also developed a process of mapping underwater habitats to better understand how whales and dolphins both influence, and are affected by, their environment. Many believe that the maps Barbara has been creating of marine and wetland habitats will change how we see the world. While John Olguin was a mentor to many, he was a father figure to Barbara and helped her to find the confidence and stamina to overcome illness and accept adversity as a small price to pay for adventure.

Among the many people Barbara met in John's Whalewatch classes was Robin Makowski who, like Brunnick, also moved to Florida in the early 1990s. While many who participated in John's classes became scientists or naturalists, Makowski, Talbot and others successfully pursued careers in the arts. With John's wife, Muriel, being an artist, John was exposed to art, as well as science, all of his adult life. It was only natural that he would give aspiring artists an equal amount of support and encouragement.

Robin Makowski was born in Chicago. She grew up in a self-described "dysfunctional home" with two alcoholic parents. After her parents' divorce, her stepfather abused her. She was a child full of potential, but with her focus squarely on just surviving each day, she had little energy or guidance to pursue her dream of being an artist. Though she had her doubts about becoming an artist, her quiet, mental mantra of "I am an artist" helped keep her dream alive. When she was 4 years old, her drawing of a horse got the attention of her father, an amateur but competent artist. Looking back, Robin would say that she was 10 years old before she realized that most people did not see things the way she did. That was about the same time Flipper splashed through the TV screen in the 1960s, recruiting her into the world of whales and dolphins. Jacques Cousteau and his ABC television specials over the years reinforced and increased her desire to learn more about these marvelous creatures. Maybe, she thought, one day she would even see them for herself.

In 1976, at age of 22, with her boyfriend who had recently been transferred from Chicago to Los Angeles, she jumped at the opportunity to leave the Midwest for California, a place where she and her friends had fantasized about moving one day. As she would quickly discover, life in California was not just about the beach, having fun, the movies, surfing and the good life – at least not for everyone. Robin worked the night shift as a waitress at the Hyatt Regency Hotel in downtown Los Angeles and, not making a lot of money, she ended up living in a roach-infested apartment in West Hollywood. But she enjoyed the opportunities California offered to nature lovers and spent days discovering the area.

One night at work, someone mentioned the wonderful experience of going out on a Whalewatch boat. Robin could not believe that she could go to San Pedro, pay $8, get on a boat and see whales close up. She did not need to hear more. She made her reservation, went down to Ports O' Call, got on the boat, and, for the first time in her life, she saw California gray whales. They seemed smaller then she thought they would be. A docent from the Cabrillo Marine Museum in San Pedro was narrating the trip and Robin plagued her with questions about the whales, about the program, and about how to learn to do what she was doing as a docent. She could not stop. Finally, she was told that if she was *that* interested, she should contact John Olguin at the Cabrillo Marine Museum.

Robin called the museum and was encouraged to visit and meet John. She remembered John as, "a warm, mid-fifties, clean-shaven, white-haired man with a road map of wrinkles on his face." Robin nervously introduced herself, telling him the same story he had no doubt heard a thousand times before, about how the Whalewatch trip changed her life. She was in no way prepared for John's answer. He replied, "I need a dockmaster at 22nd Street Landing on Monday, Tuesday,

Wednesday, Thursday, and Friday. You meet the school buses, talk to the teachers, and make sure they get on the right boats. We have meetings every Tuesday night and we work with ACS…the American Cetacean Society. You'll learn everything you need to know. Okay?" Robin's response was dumbfounded silence. John knew a sucker when he saw one. "Okay?" he repeated.

"Uh…okay," Robin replied reluctantly. It was the beginning of her not ever learning how to say "no" to John.

Through people who soon became fast friends, Makowski was offered a very inexpensive apartment in San Pedro. For a while, she commuted to West Hollywood to a job at a parrot store, but when that came to be too much, she got a job at the newly opened Grinder Restaurant on the San Pedro waterfront, where she worked for eight years. Living in San Pedro allowed her to get deeply involved with the museum, the ACS, and with other docents. Under John's guidance, Robin's true personality was allowed to emerge. The first time John put Robin in front of a gaggle of kindergartners and made her "Flap like a pelican," she was so scared that she had tears in her eyes. Like so many others, she not only learned how to speak in front of a group of museum visitors of any age, she came to love to be on stage in front of hundreds of people.

The infamous 1978 caravan trip to Baja California was a classic never to be repeated. Makowski had anticipated the trip for months, counting down the days. She met another docent, Cheré Gibson, a redhead with a red jacket, the standard uniform of the times. They hit it off and Gibson asked Makowski to ride to Baja in the van with her and Sharon Baumgart (now Marshall), who was also instrumental in changing Makowski's life and is still a close and cherished friend.

Ted Cranford's first dolphin contact at Marineland, California, in 1976.
Photo Courtesy Ted Cranford Private Archive

Ted Cranford and the blue whale skeleton at Long Marine Lab, CA. 1985.
Photo Courtesy Ted Cranford Private Archive

Chris Matheson, Barbara Brunnick and Tony Bernot (from left to right) studying killer whales around Vancouver Island in 1979. Photo Courtesy Harzen/Brunnick Private Archive

Barbara Brunnick studying Atlantic spotted dolphin in the Bahamas. 1997. Photo Courtesy Harzen/Brunnick Private Archive

Barbara Brunnick with her mentor Ken Norris. 1993.
Photo Courtesy Harzen/Brunnick Private Archive

Robin Lee Makowski and John Olguin on December 31, 2010, at John's home.
Photo Courtesy Marcos Lee

Alisa Schulman-Janiger encountering a gray whale at close range in San Ignacio Lagoon, Baja California. 1985. Photo Courtesy A. Schulman-Janiger Private Archive

Alisa Schulman-Janiger, John Heyning, Carol Ball, Bob Bonde, Barbara Brunnick, and Diana McIntyre (left to right). 2001. Photo Courtesy A. Schulman-Janiger Private Archive

Alisa Schulman-Janiger on a whale watch trip. 2007.
Photo Courtesy A. Schulman-Janiger Private Archive

Pt. Fermin Lighthouse, San Pedro, Cal

Postcard showing the Point Fermin Lighthouse around 1914.
Courtesy of Point Fermin Lighthouse Collections

Point Fermin
Lighthouse in
2006. Courtesy
of Point Fermin
Lighthouse,
Department of
Recreation and
Parks, City of Los
Angeles

The historic Fresnel lens that John Olguin and Bill
Olesen sought to return to the lighthouse, was final-
ly returned to its home after years of negotiations.
Photograph by Kristen Heather. 2006. Courtesy of
Point Fermin Lighthouse Collections

John talking with a little girl on 4th of July 2001

Marji Frank, Anne Holmes, and John Olguin (from left to right) promoting 4th of July fireworks campaign. Early 1980s. Photo Courtesy Cabrillo Marine Museum/ Cabrillo Marine Aquarium

John Olguin always enjoyed dressing up as the famous Portuguese explorer Juan Cabrillo, the 16th century adventurer after whom Cabrillo Beach was ultimately named. 1996. Photo Courtesy Alisa Schulman-Janiger Private Archive

The three of them stopped at San Quintin, Baja California, the first night, and then continued to Guererro Negro where they stayed at the El Presidente Campground. Together with their fellow adventurers and explorers, they trekked out to Guererro Negro Lagoon every day to watch and listen to the whales, their calves, and in between, the silence. They witnessed the most awesome sunset any of them had ever seen and were part of the great adventure, starring "Libby," the entangled gray whale. Bob Talbot, Chip Matheson, Rick King and a few more good souls helped the whale to free itself, which segued into a night of celebration, a whole lot of tequila, and a night in a spinning tent with Horace Staubley and a few more fellow whale enthusiasts.

For Robin, the positive dominoes of life continued falling in place. She rented an apartment in San Pedro with Sharon's mom, Chloe, who would be her landlady for twelve years. Through Sharon, she also met Mark, her husband and the love-of-her-life for the last thirty years, with whom she has two boys. Robin's artistic career also began through her association with John and the ACS. She illustrated for the *Whale Watcher*, the journal of the American Cetacean Society (ACS), and the posters she created for them were shown in the movie *Free Willy*! She got her first paid illustration job with Pam Stacey at the Cousteau Society, a friend and associate of Patty Warhol, who was the executive director of ACS at the time, and with whom Makowski became close friends. Soon, Robin was commissioned to create a poster for the Discovery Channel. The person she worked with at Discovery was also looking for an illustrator for a line of children's books he wanted to develop, and commissioned Robin to illustrate a couple of pages so he could present them to publishers with his manuscript. While the book project was too ambitious for

Kidsbooks in New York, after reviewing the illustrations, they asked for Robin's contact information for other projects for which they felt she would be perfectly suited.

Because Robin and her husband could not afford to buy a house in California, they decided in 1992 to move to Florida, where real estate was much more reasonable. In Florida, her career really took off, as Robin became involved with the Wild Dolphin Project in Jupiter, Florida, and started working as the organization's illustrator. They developed a line of pro-bono ads with her illustrations that appeared in *National Geographic, Surfer, The New Yorker* and other magazines. In 1993, she landed a position creating T-shirt designs for the American Outback line through American Artwear in Palm City, Florida, through which she became proficient at illustrating animals with fur, antlers and hooves for the first time. she also learned the tricky business of silk-screen printing, which eventually led to a job with Southeastern Printing in Stuart, Florida, in the department that produced fine art prints for artists. She then ran Blue Water Editions for almost ten years, producing more than one hundred of her own fine art images as reproductions. She also joined the outdoor art festival circuit in Florida and the Southeast and sold her own work. Makowski continues to show and sell at many art festivals, galleries and juried art shows around the country.

In 2008, Robin and Mark moved to New Mexico, bought a commercial building with a residence behind it and created Studio 54@70, a gallery and art studio. Over the last twenty-two years, Makowski has become an award-winning professional fine artist, illustrator and author of more than thirty children's books. Since leaving California in 1992, she has maintained many of her Cabrillo-family relationships and has kept up on all the gossip. If Baumgart's tenant ever moves out of her old apartment on 23rd Street in San Pedro, Robin might be back. No matter where Robin lives, she is far removed from her days as a child who had her doubts about becoming an artist, yet never forgot the "I am an artist" mantra that helped to keep her dream alive. Makowski the artist has clearly arrived, even though her life took quite a detour through the wild, but positive world of John Olguin. He helped her hone her talents and develop an even more positive attitude to help her ensure her dreams would come true.

If Robin ever does return to the cradle of her career in San Pedro, she might easily run into her old Whalewatch pal Alisa Schulman. Like for so many, John Olguin played a significant role in her life too. John instilled in her a life-long fascination with grunion and hands-on teaching techniques. John helped to fuel Alisa's scientific mind, got her firmly hooked on whales and brought her many lasting relationships.

It all started innocently enough when Schulman first came to the Cabrillo Marine Museum as a little girl with her kindergarten class in 1961. She examined several marine creatures sitting in jars on a table outside of the bathhouse. And then she hatched grunion. She filled a little jar with sand and water, shook it, and watched the baby fish pop out of their eggs. Right before she hatched the grunion, John had told all of the kids to, "Put your arms up, wiggle, and dance like a grunion!" He danced around with such enthusiasm, showing the kids what to do, that none of them realized they were learning something. It felt like play. The memory of those little grunion stuck with Alisa. When it came time to pick a project for her advanced science class in Grade 9, she chose to investigate the life cycle and mysteries surrounding the grunion. By

1978, Schulman was attending California State University of Long Beach, where she met John Heyning, who shared her interest in marine biology and her passion for whales. Both hoped to become whale scientists.

Heyning, who later became the curator of marine mammals and deputy director of the Los Angeles County Natural History Museum, had been one of John Olguin's high school museum volunteers. He invited Schulman to go with him to the Tuesday night Whalewatch class at the Cabrillo Marine Museum. Presentations by Bemi DeBus, one of the founding members of ACS, and Bill Samaras, the colorful high school marine biology teacher famous for his lecture on gray whale reproductive habits, captivated Alisa's attention. Overnight, Tuesday evenings became the special time that she spent with like-minded college students. They would sit on the floor in small groups with a "veteran" whale watcher leading discussions about the evening's topics. John Olguin would make sure that students were never in the same small groups, so that they were exposed to a variety of people, stories and experiences.

Schulman's first Whalewatch season ended in March 1979, just in time for grunion season. Many Whalewatch volunteers returned to see slides on a screen set up on the beach near the museum to learn about grunion. For Alisa, it was her first class and it reconnected her with her very first experience at the museum. When John told everyone to, "Put your arms up, wiggle, and dance like a grunion!" while dancing and showing the volunteers what to do, Alisa suddenly realized that this was the same man she remembered from her childhood. Her life had circled back to the same museum, to the same person whose crazy grunion dance had influenced her decision to pursue a career in marine biology. No doubt, she was in the right place. As it would turn out, being a volunteer at the museum would not only bring adventure but, for Alisa, it would also bring love and personal happiness.

John had compiled a list of Whalewatch volunteers who would be interested in working on any future stranded dead whales. The list was short because most volunteers just wanted to see live whales, but both Schulman and John Heyning were on the list. On July 6, 1980, Alisa had an opportunity to see – and work on – her first whale stranding. She stood on Cabrillo Beach and looked through the binoculars to see a large whale that was floating upside down in the harbor. Several throat pleats or grooves, extending from the whale's lower lip past its flippers, were clearly visible, so she knew right away that it was not a gray whale because they only have between two and five throat pleats. It turned out to be a blue whale. Even though it measured nearly fifty-eight feet in length, this juvenile male was only just over a year old.

Together with dozens of volunteers, Alisa worked tirelessly on the blue whale for about a week in the summer heat that sometimes soared to over one hundred degrees. The beach took on a quite distinctive aroma. Thankfully, after a while, the volunteers did not even notice the smell. The same could not be said for the regular patrons of a few local eateries that the crew visited at the end of their long days. Those patrons covered their noses and cleared out. As a result, John Olguin decided it would be better to provide food and drinks to the volunteers on the beach.

John and Bill Samaras were always teaming up on new projects and, this time, they decided to plan a blue whale reunion party at Bill's home later that month. They invited all of the people who had been involved in the whale dissection. Bill had noticed that Alisa seemed especially interested in one volunteer - Dave Janiger – with whom he had worked to cut up the whale. Bill asked Dave to help Alisa put her slideshow together in the backroom of his house. The time they spent at this party led to romance between Dave and Alisa, as well as life-long friendships with Matchmaker Bill and his wife, Mary.

Many of the volunteers had a very close relationship with John, who was genuinely interested in their personal lives and well-being. Over the many years that Dave and Alisa were dating, John would occasionally ask when they were going to get married. Thirteen years after the party at Bill's house, on a Tuesday night in January just before Whalewatch class was to begin, Alisa told John that she and Dave had briefly discussed marriage but had not made any definite plans. Half-jokingly, Alisa added that she was thinking of asking Dave to marry her. John suggested she do it now since there would be plenty of witnesses.

After Alisa finished presenting her short weekly slideshow review of local whales, she projected a slide of a blue whale, described the whale, and reminded everyone of the 1980 blue whale stranding. And then, she proposed to Dave, who had not been paying attention at all. More than one hundred people stopped talking and turned around to look at him. He looked up, quite puzzled and stammered out a reply. Janiger and Schulman were officially engaged, distinguished as being the only marriage proposal ever to occur during the Whalewatch classes. The couple was married in the community building that overlooked Cabrillo Beach, right where the blue whale had stranded.

Bill Samaras was a pillar of the Whalewatch program. Together with Laura Osteen, the ACS membership chair at the time, he ran the gray whale census from 1979 until 1981. They suspended it during the huge El Niño event of 1982 and 1983, but resumed it one year later. With Samaras as her advisor, Alisa Schulman-Janiger became the coordinator and director of the ACS/LA Gray Whale Census and Behavior Project. Teams of volunteers would go out to the cliffs where they had a panoramic view of the coastline to identify and count gray whales and other marine mammals from sunrise to sunset.

In 1984 and 1985, Schulman-Janiger set up a concurrent census site at the west end of Santa Catalina Island. These tandem projects provided data that verified the findings noted previously by Bill Samaras and his students: gray whales migrated along the backside of Santa Catalina Island during the southbound migration and off the mainland during the northbound migration. This unique project would not have been so successful without John's help. He organized free passage with the Catalina Express to the island for the census takers, held garage sales as fundraisers, and donated monies from the John Olguin Trust Fund to cover some of the project's expenses. John also included the census in the sign-up process at the Whalewatch meetings, making it eligible for volunteer credit hours.

When the census was in full swing, John asked Alisa if she wanted a part-time job at the Cabrillo Marine Museum as a program assistant. She was already teaching marine biology to students on boats for LAUSD's Sea Education Afloat program, following in the wet footsteps of John Heyning and another good friend and Whalewatch alumnus, Emmanuel Rosales. Emmanuel was a former high school volunteer, who, in 1981, became the first curator of the museum, which was renamed Cabrillo Marine Aquarium (CMA) in 1993.

Schulman-Janiger accepted the position and was a Cabrillo Marine Museum program assistant for three years, operating the information booth, running slideshows and giving tours. When Emmanuel was unable to accompany John on the museum's San Ignacio Lagoon gray-whale trip, he sent Alisa as his replacement. For Alisa, it was the trip of a lifetime, an opportunity to share her knowledge of gray whales while observing them up close from small boats. John's encouragement and expertise were indispensible, and his enthusiasm was always contagious. No matter how many times he saw a whale performing a behavior, he never failed to point and appropriately yell "spyhop!" or "breach!" with all of his unbridled, genuine excitement. When John offered Alisa a Cabrillo Marine Museum naturalist position the following year, she happily accepted.

While the census work of gray whales quickly became routine, there were days when Mother Nature threw in a surprise or two. On one of these occasions, the volunteers spotted some killer whales off Palos Verdes Peninsula. Alisa immediately called photographer Bob Talbot, who had firsthand knowledge of killer whales, and the two headed out in Talbot's Zodiac. They found and then spent several hours with the orcas, giving Alisa her first look at the local group that later became known as the L.A. Pod. Equipped with new data, Alisa contacted Dennis Kelly, a marine biology instructor at Orange Coast College, who had started collecting records and photographs of killer whales sighted at various locations along the California coast. With encouragement from John Olguin, Alisa and Dennis compared notes, and soon Alisa was putting together a catalogue of photos in Dennis's collection, which resulted in *Killer Whales of California and Western Mexico: A Catalog of Photo-Identified Individuals,* the only California killer whale ID guide.

All these years later, Alisa continues to direct the ACS/ L.A. Gray Whale Census Project, which is the world's longest-running shore-based gray whale project. She is one of the world's leading experts on California killer whales. Along with Diana McIntyre, she is a key instructor for Tuesday evenings' Cabrillo Whalewatch classes, the program that John started so many years ago. She also continues to teach marine biology at San Pedro High School's Marine Science Magnet Program, where she always includes fieldtrips to the Cabrillo Marine Aquarium.

These are just a few of the documented stories of the thousands of people whom John Olguin influenced and nurtured. John's unparalleled guidance increased the ranks of marine scientists, writers, photographers, and artists exponentially. His influence also spans across generations of teachers who educate individuals about the world's oceans, the many species who live in them, and the importance of respecting the magnificent creatures in those amazing bodies of water.

THE COMMUNITY
ORGANIZER

*J*ohn Olguin was always a lifeguard – on and off the beach.
For him there was no clear distinction between the two:
the border was fluid. His home-town, his community, was
remarkably important to him. John was always the first
one to step up, help people in need, and assume responsibility
for making San Pedro a better place.

One of John's life-long community projects was the
Fourth of July fireworks. As a lifeguard who was often on
duty on Independence Day, John had seen his fair share of
grown men and children come to the lifeguard station with
their fingers blown off because they had held fireworks in
their hands for too long. All he could do was administer
first aid and then send them to the emergency room. John
thought that if only professionals set off fireworks, there
would not be all of the injuries, so he inquired if the City
of Los Angeles could fund the fireworks in San Pedro. The
response was that if the people of San Pedro wanted a fireworks show on the Fourth of July, they should form a committee and raise their own money to pay for it.

In 1949, John formed a committee. He asked Bob Beck,
the editor of the local newspaper, the *San Pedro News-Pilot*, if
he could publish a story explaining what he was trying to do,

why he had committed himself to making it happen, and how he and his fellow lifeguards wanted to raise the money. John suggested that Bob include the instructions that if people wanted to donate money, they should leave their front porch lights on. A committee member would only knock on the doors of houses where the lights were on to collect a donation. The story was published and when John and his friends went out that night to fundraise, almost every house had their lights turned on.

As John would find out, not every light meant that he was welcome, but in most cases the citizens of his hometown reached into their pockets and contributed to their hometown's fireworks. Notwithstanding the generosity of many, collecting money one dollar at a time was hard work. Most people were not home before 7 p.m. and most people were in bed after 9 p.m., so they had only two hours to go around and collect. It took about two weeks to collect four thousand dollars, working five days a week.

From 1949 through 1963, John continued to spearhead this effort. The following years, the Chamber of Commerce stepped in and John was then able to lie back and enjoy the show. As the big day drew near in 1964, with no news about a fireworks display in San Pedro, John called the Chamber and they told him that there would not be any fireworks that year. No one had volunteered to chair the finance committee and organize the fundraising. Little, if anything, is achievable and attainable without leadership. For John, as a born leader, when it came to serving his community no task was too difficult or too time-consuming. John knew he needed to get back into the game, so he became the chair of the finance committee and remained in that post until he retired from the museum twenty-four years later. During the more than two decades he headed the finance committee, John always managed to raise enough money to pay for the fireworks at Cabrillo Beach.

When John retired in 1987, he wanted to make sure that the fundraising continued. By then, the Cabrillo Marine Museum had a not-for-profit arm called Cabrillo Marine Museum Volunteers, with which many of his volunteers were involved. John approached them saying that he would like to continue raising money and give it to them, if they would in turn write a check to pay for the fireworks. To John's surprise and disappointment, they declined because they felt the fireworks had nothing to do with the museum. John went back to the Chamber of Commerce and together they began to build up a fund large enough that the interest would pay for the annual fireworks.

After three years, a new law took effect that determined donations to the Chamber were no longer tax deductible. John then took his cause to the Lions Club, but they declined. Next, he proposed it to the Rotary Club, where he was an honorary member, and they agreed. When he finally passed on the torch and resigned as the chairman of the San Pedro Fourth of July Celebration in 1989, he had completed thirty-seven years of service. Of course, John continued to do the hard work of raising money by organizing a trip around Catalina Island and giving lectures at universities, schools and civic organizations.

In the spring of 2000, John decided to make wooden firecracker lapel pins that he and his friends could sell to raise funds for the fireworks. He knew just the right people who could help him: Judy Scoble and her husband, Glenn, were experienced woodshop volunteers. In 1997, John had wanted to celebrate French aviator Louis Paulhan and give away one thousand wooden airplane kits to children. On January 14, 1910, Paulhan had flown his Farman biplane on a twenty-mile flight from Dominguez Aviation Field (which is now Carson) to San Pedro, where he crossed over the ocean at the Point Fermin Cliffs, establishing a new endurance record. During the same air show, he also established a new world altitude record of 4,164 feet. It was the beginning of an entirely new frontier in transportation, which was met with great enthusiasm by more than two hundred thousand spectators and helped usher in the aerospace era in Southern California. In the 1960s, fifteen of the twenty-five largest aerospace companies in the U.S., including Hughes Aircraft Company, the Aerospace Corporation, Northrop Corporation and Lockheed were based in Southern California. These companies built commercial and military planes, as well as the Apollo command module in the 1960s. California has remained a center of the aerospace industry ever since.

It took eighty-eight years for someone like John Olguin to come along to recognize and celebrate the achievements of Paulhan in 1910. With most of the professional woodworkers working on Christmas projects at the time, Judy and Glenn came to the rescue. John organized a place with workbenches and electricity, but it did not have any heat. John rounded up money, wood and other materials, and then Glenn and some volunteers cut up many feet of wood and high school students cut the wing boards. The volunteers ended up manufacturing the airplanes, while the children painted them and added a commemorative decal. It took from December 1, 1997 until January 17, 1998 to complete one thousand wooden airplanes.

One year later, everyone was working on one thousand wooden bridges to celebrate the lighting of the Vincent Thomas Bridge for New Year's Eve 2000. And now, in the third year of the woodshop volunteer group, they were manufacturing 3,700 wooden firecrackers: cutting wood, painting the pieces red, using pipe cleaner as fuses and attaching pin-backs. John started to sell the firecracker pins for $2 a piece in 1999. For years, if you were walking the streets of San Pedro, or were at one of the local establishments or landings, there was a good chance that John would walk up to you and ask you to buy some.

As if working at the museum, training naturalists in his Whalewatch classes and speaking at countless events and occasions was not enough of a workload, John was constantly getting involved in new adventures. He just could not say no. If it benefited the community, John Olguin would get it done.

The Point Fermin Lighthouse certainly qualified, as John loved the lighthouse. It was a beautiful landmark and one of the oldest buildings in San Pedro. After the World War II, the lighthouse no longer served a purpose. It just stood there, a landmark, a relic of the past, slowly showing signs of decay. It was the early 1970s, the decade when many wanted to replace the old with something new. The Coast Guard, which now had jurisdiction over the lighthouse, had decided to tear it down so a radar station could be installed on the site. A hundred years of San Pedro's history was on the butcher block.

It was only after the Treaty of Guadalupe Hidalgo, which brought an official end to the Mexican–American War, was signed in 1848 that the California coastline was surveyed accurately and critical locations for lighthouses were identified. It was again Phineas Banning, the man who developed the inner San Pedro Bay, who petitioned U.S. Congress to build a lighthouse in San Pedro to increase safety for the ships coming to the harbor. Congress made a first appropriation to cover the cost for a survey and some preliminary plans, but land disputes made any progress impossible.

In 1871, the Army Corps of Engineers had begun construction of a jetty to form a barrier between Rattlesnake (Terminal) Island and Deadman's Island. As many as 600 men worked on the project and many lived at the construction camps set up on Rattlesnake Island, which represented the original community of East San Pedro. With this 6,700-foot-long seawall, along with another built on the west side and some dredging, ships would be able to proceed up the channel to protected docks to unload their cargo. Traffic was sure to increase and a lighthouse was needed more than ever.

Point Fermin was selected as the best location and, at last, the federal government appropriated three acres of the headland. According to an account by Bill Oleson, Jose Diego Sepulveda was deemed to have the most valid claim and received thirty-five dollars as payment. The Lighthouse Board completed the plans in 1872, and the lighthouse was completed in the summer of 1874 at a cost of fourteen thousand dollars. The lighthouse was equipped with a Fresnel lens of the 4th order and its 2,100 C.P. (candlepower) made the light visible up to thirteen miles offshore.

At the time, lighthouses were important navigational aids for the shipping industry, and the lighthouse keepers served as lookouts and first responders to approaching vessels. In 1888, the *Respigadera*, a sailing ship bound from Newcastle, England, with a delivery of coal for San Pedro, hit the reef off Point Fermin. Captain Shaw, the lighthouse keeper at the time, sounded the alarm and the community prepared to salvage the vessel. First, though, the crew had to throw their cargo overboard to lighten the ship and the rescuers had to wait for high tide to pull the vessel off the reef. As it turned out, the *Respigadera* had rescued seven people from the Gilbert Islands on a raft in the Pacific – they certainly must have thought that lightning can strike twice! The community provided shelter for the group, who were then transferred to San Francisco and from there returned to the Gilbert Islands. To this day, more than one hundred years after the ship's grounding, coal will still wash up below the Point Fermin Lighthouse after a strong winter storm.

The first keeper of the lighthouse was Mary L. Smith, a young woman who had previously been the keeper of the Ediz Hook Lighthouse, with her sister Ella serving as her assistant, at Port Angeles in Washington Territory near the Canadian border. In 1874, after four years at Ediz Hook, at the age of 34, Smith became the keeper of the Point Fermin Lighthouse, with her sister Ella once again by her side as the assistant keeper. After eight years, in January 1882, Ella resigned and the Lighthouse Board appointed James Herald as new assistant keeper to serve with Smith. What followed was a rather tumultuous three months that led to the dismissal of both Smith and Herald in April of the same year. Captain George N. Shaw and his wife replaced them, serving 22 years. They were followed by Irby H. Engels from 1904 to 1917, and then William and Martha Austin became the keepers of the lighthouse. Their daughter Thelma took over in 1925, after her parents died within two months of each other. She remained the keeper until 1927.

By the mid-1920s, the light had been twice upgraded. In 1912, an incandescent petroleum vapor lamp with a candlepower of 6,600 replaced the oil wick light and, together with a new Fresnel lens of the 4th order, extended the visibility to twenty-two miles. Then in 1925, the system was converted to electricity. Finally, the City of Los Angeles Department of Recreation and Parks took over the lighthouse operation in 1927 in exchange for the use of the three acres for a park.

Oscar I. Johnson and his wife were the last to switch the light on and off every day until the morning of December 7, 1941. After the attack on Pearl Harbor, all coastal lights along the western sea border of the United States remained dark. In short order, the light was replaced with a radar scanner aimed at detecting enemy ships.

This wonderful lighthouse, together with its history, might well have been bulldozed into oblivion had it not been for an anonymous phone call in 1973 that alerted John Olguin to the Coast Guard's plans. If John had anything to do with it, that lighthouse would always be there. He immediately drafted a letter, drove by the office of the local newspaper, the *News-Pilot*, and handed it to the editor, Bob Beck, who published it the next day. John cut it out and sent it to his congressional representative, Glenn Anderson, who made the phone calls to stop the bulldozers. Congressman Anderson had played a significant role in passing of the Marine Mammal Act in 1972 and would, once again, play a crucial role by paving the way for the lighthouse to be put on the National Register of Historic Places. Once that happened, John and his friend Bill Olesen moved on to phase two, its restoration.

After obtaining the original blueprints from the Coast Guard, they went to the City of Los Angeles and asked for permission to restore it. John and Bill were prepared to raise the funds and do all the work with volunteers if the city would give them a permit. The city agreed to issue the permit contingent upon John and Bill signing an affidavit taking personal responsibility for any accidents or any lawsuits associated with the restoration. The two men looked at each other with a smile, nodded and signed.

Bill Olesen, a boat builder for Wilmington Boat Works, knew how to read blueprints, determine what and how much

material was needed, where to get the materials, how to schedule what needed to be done and so forth. John knew everyone
in town, as well as how to raise money. They were convinced
they could do it, so they began to work on the lighthouse.
They put a pulley up on top and pulled down what they called
a chicken coop. While Bill worked on the site, John would
go around town to buy materials and raise money. No matter where he went, nobody would take his money. When told
that it was for the lighthouse, they would ask, "What do you
need and how much?" Lumber, glass, whatever it was, they
gave it to John. When John went to the five- and ten-cent
store to buy some things, the manager asked if he was buying
the supplies for the lighthouse. John replied that he was. The
manager told the clerk not to take John's money. Now that
was unheard of because the five- and ten-cent store did not
give anything away!

One of the people working on the lighthouse restoration
was John's long-time neighbor Claude Morris. At the time,
Claude was retired from the Fire Department and was working
with the Department of Water and Power five days per week.
John wanted him to help with the lighthouse, so he spoke to
Claude's boss, asking if he could work on the lighthouse as long
as needed. To Claude's surprise, his boss agreed. Claude spent
about a month working on the lighthouse. It turned out that
John had used some of his old-time persuasive leverage.

While Claude and Bill had great mechanical talent, John
did not. He was the organizer. Everything went fine except
one aspect: the original light was put in the cellar right after
the war, but it was not there any more. John found the names
and addresses of all the people who had been living there in
1941 and contacted them. Nobody knew what happened to
the light. John and Bill grew frustrated and anxious. It was

1974, the 100th birthday of the lighthouse was coming up and they were planning a grand celebration.

Bill and John met once a week over breakfast to discuss what they could do. At one of these meetings, a sea captain named Ed Fabian, who worked for the Navy at the time, walked through the door. The three men sat down together and talked about the lighthouse. Bill and John told him that they had a temporary light to put into the lighthouse for the opening, because they could not locate the original light. To their great surprise, it turned out they were having breakfast with the man who knew where it was! In fact, Fabian had delivered it to lifeguard captain George Watkins in Santa Monica so he could put it into a museum he wanted to develop on the pier in Santa Monica.

George Watkins was a friend of John's, but he had passed away. John called his son, Willie, and inquired about the light. They had removed many items from the pier to protect them from a big storm, including the light, and stored them on George's property. When the property was sold, the light went with it. As far as Willie knew, it had ended up in Ventura. John got to work and tracked it down. With a picture in hand, he and Bill went to see the man who had in his possession the lighthouse light they needed. It was only a couple of weeks before the big anniversary.

Louis Busch, a realtor in Malibu, was the man they had to see. However, when they met Busch, he was not as cooperative as Bill and John had hoped. He claimed that the lens he had in his possession came from a lightship and that Bill and John must be mistaken in believing that his lens belonged to the lighthouse. Bill and John looked at the label and it read:

This lens is of the fourth order, made in 1854 in France [a Fresnel lens]. Shipped around the Horn into

California, lit on December the 15th, 1874 at Point
Fermin Lighthouse in San Pedro.

Regardless of the evidence, Louis Busch was not going to
hand over the lens. John and Bill tried everything, including going to the admiral of the Coast Guard, but he could
not help. John went to his supervisor, but he could not help
either. Former California Supreme Court Associate Justice
Stanley Mosk, now a private attorney in the California capital of Sacramento, offered to sue Louis Busch at no charge to
John and Bill, but they did not want to take legal action. After
all, they felt he had helped to protect the lens over the years.

John went to a friend of his who worked as a fundraiser at
Stanford University. John explained his predicament and his
friend was ready to help. He would go with John and a lawyer
and explain to Louis Busch that, according to all the documentation, the lens belongs to the lighthouse in San Pedro. Then,
they would ask him how much he wanted for it. John was worried. What if he wanted a million dollars? John's friend promised to come up with the money, no matter how much it was.

All excited that they would finally get the lens back, John
called Bill to tell him the good news. Bill did not want to
have any part in this. He felt the lens belonged to the government and, even though he too appreciated the fact the Busch
had taken care of the lens, he did not want to pay him a penny
for it. He was convinced he and John could outlive Busch and
somehow get the lens after all. John was not so peculiar, but
quickly learned that Busch was not prepared to sell the lens
for any price. There was nothing John and Bill could do. They
would have to celebrate the 100th anniversary of the lighthouse without it. It was a grand event nonetheless.

As the years went by, John figured it might be a good idea
to try to get the lens before Busch died. John always put a

positive spin on everything. He was not quite sure how to go about it, but he sure would be ready when the moment was right. One day in 1984, John attended a Whalewatch meeting with about two hundred people and he noticed a distinguished-looking, gray-haired elderly gentleman. John noticed him because he was the only person in the room who was wearing a coat and tie. John thought that if ever there was a man of importance, this must be him.

When the meeting was over, John approached him. The man's name was Leon Dougherty. He was the retired president of Northrup University in Hawthorne, California, and a regional head of the Federal Aviation Administration (FAA). He had come down to the meeting because his children had such a great time whale watching that he wanted to be part of it too. John walked him into his office and, after a while, they came to talk about the lighthouse. John inevitably told him the whole story about the lens. After listening to everything John had tried, Dougherty suggested that John contact the Department of Commerce by writing a letter to Secretary of Commerce Elizabeth Dole who served as head of the department and was a cabinet secretary under President Reagan. Leon Dougherty even wrote the letter and delivered it the next morning. According to John, it was one of the finest letters he had ever read. He mailed it right away. Only after sending it did he realize that he had not made a copy for his own records.

Some time later, John received a phone call from someone at *Life* magazine, who had heard from Secretary Dole's office about John's struggles to get the lens back. John and the magazine developed a plan: they would take a picture of the original lens through the window of Busch's house in Malibu, and take a photo with many people and the lighthouse. The headline would say, "The people of San Pedro want their lens back and Mr. Busch won't give it to us." Put that on the cover of *Life* and see what happens, John was told. A photographer and a reporter from *Life* magazine came to San Pedro. They went to the lighthouse to take the photographs, but there were only about twenty-five people willing to serve as "extras." The photographer thought there were too few people, given the size of the lighthouse. He told John he needed a hundred people within forty-five minutes, so John got to work, called everyone he could think of and, within the hour, 125 people showed up.

The photographer then decided to wait for the sunset. They went out, rented torches and gave a torch to everybody. John was to stand in front of the lighthouse, some people all around the lighthouse, and some leaning out of the windows. Then they wanted some people to climb on the roof, but John thought that was just too dangerous. The photographer claimed he needed it for a good shot, so John called the chief of the Fire Department and told him he needed ten firefighters on the roof of the lighthouse in fifteen minutes. The firemen got there in less than five minutes! They pulled up their ladder trucks and, as the sun set that day, ten firemen stood with torches in their hands on the roof of the Point Fermin Lighthouse. The issue of *Life* magazine came out in August 1987. However, the picture of the lens itself was never taken and they did not get the lens back from Busch.

In the late 1990s, the Lighthouse Society appointed a committee to try again to persuade Busch to return the lens but, despite their best efforts, they were not successful. Then, Huell Howser, a quirky Los Angeles Public Television personality from KCET Channel 28, wanted to do a story on the lighthouse, so John and a few others met with him and told him the whole story. Together with Dr. Pete Lee, the director of the Maritime Museum at the time, John invited Busch for lunch and offered him a great story and television publicity. Again, he refused.

The Coast Guard also kept trying to get the lighthouse lens back. A picture of the original Point Fermin Lighthouse lens was found on file, so the Coast Guard compared the picture with the lens in Busch's possession and proved that it belonged to the Point Fermin Lighthouse. Busch had to relent, the lens was finally returned to the lighthouse on Nov. 13, 2006, over thirty-two years after John and Bill Oleson had first tried to bring it home. The Point Fermin Lighthouse Society held a dinner celebration on Friday December 15, followed by the public celebration the next day. Many of the actors involved in the drama were present, including Louis Busch and John Olguin. John's friend Bill Oleson, however, would not see the fruits of their joint struggle. He had died in 1999, but not before John had promised him that when the lens was finally returned, he would dance the sailor's hornpipe, a dance that reaches back to the 19th century, telling the life of a sailor and his duties aboard. In true John Olguin style, he had the music played by his favorite local mariachi band.

With the lighthouse saved, John found time to work on another landmark: the Vincent Thomas Bridge that spans San Pedro and Terminal Island. It is the most prominent feature of the harbor. In the 1870s, the only way to cross the main channel of the harbor from San Pedro to Rattlesnake Island was with a rowboat. It was the first ferry to speak of, provided by Captain Martin E. Lindskov. It was service upon demand, not by schedule. Then, in the early 1880s, Captain Mitchell Duffy began to offer a scheduled ferry service to Terminal Island. Over the years, he added five boats, which he named after all his children. As both sides of the channel developed and grew, a need for larger boats arose, boats that could transport vehicles. In 1911, the San Pedro Transportation Company began a ferry service that could carry horses, wagons and even automobiles.

By the later 1930s, there was growing discontent with the ferry service. In 1937, Cuthbert Olson, then senator and later governor of California, authored Bill 590, which called for the construction of a tunnel to connect San Pedro and Terminal Island. The bill never passed. Instead, a municipal ferry system was implemented on September 2, 1941, with shorter routes and new terminals at 6th Street in San Pedro and 4th Street on Terminal Island. Two ferries, the *Islander* and the *Ace*, shuttled passengers, automobiles, workers, commuters and travelers, the *Islander* during the day and the smaller *Ace* at night with only pedestrian passengers. This ferry system would continue to operate for the next twenty-two years.

In the early 1940s, Assemblyman Vincent Thomas continued where Olson had left off, but it took nine years before the financing for the tunnel was finally approved. When work on the tunnel would begin was a mystery. Engineers had convinced Thomas that building a four-lane bridge instead of the two-lane tunnel was advantageous. Consequently, Thomas reversed his position, dropped the tunnel concept and wrote a new bill for the construction of the bridge. Finally, on May 28, 1960, the ground was broken with Governor Edmund G. Brown, Lieutenant Governor Glenn Anderson and Assemblyman Vincent Thomas in attendance. Construction commenced in May 1961 and, after two and a half years and about $20-million, the dedication of the new bridge took place on September 28, 1963. Named after Vincent Thomas, the bridge was opened for traffic at 12:01 a.m. on Friday, November 15, 1963.

To the dismay of many, one could not see it at night so a local lawyer, Marty Chavez, husband of another local attorney, Juanita Chavez, started a movement in 1991 to put up lights so the bridge would be visible at night as well. John joined the effort and was instrumental in raising more than fourteen thousand dollars. They sold patches and closed the bridge three times, charging people fifteen dollars to walk across it. People mused, "The Vincent Thomas Bridge is to the harbor of L.A., what the Brooklyn Bridge is to New York." The difference between the two bridges was that the Brooklyn Bridge was fully illuminated and looked beautiful with the evening New York skyline. So why not do the same for the Vincent Thomas Bridge? The City of Los Angeles finally agreed and committed one hundred thousand to the project. On January 30, 2005, after fourteen years of advocacy, the new, bright blue lights were finally turned on.

John did more than try to protect people from injuring themselves or protecting landmarks. He used every opportunity to celebrate the heritage of San Pedro and its citizens, turning most into community events in which everyone could actively participate. Needless to say, he always found a way to play a role himself. There is perhaps no better case to demonstrate this than the celebration of the Portuguese explorer Juan Rodriguez Cabrillo.

The first celebration of Cabrillo dates back to October 15, 1920. A lengthy account by John M. Houston details that a local historian named Luther A. Ingersoll first suggested the celebration. The idea was adopted by several local historical societies and, as more and more people got involved, the simple idea of a picnic grew into a complex series of numerous events scheduled throughout the day. In the early morning of October 15, marchers for a military parade assembled on

Harbor Boulevard, north of 4th Street, scheduled to march at the stroke of 10 o'clock. However, parades hardly ever start on time, and this parade was no exception. According to eyewitness reports, it was the largest military parade ever assembled in San Pedro, even though exact numbers are hard to come by.

Various events followed during the day, which all culminated with the most publicized event of the day: the first reenactment of the Cabrillo Story. John Houston wrote:

> *If only parents and friends of the cast and production workers had attended, a full house would have been assured, but, in addition, thousands of townspeople and out-of-town visitors were lured by the announcements. Luckily, the 'Dress Rehearsal' on Friday afternoon had been also open to the public and helped take care of those who wished to see it.*

Many events followed, including a banquet on the First Street Wharf, the Great Water Parade and a street party for everyone. Some may wonder what all that had to do with history, but, as the Roman Emperors knew, the citizenry likes a spectacle.

In 1921, San Pedro extended the celebration to a three-day event, with many thousands in attendance. The pageant, performed on Friday and Saturday evenings, was seen by five thousand people alone. After a hiatus of several years, the celebration of Juan Cabrillo resumed in 1934 on Cabrillo Beach, which had been filled in and developed in 1927. After a few years, it went through an even longer hiatus that lasted until the mid-1970s when John Olguin and his staff at the Cabrillo Marine Museum revived the celebration with a vigor and perseverance that only John could muster.

John had a personal interest in reviving the Cabrillo celebration. His mother was a California Indian and John had always had an interest in Indian culture. In fact, he, his wife Muriel, and his brother Leonard once spent an entire week at Emerald Bay, near the isthmus on Catalina Island, trying to live just as the Indians once did – spear-fishing, catching abalones and living off the land. They always wondered whether the fires Cabrillo saw ashore had indeed been navigational fires. It would be difficult to prove anyway, but then an event in 1946 had provided a little bit more insight.

Benny "King" Nawahi, a 47-year-old Hawaiian musician, wanted to swim the Catalina Channel. While there are different accounts about the swim, the way John remembered it was that he, being an accomplished swimmer, was one of a hand full of people swimming alongside Benny and guiding him with his voice. It is a twenty-four mile swim from Catalina Island to the mainland at San Pedro, which took Benny and John twenty-two hours and twenty minutes to complete. As darkness fell, John saw a number of bonfires his mother, brothers and some friends were tending along the mainland beaches. John swam toward one of the fires and came ashore just below Palisades Park, west of Point Fermin. With that, the Olguin family demonstrated the successful use of fires as navigational aids. If his mother's predecessors also used fires in the same fashion and explorer Juan Cabrillo had sailed into the bay, the history of the area would have been decidedly different and San Pedro most likely would have a different name. We'll never know.

What we do know is that John's personal experiences motivated him to resume the Cabrillo celebration in 1975 and he would do so with a focus on educating children. The event consisted of many children's activities, like making a thousand little boats designed by Bill Oleson, drawing pictures of Juan Cabrillo and his ships on butcher paper, and a parade. The tradition continued with the evening performance reenacting the landing of Cabrillo and his men and their reception by local Indians, which presumably took place on one of the California Channel Islands. The Cabrillo Marine Aquarium continues to organize an annual Cabrillo event, and a statue of Cabrillo, crafted by sculptor Henry Lion, stands in front of the old bathhouse.

In the 1930s, the *Cabrillo*, a well-known vessel at the time, sailed between San Pedro and Catalina Island. She was confiscated in World War II to transport soldiers from Camp Stoneman in Pittsburg, California, down the Sacramento River to the docks in Oakland. At the time the Maritime Museum opened as part of the Cabrillo Marine Museum in the bathhouse, John began to look into the fate of the ship. No one knew where she was or if she was still in service. Finally, in 1978, one of John's collaborators, a part-time employee named John Myers, located the ship in the mud of the Napa River near Sacramento. By then, she was pretty much a wreck.

John went to his supervisor and asked him whether they could get some people to go up there, cut off as much as they could and bring it back to the maritime museum. Of course, they did not even want to entertain the idea of getting involved in something like a boat salvage operation. They told John that if he wanted to do it he could, but they wanted no part of the venture. John's "Just do it" approach had penetrated their thinking. They simply did not want to know and would deny that they had ever heard anything about such a thing.

John, of course, took their answer as encouragement, and after writing letters for almost five years, he was finally able to hire John Myers to cut off the bow of the ship and bring it back to San Pedro on a trailer. However, the bow of the *Cabrillo* was so rotten you could put your finger right through the wood. It was dry rot. Following the advice of a long-time carpenter at the Natural History Museum of Los Angeles, they used will-hold glue to put it all back together again before they painted it, and then covered it in glue one more time. Eventually, after several coats, it became as hard as cement. It is still on display at the Maritime Museum today. Some years after the *Cabrillo* had found a final resting place at the Maritime Museum, Margarite Mueller, John's math teacher at San Pedro High School visited him at the museum. When she saw the remains of the *Cabrillo*, she told John that she was 12 years old when her father built the *Cabrillo*. In fact, she broke the champagne bottle on the bow when they christened the ship.

Whatever John touched turned into gold, or at least into an opportunity to have another community event. John decided to christen the *Cabrillo* one more time. He bought a bottle of champagne and put some netting around it so nobody would be cut. They invited dignitaries and historians. Speeches were given and a photo of the ship and Mueller were on display. Then Mueller stepped up on the platform and said, "Fifty-some years ago I christened you the good ship *Cabrillo* and you shipped on the waves. One more time, I christen you the good ship *Cabrillo*." Then she broke the bottle of champagne on the remaining piece of the hull.

THE FAMILY MAN

By the time John Olguin retired in 1987, he had been married to his wife Muriel for thirty-nine years. Together, they had raised three children and were looking forward to spending more time together. Early on, John had told Muriel that he would give fifty years to his job and then fifty years to her. When John turned 50, Muriel didn't think he had another fifty years left, but then with John, you never knew. He consistently exceeded expectations.

In Muriel, John had found the love of his life and his rock; a like-minded person, who loved the ocean, loved the outdoors and shared his views on the importance of education and the community. John and Muriel also connected through the arts and Muriel's paintings. They would go to the beach together and Muriel would often sketch sea images while John would watch, listen and learn from the ocean itself. Muriel would later transfer her sketches to canvas and finish them. John, on the other hand would take what he had learned back to the museum.

Even though John spent most of his time on the beach and at the museum for the first forty years of their marriage, family – including his mother, brothers and sisters – was very important to him. For years, John, his siblings and their children would meet on Sundays at their mother's home, enjoying each other's company, sharing in each other's accomplishments, recounting childhood stories and teaching their children about the importance of family. His family provided love, refuge and support, and he would make sure that his family affairs were kept private.

John met Muriel for the first time in 1935, when he was 14 and she was 12 years old. They both belonged to the San Pedro Swim Club, headquartered at the Plunge, a public swimming pool located at 8th and Mesa streets. It was one of John's favorite places to hang out. Jack Chaney, chief lifeguard at the Plunge, had recently organized the club and had gathered a few paddleboards, a rowboat and two small sailboats that had been abandoned on Cabrillo Beach. Jack had been eyeing the sailboats for a while before he finally asked C.P.L. Nicholls, the supervisor of Aquatics, for permission to take over the care and use of the two boats. Nicholls granted the request by assigning them to the club. The only condition was that the club was to be responsible for maintaining the boats in first-class condition and hold the city free of any liability. The city also reserved the right to use the boats for any group, or event, it saw fit, upon the request of C.P.L. Nicholls or Ernest B. Ehrke, director of Cabrillo Beach.

Club members could use any of the equipment, including the boats, but to ensure that everyone had an opportunity to enjoy the benefits, they could be used for only two hours at a time. John was an early-morning riser and would go to the Plunge at 7 a.m. because nobody else wanted to go sailing that early. He would take one the sailboats, the *Cutty Sark*, out to the Point Fermin Lighthouse and, when the wind picked up later in the morning, he would sail it back. John loved it, but he also would have loved to have some company. So, he asked if anyone wanted to meet him in the early morning and go sailing and the only one who raised her arm was

Muriel. That was not really what John had in mind, though, so he tried to talk her out of it. Muriel was committed, so there was no turning back.

They began to meet in the early morning. John would come by himself and Muriel would be dropped off by her father, Harold Groat, who was in the law enforcement division of the Fish and Game Commission in Los Angeles. He also happened to have a few big guns in his car that scared the heck out of John, even though he tried to convince himself that Muriel's father was a nice and kind man. They would then sail out to the lighthouse. He would hold the tiller, she the sheets, and when the wind started to blow they would sail – two young teenagers with no worries and with parents who did not seem to have any either. Occasionally, they even took Muriel's 10-year-old brother Bud along (his real name was Clarence).

John came to like Muriel a lot and eventually he wanted to ask her out, but Muriel's mother objected. They continued to sail together for a while but then lost contact. They met again a few months later on the morning of New Year's Day in 1936. Calling themselves the Polar Bears, this group of fearless swimmers went swimming at noon that day, despite the chilly January water temperatures of fifty to sixty degrees. It takes some courage to dive into the cold Pacific Ocean, even for a few minutes. But the post-swim warmth and treats of hot chocolate and cookies made it all worth the effort. It was the beginning of a long-standing tradition that continues today and John and Muriel have participated in most of the New Year's Day swims ever since.

Yet, despite some encounters here and there, John and Muriel would not see much of each after their Polar Bear adventure. Muriel's family moved away from San Pedro, first settling in Wilmington, where she attended Banning High School, and then later to Long Beach, where she attended Wilson High School and eventually graduated in 1941. It was only in 1947 that Muriel and John would meet again.

By then Muriel was trying to put her life back together. She had contracted tuberculosis a few years earlier and spent a year in a sanatorium. While undergoing treatment, her husband at the time, Kurt McKeaver, divorced her. Not surprisingly, Muriel went through a serious bout of depression, which continued even after her release from the sanatorium. One day in 1947, she decided to drive to Cabrillo Beach where she saw a handsome young man whom she thought was John. It turned out it was his brother Leonard, but she did reconnect with John on the beach that day. It did not take long for John and Muriel to begin dating.

With none of the Olguin brothers married at the time, dating one of them came with its challenges. At that time, Roy, Alfonso, Albert, Leonard and John were all lifeguards and the five boys had any number of rules that would be difficult to fathom for any outsider. One of these rules was that if, for example, one Olguin had money and bought something like a new shirt, it was his to use the first time. After that, it went into the closet and whoever needed a shirt would wear it. It was sometime that same year that John decided he needed new pants. He wanted to look nice when they went out because Muriel always looked beautiful and he did not want to embarrass her.

Occasionally, they would go to Catalina Island, 24 miles across the channel, to dance at the casino. They would leave at 6 p.m. by water taxi, dance until 1 a.m., and then come back at 2 a.m., and go to work the next day. John had just bought new pants, a new coat, nice shoes and a tie, and was gleaming in anticipation of showing off his great style to his girlfriend, Muriel. The boys worked all day on the beach, but John stayed behind to put things away while his brothers left for home. When John finally got home, one of his brothers wore his brand new pants, his other brother was wearing his new coat and all of them had taken possession of his best ties. So there he was, having just spent his hard-earned money on a new outfit, having no choice but to put on a bad pair of pants and use a sock to make it look like a tie. When Muriel arrived, she was in utter shock. She pleaded with John and his brothers, but to avail. At the end, they all went to Catalina and had a great time anyway. That's according to John's memory. Muriel doesn't remember it that way.

John was working full-time on Cabrillo Beach and in 1948 he was promoted to lifeguard captain. Now earning enough money to raise a family, John asked Muriel to marry him. The two were married on June 12, 1948, at the Mission Inn, an old, beautiful hotel in Riverside, California. John's mentor, Jack Chaney, who had helped John become a lifeguard more than ten years earlier and had been one of his best friends ever since, served as best man. From there, John and Muriel went to Northern California for their honeymoon. John would later joke that the only reason he married Muriel was because he had to; they were together so much that it was the only way he could get a good night's sleep.

They had rented a house in the 500 block of 2nd Street and had begun to furnish it before going off on their honeymoon. When they returned, they settled instead into the cozy San Pedro Lighthouse residence, located at 807 Paseo del Mar, on the cliff next to the Point Fermin Lighthouse. John could not be happier. Before he was married, his mother used to ask him, "When are you going to work?" She would think of the people on the beach having fun and wonder when John would make something of his life. John would always tell her that he was paid to have the time of his life: swimming, rowing, canoeing and rescuing people. John did not want to wait until he was in his seventies to have fun and enjoy life. That was not for him. Now that he was married, his mother finally appreciated her son's work and stopped asking him her usual questions.

In time, John and Muriel would become the proud parents of three children and four grandchildren. Viola, their first daughter was born on January 14, 1950, and just over a year later, their second daughter, Monica, arrived on May 29, 1951. Their third child, John Cabrillo, was born on October 4, 1954. By 1955, the Olguin family had moved into their new house on Patton Avenue. Vi and Monica started to attend White Point Elementary School. Like their father, they would later attend Dana Junior High and eventually graduate from San Pedro High School. Viola would pursue a career in recreation therapy, while John Jr. would become a successful plumber. Monica earned a master's degree in educational administration and followed in the footsteps of her Uncle Leonard, expanding her career into bilingual, cross-cultural, and multi-subject teaching.

For the first ten years of their marriage, Muriel was a homemaker and continued to pursue her passion for the arts. Muriel had drawn and painted since early childhood and she would develop her talents into a career of her own that she managed to blend with her family roles. Besides working on paintings, she designed banners, Whalewatch patches and the signage that John wanted to use at the museum. When Viola and Monica were old enough to attend kindergarten, Muriel decided to go back to Long Beach State University and earn her Master of Arts degree. She would often take John Jr. along, until he was old enough to join his sisters at White Point Elementary. Muriel later taught art at various schools, including Lunada Bay Elementary School in Palos Verdes and Hudnal High School in Inglewood. At heart, however, she was always an artist. Even while working in the schools, she would often draw children in her classes and give them the sketches to take home.

Muriel's first studio was at home. In 1969, she moved it to a garage next to the Tender Trap, a bar located on Pacific Avenue, between 17th and 18th streets. She would stay there for about three years before moving into a building situated at the upper reservation of Ft. MacArthur, which would later develop into the Angel's Gate Cultural Center. After working in a studio in Wilmington for a while in the early 1990s, Muriel returned to San Pedro. She has been working at The Loft, an old commercial building on 4th and Mesa, since 1997.

Most of her early work depicts sea images. In the 1980s, Muriel began painting in oil and acrylics. She would often take advantage of the live models at Angel's Gate Cultural Center. Then in the mid- to late-1980s, she broke away from realism and began to explore the symbolism of her dreams and the images she encountered while working on the canvas. Over the decades of her successful career, Muriel has exhibited her artwork widely, including in public places across San Pedro.

Both Muriel and John had larger-than-life manifestations of their passions. In Muriel's case, her art talent was not limited to just canvas and average-sized works of art. She also painted murals on buildings. The American Cetacean Society national headquarters at Point Fermin Park, on the cliffs at the edge of the Pacific Ocean, is graced with one of her murals. At the opposite end of San Pedro, the Bandini Street Elementary School, one of the oldest in town, also displays her artistic talents in a large mural that is popular with visitors to the campus.

Throughout his career, John worked all day on the beach as lifeguard captain and as the museum director and would often come home late. Many evenings, he would be giving speeches or presentations around town, or conducting meetings about a variety of community affairs, issues and opportunities. Little time was left for Muriel and the children, which created a dilemma for John. The spectacular, jovial and beloved master of the Cabrillo Marine Museum was really a man of tremendous contradictions. Most people never saw that side of him, however, because behind this unbelievable man was an even stronger and more supportive force of nature, Muriel.

For all the love that she and John had, his workaholic personality took precedence over his conscious understanding of how much Muriel sacrificed at times to be both the mother and the father figure during John's wanderlust. Muriel knew how important it was for John to feel that he was a better dad than his own abusive father had been. Yet, John was seldom home. Muriel, John's rock, was actually much stronger and independent than most people realized, including John. She knew John meant to do more, that he meant to carry his share of the load at home. Muriel found some solace in the fact that John made a very conscientious effort to hug and play with his children, and to sit down to tell them stories when he was home.

The stories John told his children did not come out of a book, he told his own. He would talk about the sea and the wonders of all living things, to instill an appreciation for the world in his children. His stories included those from his time in the Army and the war, but he omitted the horror and instead shared vivid accounts of how he and his comrades had used their helmets to cook food. John was a great storyteller who could turn anything into an interesting, and often funny, story that his children loved to hear. These stories made for wonderful evenings that live on as precious childhood memories for the Olguin children. Yet, while the children could see John as a great storyteller dad, Muriel needed John to focus on being home more often as her husband.

When Viola and Monica were attending grammar school, John would take them there in the mornings on his bicycle on his way to work. Muriel and the children would also often come to Cabrillo Beach to enjoy an afternoon in the sun. All the lifeguards knew them, so there were many eyes keeping the children safe. It was a wonderful balance, as they were able to play, see their father at work, and witness how he was interacting with children visiting the museum and the people on the beach. If there was not too much going on, John would spend more time with them. They all swam in the ocean year-round, carrying on the family tradition that started with John and his brothers sneaking down to the ocean as youngsters and later working as lifeguards on Cabrillo Beach together.

Even though John and Muriel did not have as much time for each other as they would have liked, they had something many couples do not have: a shared passion for the ocean and rowing. Swimming and rowing were the first activities that John and Muriel shared when they were just 12 and 14 years old. Ever since they were married in 1948, they had taken advantage of any chance they had to get out on the water. When they talked of rowing, they did not mean a glide across the lake at MacArthur Park in downtown L.A. The Olguins rowed the open seas, winter and summer, rain or shine. Rowing on the open sea in a fifteen-foot rowboat required confidence and trust in each other. To reach any destination, the oars had to be pulled through the water in unison and harmony; otherwise, they would not get anywhere.

John and Muriel were masters in the art of rowing. They enjoyed the calm of the ocean and fought through storms and high seas. The experiences helped them get through some tough times in their personal lives too. For John and Muriel, the many hours of being in a boat were times that replenished their souls. They saw rowing as the fastest way to get away into the wilderness. With their boat filled with a thermos of coffee, sleeping bags, warm clothes, a tarpaulin, a guitar and their little poodle, Pico, they would set out to sea. Their many trips became legendary.

Rowboats can go where sailboats cannot go. Rowing also requires a different attitude than sailing. In John's mind, there was an important but fine line between a sailor and an oarsman. A sailor will plow through the sea and sail hard on the wind to make his or her way. An oarsman, on the other hand, must never fight the sea. He feels every swell and can only survive if he follows the sea. It requires much more discipline. The wind does not propel the oarsman forward, rather the strength of his own body and the synchronized movement of the arms keep the boat on course. The rewards are equally awesome, though: closeness to the water and the ability to see fish, sea otters, dolphins and whales at close range.

When rowing, there is an estimated time of arrival, but it really does not matter when you arrive. That is not important. It is important that you are safe, warm and eventually arrive at your destination. "You don't row hard, you row steady," John would say. John and Muriel had learned early on that discipline and pacing themselves were essential. They would row for fifty minutes, followed by a ten-minute break during which they stretched out and did what they could to relax. Under good conditions, they could make about three miles per hour. At times, John and Muriel used a triangular nylon sheet as a sail, catching the wind and providing some relief.

In the early years, the couple would often enter the surf with their rowboat just west of Point Fermin, below their home. Rowing out for some distance, they would anchor and have a picnic, sunbathe or sometimes nap before returning to shore. They also rowed to the isthmus at the west end of Catalina Island, which took six hours from the Cabrillo Marina. The first time they went, their neighbor Claude Morris, who was a firefighter, followed them in his motorboat.

John's friend Forrest Taylor had a beautiful rowboat whose design dated back to 1884. Forrest described it as "so sweet." He worked as a lifeguard with John for a couple of years, but then moved on to become a firefighter. Forrest knew how much John and Muriel loved rowing, so he offered them the use of his boat as often as they pleased. Many of the couple's Saturdays were spent rowing around Palos Verdes and San Pedro Bay in Forrest's wonderful boat.

Built by San Pedro Boat Works, Forrest's boat was 15 feet long with a four-foot beam; its round bottom lifted the boat when a wave hit while its sharp bow deflected water away. Weighing a little less than 190 pounds, the boat drew only three and a half inches and had removable wheels that allowed John and Muriel to launch and beach it easily. In a perfect balance, it was light enough that John could get it on and off his flat-bed truck, yet sturdy enough for heavy seas. Its design and construction out of fiberglass worked well to absorb swells and made it close to unsinkable. Equipped with two fixed seats and two flotation tanks, it provided just enough space for the essentials that John and Muriel would bring on any of their many journeys.

Eventually, John persuaded Forrest to sell it to him. The boat changed hands in the 1960s and John and Muriel named it the *Pico Maru* and continued to use her to row open oceans, coastal waters and lakes all over the world. As a lifeguard, John was acutely aware of the challenges and dangers the ocean could pose. While regular practice was essential, equally important was his understanding that one could not fight the sea, but instead had to go along with whatever nature would throw at them. John outfitted each oarlock with an extension so he could stand up and do some push rowing to relieve his strained back. The extensions were also useful when passing through areas of high traffic, such as when passing through ports or marinas, since standing up provided a much better view of the surroundings.

When John spoke of their rowing adventures, he was the first to tell you that they knew what they were doing. The Olguins were always prepared for whatever was to come their way. A battery-operated light provided the opportunity for them to row at night and sleep during the day if weather conditions made it necessary. They also carried flares, sleeping bags, warm clothing, compass charts, a watch, three anchors, foul weather gear, and food and water for a week. From brewing coffee to making a sandwich or rowing to shore to cook a burger, they had what they needed.

Above all, they had respect for nature and its forces. They always ran with the storm, not against it. At times, the experienced rowers found it outright exciting when a storm would start brewing over them. One time, they saw a storm coming and were so anxious to get *into* it that they rushed down to the ocean and jumped into their rowboat. Using one oar for a mast, they rigged a small sail and went along the coast for forty-five minutes, riding the storm all the way. Then they went ashore, called for a pick-up and went back home.

When the children were old enough, John and Muriel took them on many family canoeing and rowing adventures. On one canoe trip, a storm hit and they had to paddle for ten hours without a break. The kids vowed to burn the canoe, but they did not. Eventually, they loved canoeing and camping just as much as their parents did. On another trip with only their 13-year-old son Johnny, they paddled from Oxnard to Anacapa Island, one of the eight Channel Islands situated off the California Coast. They camped at Frenchie's Cove and the next day continued to Santa Cruz Island. While on their way, a big wave swamped their canoe. Everyone was all right, but John's jacket, with his car keys inside, fell into the ocean.

John took a sighting on where the jacket had sunk to the bottom. Then they paddled back to Frenchie's Cove where John met a couple of SCUBA divers, whom he offered twenty dollars to dive to look for his keys. They told John they would do it for free, so they all went back to the place John thought was the exact location. The divers went under the water and, within minutes, came up with John's jacket and the keys. The rest of that day and the next, the wind blew so hard that John, Muriel and Johnny could not paddle back to Oxnard. The third day, an Island Packer boat offered to take them back to the mainland free of charge.

Over the decades, they rowed around the Virgin Islands, around San Miguel and Santa Rosa in the Channel Islands, around Fiji, in stages from Gaviota to San Diego, the Gulf Islands, a bit down the Amazon in Peru, in Puget Sound in Seattle and part way down the Russian and Snake rivers. They also rowed lakes in Minnesota, followed a trail into Canada and back, portaging where necessary, and made it from Juneau to Ketchikan in Alaska. In addition, over a period of nine years, John, Muriel and their children rowed the entire length of Lake Powell. John and Muriel also completed more than a dozen round trips to Catalina Island, covering forty-eight miles. It would take them about six hours one way, but when they were older and did not work as hard, it took ten hours. Trips to Avalon for steak dinner were also part of their repertoire, where they would sleep in the boat and return to San Pedro the next day.

Throughout their voyages, John and Muriel had their fair share of mishaps and bad weather, but it was all part of the adventure. John always felt responsible and sometimes wondered why Muriel would not be upset. She, on the other hand, would work the oar and keep quiet. On one of their many rowing trips to Catalina Island, they found themselves in a storm blowing thirty-five miles per hour and creating huge swells just eight miles short of their destination. It was late afternoon. The entire ocean was white and soon they found themselves in total darkness.

Struggling to keep the boat on course, Muriel eventually gave into her fears, curled up in the boat and went to sleep with her head away from the wind to make sure the wind did not blow into her sleeping bag. John worked the oars by himself for a few hours, keeping the *Pico Maru* pointed into the waves and making sure she would not capsize. At about 1 a.m., the storm finally let up, the waves disappeared and John and Muriel found themselves on a flat, calm ocean. With the worst over, Muriel took over the oars, allowing John to take a rest. Shortly thereafter, they arrived tired, but safe, on

Catalina. When John later recounted this story, it was so vivid that the audience felt like they were in the rowboat with him.

Interestingly, Muriel's accounts of their common adventures were often a bit different from John's stories. John's Mexican heritage, the "Macho Man genes" in him, just would not allow him to admit any form of defeat, weakness or dependence on others, under any circumstances. And certainly not in front of his wife. Throughout his life when he was denied permission to do something or buy something, he would find a way to get what he wanted because he was incapable of accepting loss of control.

One of their famous narrative disagreements relates to an incident where they were stuck on the ocean because the wind was blowing so hard they simply could not get ashore under their own powers. Fortunately, another boat came by and offered to give them a ride, which John and Muriel happily accepted. Then that boat suffered an engine failure and ended up being towed to port by the Coast Guard. When Muriel would tell the story, she would often say that the Coast Guard rescued them, but if John were around, he would immediately interject and make clear that it was the other boat that had to be rescued, not him and Muriel. John was a lifeguard and he just could not accept the idea that he had to be rescued by anyone, especially not the Coast Guard. Furthermore, for a Silver Star-winning Army veteran, it would almost be blasphemous to suggest that he, a soldier who had served under General Douglas MacArthur, needed the Coast Guard to save him.

John and Muriel were master rowers and their recreational home away from home, the ocean, never mastered them. So how could John possibly need someone else, especially another military unit, to protect him and Muriel? John was more than capable of being in charge and taking care of his loving Muriel and himself. John used to get amused when well-meaning but ill-informed people would approach them in the Catalina Channel and attempt to rescue them when they were out on an ocean adventure. People often thought Muriel and he were in trouble, but he would quickly explain that they were perfectly fine, just on one of their voyages. With very few exceptions, they always were. They would continue the rowboat trips to Catalina into their seventies and were in such wonderful physical shape that they successfully completed their last voyage to Catalina Island when John was 75 years old, the same year they also climbed Mount Whitney.

Other adventures were fraught with both excitement and challenges. On their trip from Monterey to San Diego, they started out rowing along the coastline and dropped anchor in the middle of a kelp bed at dusk. That night, a couple of sea otters climbed into the boat. John and Muriel had some great fun and took some photos. John told that story for years at Tuesday-night meetings at the museum. On another voyage, they slept onshore near Balboa only to awake with their oars stolen. They bought new oars and continued on their way, but would not sleep ashore again.

Many people can envision themselves flying to the Caribbean and sailing from one island to another, but it takes true oarsmen, like John and Muriel, to do the same in a rowboat. They flew into St. Thomas, their own oars in tow, rented a motorcycle and went to all the marinas in search of a suitable rowboat they could rent. They eventually found a rowboat they liked and talked to the owner about renting it. After the owner asked John and Muriel where they were going, he expressed concern that it was too dangerous for people to be rowing to as many islands as the Olguins were planning.

With the help of some newspaper clippings about themselves, John managed to persuade the owner to rent them his boat.

John and Muriel brought water and dehydrated food that they could cook in the rowboat or go ashore to cook on the beach. When they found a store, they would replenish their supplies. They rowed at night to avoid the trade winds and had a flashlight and a sailing guide, so there was no problem plotting their course from one island to the next. John knew a sailing captain named Ed Fabian who had a house on one of the islands. He insisted that they use it when they arrived, but when they found the house, they tied up to the dock and slept there. The next morning, John and Muriel explored the island and then got back in their boat to continue the adventure.

It was very tough rowing at times, but by pacing themselves, they made it to the next island where they landed on a beautiful empty beach. The Olguins relaxed in the solitude until a large sailboat sailed in and dropped anchor. Small boats then began ferrying people and supplies to the beach not far from where John and Muriel were relaxing. The large group set up tables of delicious food and someone came over to invite John and Muriel to join in their feast. Once they all ate and relaxed, the big group packed up their stuff, pulled anchor and sailed away. John and Muriel slept on the beach that night and then continued their voyage.

On another day, they saw a small crowd of people on the beach of a small island. They made for shore and found a hotel, but it was three hundred dollars per night per person. John made dinner reservations at the hotel restaurant and that night they had a great time enjoying their fantastic, but expensive, meal while talking with many of the hotel guests. When it came time for bed, everyone went to their expensive rooms except for John and Muriel, who returned to their rowboat to sleep. The next morning they had breakfast in the restaurant with their new friends, said goodbye and began pulling themselves away and toward a new adventure.

John and Muriel loved the outdoors and were no strangers to sleeping outdoors. In 1965, after returning from a camping trip, they moved their bed at their home outside. The bed stood under a canopy, providing some protection from the elements, and when it rained, they put a tarp over it to stay dry. If it was cold, and Southern California nights can be chilly in the winter, they would add some blankets and keep each other warm. Their "bedroom" was an incredibly special place where they could hear sea lions bark, watch the whales go by, see comet showers in the sky and smell the roses. They never moved their bed back inside their house – they could never turn their back on their special relationship with nature.

Like most people, John and Muriel experienced ups and downs in their relationship. John was out many nights giving talks and speeches to countless groups and organizations and he had always been a flirt, a charmer. The more opportunity and support Muriel gave him to succeed and live his dream, the more the strong and independent Muriel wanted him to be at home and to spend more time with her. If she knew, or could find out where he was, she would occasionally lose her patience and actively try to get him home. John's rock for their entire marriage was slowly developing cracks in her armor.

One of those particular evenings, when Muriel wanted John to stay home, involved their neighbor Claude. John had gone over to his house for a visit, but once the two started talking the time would often fly by. The phone rang and Muriel was on the other end asking Claude to, "Please tell John that he is wanted on the phone." Claude passed the message on to John.

Above: John and Muriel Olguin visiting Yosemite on their honeymoon. 1948. Photo Courtesy John Olguin Private Archive

LEFT: *John and Muriel Olguin during their honeymoon. 1948. Photo Courtesy John Olguin Private Archive*

ABOVE: *John and Muriel Olguin at a Lifeguard Luau party in the old Cabrillo Beach Bathhouse. 1952. Photo Courtesy John Olguin Private Archive*

LEFT: *John, Muriel, and Vi during a Junior Lifeguard celebration. 1950. Photo Courtesy John Olguin Private Archive*

ABOVE: *John and Muriel Olguin rowing on the Thames River in England. 1954. Photo Courtesy John Olguin Private Archive*

RIGHT: *Muriel Olguin posing for John during their trip to Europe. 1954. Photo Courtesy John Olguin Private Archive*

ABOVE: *John and Muriel in their rowboat, the Pico Maru, with dog Pica. 1975. Photo Courtesy John Olguin Private Archive*

LEFT: *John and Muriel's children Vi, John Cabrillo, and Moni (from left to right). 1954. Photo Courtesy John Olguin Private Archive*

John and Muriel in their rowboat Pico Maru, the legendary skiff that served as their oceangoing home on their many trips, including their frequent 48-mile round-trip adventures to Catalina Island. 1975. Photo Courtesy John Olguin Private Archive

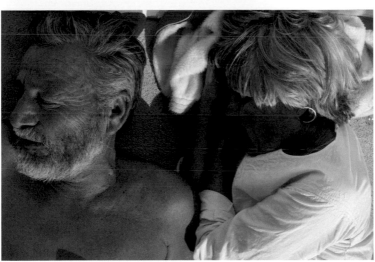

John and Muriel resting in Baja California. 1984.
Photo Courtesy A. Schulman-Janiger Private Archive

John and Muriel at the wedding of Julie Wickman and Emmanuel Rosales. 1984. Photo Courtesy A. Schulman-Janiger Private Archive

The Olguin siblings: Roy, Gus, John, Alfonso, Leonard, Albert, Ester, and Belia (from left to right). Early 1980s. Photo Courtesy John Olguin Private Archive

TOP: *John, Muriel, and their son John Cabrillo. 2007. Photo Courtesy John Olguin Private Archive*

MIDDLE: *John, Muriel, and their daughter Moni at the Grand Grunion Gala. 2007. Photo Courtesy John Olguin Private Archive*

LEFT: *John and his daughter Vi. 2008. Photo Courtesy John Olguin Private Archive*

John and Muriel in their eighties. 2006. Photo by Taso Papadakis

Vi Olguin, John Cabrillo Olguin, Moni Olguin, John Olguin, and Muriel Olguin (from left to right). 2009. Photo Courtesy Cabrillo Marine Museum/ Cabrillo Marine Aquarium

The two men wondered how John could be wanted on the phone when Muriel was calling from the only phone they had. John wasn't reading the warning signs of a wife who was asking for her time on his agenda. Despite shrugging his shoulders at what he saw as a somewhat bizarre call, John went home to see what Muriel wanted.

Muriel did not only want John to be home more often, she also wanted him to help around the house. At times, Muriel grew very frustrated; and one day in the mid-1980s, she decided she had suffered enough. When John came home from work, the house was empty. Muriel had left. She was sending him a message, once and for all, that there was more to their life than just John's satisfaction and the fulfillment of his dreams, no matter how real and important they were.

John knew immediately what this was all about and, for a moment, he was tempted to find out where she had gone. Instead, he decided to play it cool and pretend not to care. In reality, John was devastated, and he didn't have a clue about how to deal with Muriel's walkout. She had never done something so rash like abandoning him. She had always been there for him. She was the strength he relied on when he went out and took risks. She was his good luck charm – everything worked when Muriel was there for him. Sure, she asked for attention over and over and over, but John knew she understood that what he was doing was SO important. Now she was gone and he had to deal with it.

Over the next couple of weeks, he worked on everything he had promised Muriel so many times, everything from painting the house to weeding their garden. Muriel came by once or twice to get some clothes, but the two did not say much to each other. John could not say anything to her that he hadn't said before. More promises to Muriel would just fall on deaf ears. Neither of them was comfortable with the awkward moments and the split, but they both stood their ground because Muriel was tired of compromising and John knew that at this point his smooth talking would get him nowhere. Muriel left with her clothes and John was still in the doghouse.

After another couple of weeks, they ran into each other on Harbor Boulevard. Muriel nervously asked John what he was doing. She had noticed that John had painted the house and tended to the garden. He seemed to have gotten the message that he needed to meet Muriel's needs as well as she met his. Yet, she wanted to see if John was still going to ignore her daring and bold decision to walk out on him. John sensed this was an opening to reach out to the only person that made his life whole, so he replied that he was about to go and see a movie and asked her if she wanted to come along. She did. The "Cold War" between them ended much faster than it had developed. They went to see the movie and then went home together, this time for good. All was forgiven.

John was a romantic and his love for Muriel was still strong late into their marriage. He was a reformed man, a lucky man, and he knew it. He would take care of business and be more responsive to Muriel's needs now more than ever. He was not shy about expressing his feelings and thoughts to Muriel. In a letter dated April 30, 1997, John wrote to Muriel, who was in New York for a week: "Your phone call in the morning started my day on the right note ... I am in ecstatic anticipation of your homecoming on Saturday night. The candles will be lit, a piece of chocolate will be ready and I will be set to show you how much I love you." After almost fifty years of marriage, John was still deeply in love with Muriel.

John was always an easy-going soul. He never required much in life. His shoes always looked worn and so did his out-of-style clothes. When Muriel had her motorcycle, he would often use it to get around town. He used to say it only cost him three dollars every two weeks to run it. He did not need a lot of money. He could live on rice and beans. The only thing he really needed was a cup of coffee in the morning.

John always seemed to be happy and content. His smile was as genuine as his beard and together they made him look like Santa Claus or Ernest Hemingway. His daughter Monica cannot remember ever seeing him depressed, but remembers that his personality bugged her at times as a kid. He hugged them all the time and made them kiss all their relatives. Now, years later, she enjoys the closeness with her family. Monica believes that people gravitated toward her father because the warmth he radiated was missing in their own lives. John also had a great sense of humor. In the middle of a presentation, he would ask "Is Muriel here?" If the answer was no, he would go on, "Okay, then I can tell this story" and he would tell a joke. He wouldn't tell an off-color joke, just one that long-suffering wives hear many times.

When John retired, he knew life would be different. During the years he had worked, he would wake up in the morning and be out of the house in no time. Muriel often asked him to help around the house, but John had been so occupied – maybe obsessed is a better word – with being a lifeguard, heading the museum, giving lectures, or going on trips that he never had time to help. Now, after retirement, and after reconciling following Muriel's stunning walkout, John knew that it was his turn. He was finally in a position to return the generosity Muriel had showed him through her years of unselfish service.

Their daily routine changed quite a bit after John retired. Muriel would leave in the morning to go to the YMCA to exercise and then to her studio where she worked on her paintings. The newly energized John would make the bed, sweep, mop, vacuum, do the laundry, shop and cook. When Muriel came home at six or seven o'clock in the evening, he would often have dinner on the table and maybe even a candle lit. It was a completely new experience for John. Muriel loved it. John had to learn what Muriel liked to eat – corn, broccoli, squash, baked potatoes, peanuts, almonds and salad – and what she did not, which included meat or gravy. Finally, in the autumn of their lives, they had time to relax and have dinner together.

Of course, John did not always do the dishes. And maybe he did not do everything all the time. But he did do most of the housework after he retired. Muriel never expected perfection from John, just the attention she deserved. Of course, John also found the time to do other things that he wanted to do. Each day he would complete the housework quickly, so he could go to the beach or go swimming. His desire to swim in the ocean was with him his entire life.

John knew that it was important to improve the quality of time with Muriel. By his retirement, their marriage had already lasted forty years, and for it to continue they needed to make an effort on an ongoing basis to do things together. Now that their age limited their rowing adventures, John took up the art of painting and Muriel would provide support and guidance as needed. Muriel had a reputation among the artist community of being very kind and generous with her time. She would often share her technique or reveal some of her secrets in an effort to help others to advance their craft. John and Muriel went on painting trips together, during which they would produce two very different interpretations of the same setting. John often said that one of Muriel's greatest gifts to him was how she taught him to see things as an artist sees them. When he first met her, she would say, "See that?" Then she would explain the colors and shapes so he could see what she could. She opened up a whole new world for him, too. Some of his artwork is hung around the house now too, even though it is dwarfed by Muriel's large, colorful interpretive pieces.

The issue of John's absence from home had always been an undercurrent for him, although it took John a long time to address it. During their long marriage, he couldn't escape the memory that Muriel occasionally would get frustrated with having to share him with the museum and the entire community. Muriel enjoyed her own career, but at community functions, the couple usually appeared together because they cared deeply about the desires and successes of one another. The couple had accepted the fact that John, through his work, had opened up a world that Muriel would probably not have chosen for herself. Yet, she had to incorporate it into her daily life. John would always say that there is only one artist in the family, but that was not entirely true. They were both artists and stars, and everyone knew it.

Thousands of others, before and since John began his love affair with the beach and the ocean, have felt blessed to live in the working-class town of San Pedro. With its beautiful cliffs, the community literally sits on the edge of the world. San Pedro never became an uptight, high-priced and exclusive enclave like Newport Beach, Santa Monica or Malibu, with its long list of famous stars and movie moguls. San Pedro's success as Small Town America in the Big City of Los Angeles has been achieved by local people, who always put the community first. This little town had it all, indeed, but John and Muriel always felt they could give a little more.

A town that once had a waterfront with the reputation of being the toughest in the world, San Pedro was lucky to have folks like John and Muriel Olguin. These two remarkable people took what they learned from each other and shared it with the world. By doing so, they influenced literally millions of people. Yet for the Olguins, it was never about getting credit for their extraordinary contributions to the community and so many people's lives. When asked about their accomplishments, John would always say that it does not matter who gets the credit. He considered it a privilege to live in a community that had it all: ocean, whales, the harbor, commerce and wonderful people. Muriel felt the same way.

The San Pedro that John loved, and gave so much of his life to serve, always paid back the people with a wonderful sense of belonging and a local sense of pride that money could never buy. That was more than enough payback for its grateful and down-to-earth residents John and Muriel.

TURNING THE TABLES ON RETIREMENT

John retired from his job as co-director of the Cabrillo Marine Museum in 1987. Characteristic of his fun-loving lifestyle, John went out not with a whimper, but with a bang. Word of John's retirement spread and eventually reached the Air Force, which had moved into San Pedro in 1982 and taken over Fort MacArthur right above the Cabrillo Marine Museum. In those early days, people were resentful of the Air Force because they were taking over choice property and putting up buildings on all of the prime acreages right above the beach. Three hundred families moved in, they put a fence around the project, guards were placed on duty, and nobody could move in or out of the compound without being checked. Many residents of San Pedro were not pleased.

John thought the Air Force would be an asset to the community, so he invited all the families and the commanding officer down to the Cabrillo Marine Museum auditorium for a wine-and-cheese event. He also invited the chief of police, the postmaster, local ministers, managers of the gas and telephone companies, and anyone else who was "somebody" to attend. John encouraged everyone to speak for five minutes, including the L.A. City Councilwoman at the time, Joan Milke Flores. Each person gave a talk and welcomed the Air Force to San Pedro. The Air Force remained grateful to John and when news swept across town that he would retire, they offered to hold a retirement function at the Officers' Club overlooking the ocean. Everyone went all out to make it a memorable event and, in true John tradition, they turned it into a fundraiser to pay for the construction of a gray whale model to hang from the superstructure in the courtyard of the Cabrillo Marine Museum. The event, which was called the "Grand Grunion Gala," took place on April 4, 1987 and raised thirty-five thousand dollars. Since then, the "Grand Grunion Gala" has remained a major fundraising mechanism for the museum.

Since not all of the volunteers or John's friends could afford to pay the one hundred and fifty dollars to be at the gala, John made additional plans for another, very different, retirement party. John chartered one of the Catalina Cruises boats, took everybody who wanted to go whale watching out in the morning and then to Cabrillo Beach for a potluck luncheon in the afternoon. Anybody and everybody who wanted to celebrate John could attend. Some of the restaurants in town, where John had been eating for years, provided delicacies including casseroles, Chinese food, salads, cakes and other potluck favorites. A series of farewell events followed, including some that raised funds for activities John had supported over the years.

John's last day at the museum was April 11. The day started out with a Whalewatch trip and ocean viewing of the Point Fermin and Point Vincente lighthouses. There was a community potluck and evening fireworks. The day's events included whale dynamics, grunion and jellyfish dances and the famous

"Do it! Do it!" presentations. The Goodyear blimp came by with a big "Happy Retirement" sign, and the historic *Ralph J. Scott*, known as L.A. City Fireboat 2 put on a spectacular water display just offshore.

A few months later, the auditorium at the Cabrillo Marine Museum was named after John. On November 14, 1987, Georgeanne Rudder, assistant general manager of the Department of Recreation and Parks at the time, performed the official dedication and revealed a bronze relief in John's likeness. The dedication reads:

> *This auditorium is dedicated to John M. Olguin, director emeritus. Retired April 11, 1987, after 50 years of unselfish and extraordinary service to Cabrillo Marine Museum and the community. Like the Ocean, he has touched people all around the globe. Neither the community nor Cabrillo Marine Museum would be what they are today without John's commitment, enthusiasm and guidance.*

When John retired, the museum was a $3-million facility run by twenty-four paid staff and more than five hundred volunteers, with three hundred thousand visitors annually. It is John's greatest legacy to San Pedro and the ocean, shaped by his personal approach. Where else do guides dress up as sea otters or lobsters and make children dance like a jellyfish?

John had made sure his work continued, as it was always very important to him. He often said that if you start something and it dies because you die, or quit, or retire, than it was not worth anything. He did not have to worry. Susanne Lawrenz-Miller, Larry Fukuhara, the entire staff and the volunteers would not let that happen. John himself was not prepared to let it all go. He was too invested and felt that he was still a pretty good fundraiser and could help the museum and other causes.

In 1993, Cabrillo Marine Museum changed its name to Cabrillo Marine Aquarium to highlight its living collections and in anticipation of future expansion as a public aquarium. The volunteers organized a not-for-profit group called FRIENDS of Cabrillo Marine Aquarium, which has its own board of directors. In 2001, the first expansion phase of the Aquarium was approved and, as in the past, John helped to solicit funds and contributed some of his own. The groundbreaking ceremony took place on July 19, 2002, and on October 23, 2004, the new $10-million expansion was opened to the public with a new Exploration Center and the Aquatic Nursery. A year later, the Virginia Reid Moore Research Library opened its doors and, in the same year, the Aquarium received the prestigious Munson Aquatic Conservation Exhibit (M.A.C.E.) Award from the Association of Zoos and Aquariums (AZA) for its Aquatic Nursery exhibit. The year after, the new Exploration Center won the coveted M.A.C.E. Award. John Olguin's half-century of devotion to the ocean, the beaches, and marine science was being recognized outside the San Pedro community in a big way. His Cabrillo Beach dream had made the "big time."

In 2006, Dr. Susanne Lawrenz-Miller retired and exhibit director Mike Schaadt was named the new director of the aquarium. In 2010, the aquarium celebrated its 75th year of "engaging all visitors in education, recreation and research to promote knowledge, appreciation and conservation of marine life of Southern California." And what a seventy-five years it had been. Most of the programs John developed during the 1950s, '60s and '70s are still ongoing, even though they have evolved to keep up with the times.

During the school year, volunteers and staff of the aquarium may welcome as many as four thousand children per week and guide them through learning stations set up on Cabrillo Beach. They learn about grunion biology, are shown a preserved adult grunion in a jar to see the size and they all do the grunion dance. In the late winter and throughout the spring, they get to hatch grunion eggs in baby food jars and sing happy birthday to them before they are released into the ocean. The children learn about ocean pollution, one of the greatest threats to the planet, and are shown images of sea lions and birds with plastic six-pack rings around their necks to illustrate the dangers and impact of our human throwaway society.

Then there are tide pools and sea creatures, such as sea stars and anemones, and of course, lessons and stories about whales and dolphins. They learn about sea jellies by dancing like a jellyfish while simulating the movement and eating habits of a jellyfish. After their time at the beach, they pass through the aquarium itself, interacting with its exhibits before boarding their buses to return to their schools. For many of these children, they might have just experienced their first-ever visit to the beach, to the edge of the world, John Olguin's decades of innovation and education having planted a seed of curiosity that will forever live in their hearts and minds.

Between October and the end of March every year, Tuesday nights are still the time when Whalewatch volunteers and naturalists meet at Cabrillo Beach, though the participants are now college students and no longer high school kids. The Whale Fiesta is still going strong, even though it was moved from the end of whale watching season in June to its height in January. It is held on the beach, right in front of the Cabrillo Aquarium, and hundreds of people still participate in building a life-sized whale out of sand, while thousands more enjoy watching the event.

From March through the end of July, the aquarium conducts bi-weekly public "Meet the Grunion" events on the beach at night. Public tide pool walks in Point Fermin State Marine Park are conducted at low tide periodically throughout the year. The annual trip to Baja California to see gray whales has been on the schedule for more than thirty years now, and each October the Cabrillo Marine Aquarium embarks on an adventure to San Miguel Island, the most remote of the Channel Islands. There, everyone watches a reenactment of the landing of Juan Cabrillo, hikes up to the Cabrillo monument and explores some of the natural history of the island. And, of course, they always keep an eye out for marine mammals and other sea life when crossing the channel.

While a new generation had taken on the responsibility for the programs, John would still go down to the beach almost every day after his retirement. You could find him, often surrounded by a group of children, performing the grunion dance and sharing his fascination and love for the ocean. You could remove John Olguin from Cabrillo Beach through retirement, but you could not remove Cabrillo Beach from the heart and mind of this former lifeguard, Army hero, museum director, and ambassador of nature, sea life, the environment, and curiosity.

By the time John retired, his reputation had approached mythical proportions. He was as valuable an asset as the community of San Pedro has ever had. John always worked to give back to the community that gave him so much. He often spoke of it in terms of having four families. The first was what most of us consider our families, his wife and children. The second was his siblings, his uncles and aunts. The third family was his church, which he considered a private matter and did not speak much about in public. And last, but not least, he considered the entire community his family. He worked his entire life to care for and love all four families.

Life after retiring from the museum would provide many opportunities for John to continue his support for multiple segments of the community and the people of San Pedro, including raising funds to support the hungry, the poor and the homeless. John is living proof that one does not have to be a billionaire philanthropist living up on a hill somewhere to contribute to the community and to change the world. John felt that a modest person, with dedication and a strong community network, could achieve just as much as a rich one. He proved that, by building an entire museum with five and ten dollars at a time, using some of his own money and raising money through the community for as many good causes as he could.

When John grew up, he wanted to be a lifeguard because he loved the beach, the ocean and people. Once he was a lifeguard, he knew he would always be a lifeguard, because for John being a lifeguard was always much more than just working on the beach. If somebody was in trouble, it was a lifeguard's job to do what it took to help. But it was not a job; it was a passion. John felt that throughout his career, his opportunities to learn had been endless. Despite his struggles with bureaucracy at times, John felt greatly indebted to the City of Los Angeles for providing him with those opportunities. Being paid to learn things, that arguably one in his position should have known to begin with, was in itself a great privilege.

One of the programs John was determined to continue through his retirement was the trip around Catalina Island. He had first proposed such trips in 1981 after one of his rowing adventures with Muriel had taken them from San Pedro around Catalina and back in five days. Visiting the far side of the island was such a wonderful experience that he decided to share it with the public. Originally intended as a fundraiser for the museum, he eventually took the idea to the American Cetacean Society, which agreed to sponsor the trip, leaving the organization to John.

Together, they raised a few thousand dollars that went to support the national headquarters of the ACS at Point Fermin Park. Now no longer on the payroll of the city, John wanted to continue these trips under his own name and use the revenues to support charitable projects and organizations. But by then almost everyone had been on a whale watching trip at one time or another and it became more difficult, even for John, to get people excited about going out to see whales. John had to pay for the boat in advance, and he had promised Muriel that he would not use any of his retirement money. It turned out to be more difficult than he had expected.

As we already know, John looked at obstacles as a challenge, not as a deterrent. John went to the Boys and Girls Club and asked how many of their members would bring someone else to go whale watching if it was free. John was looking for about 150 participants. Within minutes, he had 150. It was only a matter of when he wanted to take the youngsters out. Then John went to the business people in town and asked them to sponsor one or two boys or girls at twenty-five dollars per person. They were prepared to do that. John asked the Lions Club to sponsor ten, and they did. He asked the Rotary Club to sponsor ten and they did. By the end of the week, he had 150 youngsters going whale watching.

The problem then was transportation, but luckily, the Boys and Girls Club had buses to shuttle the children over to Long

Beach. It worked great, so the next year John decided to focus on Mexican children, as many of them had never even been on the beach let alone on a boat. He went to the Barton Hill School and took all of the Grade 6 students out. Eventually, almost every school in San Pedro was included: Point Fermin School, Cabrillo Avenue School, Leland Street School and 7th Street School. He worked with the teachers and leaders of the groups to get the kids to write letters of thanks to the sponsoring businesses, which really helped when it came time to raise money for next year's whale watching trips.

Eventually, John would run two trips, one in February and the other one in March. One for ACS and the other for his charities like the Hunger Walk/Run, or CROP, a joint effort by twenty-two churches through the Council of Churches. He would also offer free whale watching trips to anyone who raised one hundred dollars. Of all the money raised, 25 per cent would go to local social agencies in San Pedro, while the rest would be used to help feed people in Africa, India or other places in need.

Retirement also brought new adventures that seemed so unlikely that one wondered what else could possibly happen in John's life. On New Year's Day in 1995, John was walking out of the water when a woman asked him if she could take his photo. Of course, John had no objections. Afterward, John gave her his phone number and left. He did not give it a second thought. A few days later, John was cooking enchiladas for a hundred lifeguards and their wives, who were having a reunion the next day. The phone rang. It was the photographer, and she asked John if he could come to Malibu so she could take some more photos. John did not want to go all the way to Malibu because he was up to his neck cooking enchiladas for the reunion dinner. But once she offered him three hundred dollars, he dropped the enchiladas and drove to Malibu. It occurred to him that he had not even asked what the photo shoot was about. He had been a museum director and lifeguard captain, so he did not want to be associated with smoking or anything people would consider inappropriate.

When John arrived, three women were waiting for him. They led him to a van and, before he knew it, they were powdering his nose, trimming his beard and combing his hair. It took him a while to gather his thoughts, but finally he inquired what the photos were going to be used for. The women told him that they were for an advertisement for a financial institution that would be in a number of national and international magazines. John was impressed. He put on a wetsuit, stepped out of the van and, for about four hours, they took photos of John holding onto a paddleboard with the wind gusting around him at howling speeds. The ad came out in several different publications and John received phone calls from friends across the nation. Once again, John used the attention to raise money for charitable causes.

One of these causes was the day-care center for seniors in San Pedro, a project the Ecumenical church organization had been working on since 1989. Back then, John was asked to serve on the board of directors but he declined. He was happy that he did not have to go to meetings anymore because he knew that they would likely tie him down once a month. He did not want to restrict his time like that, but he liked the idea because there was no place where retirees could go and spend some time together and be cared for during the day. So, John agreed to help raise funds. He called up some of his friends, explained what it was about and promised to match whatever they would contribute. One of his volunteers at the museum wrote a check for a thousand dollars, so John wrote one too. At the end, he had raised six thousand dollars from the community, which he matched with his own money. Of course, twelve thousand dollars was far from what was needed, but it was enough to hire a grant writer, who, in turn, brought in more funds.

In January 1996, it became clear that the Salvation Army was also thinking about providing day-care services for the elderly. Once the two parties met, it was obvious that pursuing the project together was mutually beneficial. After receiving several substantial grants, the day-care center opened on July 19, 1996, under the name Sage House. Sage, as in *wise through reflection and experience*, was a suitable name for this new facility. Still running today, the Sage House is at the corner of 2nd and Bandini streets in San Pedro, a two-story building with the senior day-care center downstairs and the headquarters of the Salvation Army upstairs.

John was always creative when it came to raising money. Having something to give to each donor was an important component of his efforts: Whalewatch patches or wooden firecrackers, for instance. When he heard that his friends who had a store that sold shells had gone out of business, he found out that they had little heart-shaped shells. He would have paid for them, but the owners gave them to John free because he was going to use them to raise money for good causes. Another friend and his two sisters put them in little boxes and gift-wrapped them. They became another token of appreciation to those who contributed to one of his many causes.

As we know, John loved to be around children, teaching and engaging them into learning something new. In the early years of the museum, a little girl had come to John and told him she wanted to have her name in the museum. Instead of sending her away, John explained that if she went out and found a seashell he did not have at the museum and brought it back to him, he would add it to the collection with her name attached to it. The little girl returned some time later with a seashell and, as it turned out, it was indeed a new one. John kept his word and the girl got her wish. With his departure from the museum, his daily contact with children ceased, but he continued to receive invitations to speak to students at schools in the Harbor Area.

For some of these speaking engagements, John would team up with Geoff Agism, an accordion and banjo player from New Jersey who had been living in San Pedro since 1967. Agism loved how San Pedro was not like a run-of-the-mill beach town, where you were always looking for action. San Pedro was much more of a hometown with a conscience. The people were concerned about what they were doing in support of the museum, the poor and the hungry. Geoff was not much of a beach person; his light skin gave him sunburns instead of a tan, which did nothing for his already low self-esteem. However, he loved the museum, with its maritime exhibits and maritime history.

All his life, Agism had had trouble fitting in and making friends. In San Pedro, he felt people were open-minded and welcoming. Nevertheless, it took a while to feel comfortable and make friends. As Agism would later admit, it was not because of the people in San Pedro, it was because of his own expectations. Being from the East Coast and used to rejection from most cliques, he expected that he had to be something that he was not. It took him a while to realize that he could just be who he was. He later said that it was almost like having a second childhood, with John Olguin, Bill Samaras and Bill Oleson as his godfathers.

On one occasion, John had a speaking engagement at the Historical Society, so he asked Geoff to come down so that when people arrived the auditorium would not be empty. John suggested that they should both be on stage playing and singing some shanties. Like so many other of John's ideas, it worked great. In fact, it was so well received that John decided that every time he would talk at the Rotary Club, he would ask Geoff to come along. He also began to pay Geoff twenty or twenty-five dollars.

In John's typical fashion, it did not take him long before he was expanding on the idea. He spoke with friends and they suggested that he and Geoff should perform and educate at the elementary schools, two sessions in the morning and two in the afternoon. John liked performing and doing the talks, but did not want to make it full-time. Instead, they arranged with three universities, San Diego State, Arizona State, and the Christian University, to deliver two three-hour talks to teachers, so they could share the information with their students. John would talk about his "Do-it Do-it" program and then he would introduce Geoff and they would continue the program singing songs and talking about ships and the maritime world.

It worked out perfectly. At first, they just made twenty-five dollars, later fifty dollars, until finally they were getting a hundred dollars each. They traveled all across Southern California, with engagements only once per week. The teachers were enthusiastic because John would talk about ships in San Pedro, early whalers, and of course, he would always engage the audience. Geoff would contribute to the experience by playing songs those sailors would have listened to, or sung, on his accordion and banjo.

What was so wonderful about John as a teacher is that he

always taught with his entire body. He would appear onstage, dressed like a tough laborer at sea, with a white oilskin, a hat, jacked hip boots, and a tatoo, artfully fashioned on his arm by Muriel. As he described how ships get in and out of port, John would act out the entire story, playing different characters that one would have encountered on sailing ships in the early days of the Port of Los Angeles. He would wear a captain's jacket and hat, a topcoat, shirt and tie, while talking about the skill set the captain would need and the responsibilities that rested on his shoulders. Then, he would peel off those clothes, kick off the boots and he would be barefoot in trousers and a shirt talking about the simple seamen that shouldered most of the labor. John told fantastic stories of what those sailors did on their voyages to and from San Pedro. He talked about what they did to get their ships out without steam, using a capstan (a rotating machine with a vertical axle used on ships to apply force to ropes and cables) and anchors.

With Geoff playing shanties, John would explain the importance of the shanty man. The shanty man was an individual standing at the head of the rope, with the other sailors standing along the rope behind him. He would start to sing to provide some beat or rhythm to the work they were about to perform. If there was really heavy work, like lifting up an anchor or taking the ship away from the dock, he would play slow, melodious songs and the sailors would walk slowly, winding the rope around the capstan. If they had to put the sails up, well, then he had to play a fast shanty.

Because many in the audience would not know what a capstan was, John would wrap a rope around one person and hand the other end to a few others. Then he and Geoff would intone some of those melodies and the audience could experience how a capstan actually worked and how all the different parts fell into place. That had always been John's style of learning, whether it was bringing a whale to life with 1000 people acting out its movements in a parking lot, or making youngsters understand how the way of life for people has really changed over the decades.

During his working years, John Olguin taught millions of children and adults who participated in the museum programs. More than twenty years into his retirement, he had spoken with and taught countless more. When people saw John coming down the road, they sometimes might have wanted to hide, as John was relentless in the pursuit of making his hometown, and by extension, our world, a better place. But no one wanted to miss that journey, so the people of San Pedro continue to give to John and his causes.

At age 89, in 2010, John had hardly slowed down. He continued to be a life-changing catalyst and speak about the importance of the ocean to everyone who would listen. Long after his own grandchildren had grown up, John would still go down to the beach, often taking a bag filled with aluminum cans, license plates, gearshifts, Frisbees with holes and red cups, all of which he used to build a truck out of sand. Children would quickly gather around to see what he was doing. He would often sit back and let them play. The only time he would disturb them is when, and this only happened once in a while, one would attempt to leave with his stuff. He would not shout or get angry if that happened, he would just say, "Oh, I think you have had enough." That's it. John would be back another day.

No doubt, the dominoes will keep falling long after we are all gone. Stories of John Olguin will continue to be told on Cabrillo Beach, in bars and restaurants across San Pedro, on the docks, and in countless homes and offices for many,

many years to come. Who knows what people will think a few generations down the line when they hear stories of this larger-than-life Mexican-American man and all that he accomplished over the years. Hopefully, this book will lend credibility to future storytellers, because he did do it all.

POSTSCRIPT

*F*ollowing a tradition that reaches back to the mid-
1930s, the members of the New Year's Day Polar
Bears were gathering on the Cabrillo Beach on
January 1, 2011, when the first rumors emerged that
John had passed early that morning. Quickly, rumors turned
into certainty.

John had not been feeling well for a few days, with flu-like
symptoms. He felt strong and well enough to go out to the
Korean Bell in Angel's Gate Park overlooking Point Fermin
for the traditional ringing of the bell on New Year's Eve, but
he left unusually early, went home and straight to bed. He
woke up the next morning, looked out to the ocean from his
outdoor bed, went back to sleep and died shortly thereafter.

Within hours of the news, countless voices were talking
all over town. People were reminiscing about John, the life
he had lived, and all the good he had done. Multiple stories
recounting the milestones of his life began to appear in local,
citywide and national newspapers, including the *Daily Breeze*,
the *Los Angeles Times* and the *Wall Street Journal*. Community
leaders and groups sent out letters and statements paying
tribute to his life and his work, and a flood of messages were
posted on the Internet and social sites from individuals sharing their memories and honoring the man who had touched
millions of lives. A Facebook page called "San Pedro Stands

up for John Olguin" emerged within forty-eight hours, with hundreds of people joining the call, assembling at Point Fermin Park, and lining Paseo del Mar to watch the sunset and share stories about John.

John Olguin was laid to rest on Saturday, January 8, 2011, in the Green Hills Memorial Park on Western Avenue in Rancho Palos Verdes, right on the San Pedro border, a place he had chosen for himself so that he could watch the whales pass by for eternity. He is survived by Muriel, his wife of sixty-two years, his daughters, Vi Olguin and Moni Olguin Patten, and his son, John Cabrillo; his four grandchildren, Micah, Tenaya, Molly and Michelle; his four siblings, Dr. Leonard Olguin, Albert Olguin, Esther Olguin Riggs and Belia Olguin Smith; and numerous cousins, nieces and nephews.

A public memorial celebration arranged by *FRIENDS of Cabrillo Marine Aquarium* was held on January 22 in front of the aquarium right next to Cabrillo Beach. It was a wonderful, sunny afternoon and more than a thousand people came to share in the communal experience of reliving some of their own memorable moments with John and hearing about others. While his achievements were and will long be remembered, his true legacy is the remarkable way in which John led his life: the exquisite balance between a profound commitment to his work and an equally profound dedication to his family, friends and their community.

A few weeks after his passing, the Los Angeles Unified School District's Board of Education, acting on a motion from Harbor Area board member Dr. Richard Vladovic, a long-time friend of John's, honored San Pedro's most beloved citizen and his wife, Muriel, by naming the new annex to San Pedro High School the John M. and Muriel Olguin Campus. The annex campus, expected to house some eight hundred students from the crowded and aged San Pedro High School, is set to open in the fall of 2012. It is a well-deserved recognition of John and Muriel who, both in their own ways and together, made dreams possible.

Perhaps not so coincidentally, and maybe more a product of fate or divine intervention, the John M. and Muriel Olguin Campus is built on high ground located at the west end of the former Upper Reservation of Fort MacArthur, now called Angels Gate Park. Students attending the school, for generations to come, will be able to look out the windows along the south side of the school buildings and get a clear view of the San Pedro coastline where John Olguin's beloved whales travel on their annual migration route. Students will also be able to see Point Fermin Park from the campus and its famed lighthouse that John helped restore.

The spirit of John Olguin lives on.

Authors' Reflections

I first came to the Cabrillo Marine Museum in 1984, during my very first visit to the U.S., delivering a speech to the Los Angeles Chapter of the American Cetacean Society. I did meet John, then, but we did not have a chance to get to know each other. Fifteen years later, my wife, Barbara, who was one of John's students back in the day, went to San Pedro to pay John a visit. By then, I had heard many stories about John and the museum, or aquarium as it was now called, and I was looking forward to meeting the man himself.

It was a wonderful experience: he treated me like a long-time friend, sharing stories of the past and he was sincerely interested in my work. Then, I told him about how I had met Barbara, my research on dolphins in Portugal, and my work on environmental and sustainability issues. He was interested in all of it. A couple of hours went by and when Muriel arrived, the four of us continued to have a wonderful, animated conversation over a cup of tea, about whales, the museum, the ocean, the arts, and life itself.

John turned out to be the man I had envisioned, and much more. I was excited, because we had taken the trip to San Pedro to ask John if he would give us his blessing to write his authorized biography. After talking to him for a few hours, I knew that writing this book would be a wonderful adventure with countless hours of storytelling, inquiries, recollections and reflections ahead. He seemed hesitant for a second, but then a big smile lightened up his face and a resounding "Yes" filled the room.

And so it began. John opened his entire archive to us and, over the next several years, we would spend hours and days with him, Muriel, their children, friends, colleagues and neighbors, sifting through all the documents and photographs. Books like this often take more time than anticipated and John's biography was no exception. It was completed a few years late, but not too late for John. By the end of December 2010, John had read almost the entire manuscript and was full of praise for everyone who had worked on his life story. He was looking forward to the book being released and ready to go to work and sell it. "Let's do it!" we would say together every time we talked about it. He sure did everything he could and I hope that I did too.

—*Dr. Stefan E. Harzen, Chairman,*
The Taras Oceanographic Foundation

~~~

I lost my father when I was a small child and did not have a strong father figure during my adolescence. When I followed my passion, it directed me to San Pedro and into the influence of John O. I was entranced by his many presentations, his stories and his persona. Over the years, he and I spent many hours together, and he was always supportive and interested in my activities. He was the perfect male role model for me, and for that, I loved him. Of course, I listened as he told and re-told the stories of his life, and in the back of my mind I kept thinking, "Someone has to write a book about this guy and get these stories down on paper." I always assumed someone else, a professional writer perhaps, would also see the benefit in such a project. As the years went by and there was no biography, my husband and I decided we had better "do it" before it was too late.

When we approached John with the idea, it was as if we had put fire to a fuse. John was very excited about the prospect and I was honored to my very core that he trusted me with the privileged responsibility. Stefan and I interviewed

John and Muriel, as well as many of John's friends and asso-
ciates, at length. Everyone was very forthcoming and shared
parts of their lives that were surprisingly candid and human.
For the first time, I heard the "back story" to the tall tales that
I had heard from John over the years. The more I learned, the
more amazing the man became.

It took a while, and a lot of help from everyone, but we got
the task done. John read each chapter and was happy with the
result. Shortly before he died, John and I had an opportunity
to sit and talk about our friendship. I am so very grateful we
had that evening where I was able to tell him just how important his influence had been on my life, and he told me pri-
vately how proud of me – and the book – he was. I guess that
has always been my goal: to make John proud of me, because
I was always so proud to be his student and friend. I know
John is smiling down on us now, telling everyone in heaven
they have to buy a copy!

—*Barbara Brunnick, Ph.D.,*
Research Director, Palm Beach Dolphin Project,
The Taras Oceanographic Foundation

~~~

My first visit to Cabrillo Marine Museum (CMM) was my
kindergarten field trip in 1959. Although I don't remember
John Olguin specifically, I have vivid memories of holding a
baby food jar of seawater with a little sand at the bottom and
lots of baby fish furiously swimming around inside. I remember the smell of the huge eucalyptus trees of Cabrillo Beach
and the excitement of my classmates as we walked around
the museum. This experience was one of many in my life that
tugged at me to devote my life to learning more about the
ocean. I have thought about that memory many times as I
pursued my dream of "getting paid to work at the beach,"

which I did for the first years of my career at California State University Long Beach and then the bulk of my career at Cabrillo Marine Museum/Aquarium.

During the first week of working as the Exhibits Director at CMM in 1989, John gave me some simple advice that has served me well over the years. "Keep peace in the family," he said. That impressed me a great deal and guided me as I performed my duties of working with the family of staff and volunteers at CMM. John recognized that an important strength of CMM was the dedication and devotion of those who work and volunteer there. He also recognized that, like in most families, there would be disagreements. His sage advice was to remember that keeping the family peaceful was critical in keeping it functional.

John was one of the best storytellers I have ever met. Over the twenty-two years that I knew him, he told stories about his life, the lives of ocean animals and stories about the town he loved, San Pedro. There was no end to his stories and I heard even more in the process of collaborating on this book. I will always cherish the time we spent together. It was absolutely amazing to me that he was able to recollect events of his life and describe them so vividly and accurately. Even in his 89th year, he had a remarkable memory.

I will never forget this man of the ocean. Every time I swim at Cabrillo Beach, hatch grunion, touch a gray whale calf in a Baja lagoon, or drive over the beautifully lit Vincent Thomas Bridge at night, John will be beside me telling me some new story I have never heard before. John was committed to ocean education and, if he were still with us today, I would tell him not to worry; thanks to his teaching and great example, all of the Cabrillo Marine Aquarium family will keep doing it!

—*Mike Schaadt*
Director, Cabrillo Marine Aquarium

Community Reaction

Following John's passing, many people who had met or known John picked up a pen and began to write down their reflections. We begin with memories of Janice Hahn, a long-time friend and supporter of John and the Cabrillo Marine Museum/Aquarium, as well as a Los Angeles City Council Member. Her tribute is followed by other people's recollections, some of which were first published in the local newspapers *Random Lengths* and *San Pedro Today*.

~~~

It is hard to imagine San Pedro without John Olguin. He was like a grandfather to everyone; he was a cherished friend who taught us all to love the ocean and its animals – from the tiny grunions to the mighty whales.

One of my many treasured memories of being with John is from years ago, after I was elected to the Los Angeles City Council, when John insisted that I join the Cabrillo Beach Polar Bears. John co-founded the group in 1953 and the "Polar Bears" – a crazy group of people who swim in the ocean everyday and have an annual New Year's Day celebratory swim – have been a dynamic fixture of Cabrillo Beach ever since. With trepidation, I showed up at the beach. John held my hand and marched me into the frigid ocean. As the first wave approached, he put his hand on my head, said, "Hold your breath," and promptly dunked me under the water. His wife, Muriel, was afraid he was going to drown me, but I had nothing but trust in that steady hand pushing me under the wave.

I personally knew John for many years, but had heard of him much earlier. In fact, my brother, former Los Angeles Mayor

Jim Hahn, went on a field trip to Cabrillo Beach when he was a boy. Jim remembers seeing card tables set up on the beach, each one stacked with glass containers filled with sea life. It is humbling to imagine that John's simple system of jars on card tables would eventually be housed in a building designed by renowned architect Frank Gehry and grow into one of the most renowned educational aquariums on the West Coast: the Cabrillo Marine Aquarium. Without John Olguin's steadfast determination, hundreds of thousands of children from across the Los Angeles area would not have had the unique opportunity to discover marine life at the educationally rich Cabrillo Marine Aquarium.

I remember John telling me the stories of his days as a lifeguard, watching kids constantly burning their fingers while lighting illegal fireworks down at Cabrillo Beach every Fourth of July. In response, John began the annual fireworks show at the beach that has grown into one of the best and biggest in Los Angeles. Kids no longer have to put themselves at risk to enjoy amazing fireworks every year.

For those of us who knew John well, this book will be a reminder of his greatness. For those who did not, I am confident that John's story will serve as an inspiration to anyone who reads this book.

—Janice Hahn, Los Angeles City Council Member

~~~

"He was the captain of the ship, the last of the legends of San Pedro. It'll never be like it was. *Random Lengths* doesn't have enough paper to print all the things that he's done for the community."

—Debbie Marr, artist and author

~~~

"I would say he was the single most effective educator I've ever encountered. Deep creativity. Boundless energy, and no boundaries – these were some of the qualities, born of love for his environment and community, that made John Olguin a man that I, and countless others, will always love and revere."

—*Dr. Susanne Lawrenz-Miller, Director,*
Cabrillo Marine Aquarium 1987–2006

~~~

"I heard about it (John's passing) within a few hours because I'm on the 'Pedro Grapevine. John was a great influence in my life and I am grateful to have worked with him for many years. He ranks high for me among the unforgettable characters, a very lovable guy that imparted enthusiasm to everyone else. He was the definition of charismatic. And he could get you to do anything. I was fortunate enough to name a new local species of sea anemone after him and when I showed him the scientific paper he was thrilled. He had a golden tongue and lived life with a passion that all who experienced him felt. His death closes the door to a whole chapter of San Pedro History."

—*John Ljubenkov, marine biologist*

~~~

"John Olguin was the ultimate San Pedran – among the last who were totally committed to the betterment of the community. He also introduced me to tortilla soup."

—*Art Almeida, San Pedro Bay Historical Society*

~~~

"John Olguin will be remembered as a legendary figure of San Pedro Bay. My image of him is the King of the Beach, the Ernest Hemingway of California. His love for San Pedro, for the ocean, for the environment and his community to giving back to the community was truly unparalleled. I will miss him immensely and will always treasure our friendship."

—*Dr. Geraldine Knatz, Executive Director, Port of Los Angeles*

'Hey John, can I borrow a paddle board?' 'Sure son, have it back by 5.' That was Johnny O. He loved sharing the ocean with everyone."

—Jerry Butera, local musician

~~~

"John's spirit embodies all that is right in a human being, with humility at the core. We are fortunate to have received the many gifts he gave. He passionately engaged in so many worthwhile endeavors for our community. No project was too great or too small. I will always remember him at Christmas season out in the cold in front of the market ringing the bell for the Salvation Army."

—Camilla Townsend, President,
San Pedro Chamber of Commerce

~~~

"John brought with him a sense of normalcy, tradition, and in many cases an old school approach to getting things done. All of us can learn from his shining example of keeping it simple, treating everyone with mutual respect and always operating with the highest level of trust and integrity. We can also honor him by carrying on his legacy of serving others, volunteering, and especially teaching our youth."

—Anthony Pirozzi, Chairman,
San Pedro Chamber of Commerce Board of Directors

~~~

"Icons and legends are often best observed from afar because many times, when you get closer, the shine disappears and you come to learn that your heroes aren't maybe so deserving of the accolades they have received. With John, it was just the opposite. The more often you met him and spent time around him, the more you came to respect and to love him. He disarmed the cynic in all of us and showed us how much difference a single human being can make by sheer effort, determination and grace."

—*Jack Baric, filmmaker*

~~~

"John managed to accomplish more than any politician or committee that I have ever known. The reason is because he lived by the "just do it" motto that he often repeated. I can only imagine how much our community could accomplish if we deserted all the talking and adopted John's walking the talk philosophy."

—*Jennifer Marquez*

~~~

"Mr. Olguin was a good natured and civil man who never had an unkind word for anyone. His devotion to his community in so many spheres has lifted the collective spirit of San Pedro. We can never watch another fireworks show without looking to the heavens and remembering this kind and gentle man. A true San Pedro saint."

—*Joe Buscaino, Senior Lead Officer,*
Los Angeles Police Department Harbor Division

~~~

"Mr. Olguin is best known for his ability to teach kids and the community about the ocean. Getting the people to learn and be excited about our local marine life was the foundation of the Cabrillo Marine Aquarium. Teaching kids about the ocean on land was just one part. Whale watching became a thriving industry along our coast well after Mr. Olguin would take boats out into the channel for a dramatic display of the world's largest mammals."

—*John M. Mavar,*
Member, Northwest San Pedro Neighborhood Council

"Fifty-seven years ago, John Olguin touched my life with his displays in the Cabrillo Beach bathhouse. For the last 25 years, he would visit my office and never leave empty-handed. We all loved this man and Muriel. I once took them to an airshow and he was child-like in wonderment. Muriel was moved to paint a recollection of that day and the painting is in my office."

—Dennis C. Lord

~~~

"What a tremendous loss for all of us. I am truly heartbroken. What a wonderful gentleman he was."

—Silvia de la Pena

~~~

"This is very sad news for San Pedro. I didn't know him very well personally, although I live just around the corner from the Olguins. His legacy will live on forever through his work. Who can't do the Grunion Dance and not smile? Thank you, John, for all you did. It's up to us to carry it on."

—Elizabeth Warren

~~~

"He was as San Pedro as it gets! Bigger than life! That is really a true loss for our town."

—Denise Marovich-Sampson

~~~

"After having heard his name around town for many years, I finally met him, quite by chance, a little over a year ago. What a nice fellow. He will be remembered."

—Joan Francis

~~~

"A wonderful man. So many of my childhood memories involve him and his huge personality. So grateful to have learned from him."

—Aleece Jones DePuey

"I will miss John's smiley face and his total commitment to our community of San Pedro."

—*Andrea Marincovich Clark*

~~~

"Mr. Olguin's 'stop and chats' were the real deal."

—*Andrea Hegybeli*

~~~

"John was instrumental in organizing a 'march of a thousand drummers' to herald in the new millennium, the year 2000. The event took place not too far from the foot of the Vincent Thomas Bridge. It was one of those days, where throughout the day, anywhere in the city where a celebration was to take place, it rained. So it did just that in San Pedro that late afternoon. Not to be deterred, we waited for John to bring on his marching drummers, wet from the occasional drizzles that we feared would turn into a torrent. Just as we heard the coming drummers the clouds started breaking, with a spike of sunlight bursting through every now and then. His big grin was visible from a distance. John came closer to us, as we stood by the bandstand, arms moving as he gestured, marshaling his troops forward."

—*Slobodan Dimitrov*

~~~

"We all know that John's passing has left a huge hole in the heart of San Pedro. What if we all make a pledge to do at least one thing for the community each year in honor of John? We could call it doing the JO. I think that would be the greatest honor we could pay to this great man, to carry on his work."

—*Darlene Zavalney*

~~~

"As one of the Junior High docents, John Olguin greatly impacted my life, my love for learning and my love for the sea and all its creatures. There are too many memories and at the mention I am sure we all have the flashes of the man and the legacy."

—Jennifer Vandivort

~~~

"I live in England now so won't be at Point Fermin. I'll be thinking of John on Sunday. His enthusiasm and love of all life shined through and enlightened everyone lucky enough to meet him. I loved the little museum where my sister used to volunteer. The grunion runs were exciting, and I don't think anyone else would have been able to get me to touch an anemone or dance like a jellyfish."

—Nancy Bunyan

~~~

"My John Olguin story begins in 1969 when a friend invited me to attend John's Wednesday afternoon marine biology class at the Old Cabrillo Beach Marine Museum. High school students from across the South Bay came together weekly to learn about the tide pools, the museum displays, public speaking, and themselves. John chaperoned volunteers to the first Earth Day Celebration at the Long Beach Municipal Auditorium, took busloads of teenagers to Sea World, and introduced us to ecology, team building, and story telling. John had a unique way of nudging everyone out of their comfort zone. Though I am prone to sea sickness, John urged me to be a naturalist on the Whalewatch boats. John hired me to be a summer tour guide, my first 'real' job and encouraged me to be a teacher. I have heard his voice in mine many times. All lessons about whales and conservation begin with John's stories and gestures.

John Olguin is my hero. He is a National Treasure."

—Majella Almeida Maas

"I met John Olguin in 1969 when a science teacher at Dana Jr. High School took me to meet him. My father had passed away young, so John became sort of a father figure to me. He inspired my love of the ocean I still have today. We kept in touch after my school years via whale watching or Channel Island trips. Then in his retirement, there was John Olguin at San Pedro High School football games. Next thing I knew, I'm driving him to the games, and enjoying a lot of private time once again with him. This is time I'll cherish forever, and never forget. During a long drive to an away playoff game, he did say how he wanted to be remembered. He simply said 'Just a man that did the right thing, and left this world a little better than it was when he came into it.' Well Johnny O, you not only made the world a little better by yourself, but you also inspired an army of people that in their own way, are trying to do the same thing. We'll never forget. We all say Thank You, and God Bless."

—Lloyd Champion

~~~

"Someone wrote on the *Daily Breeze* obituary that they were in shock when they heard of John's passing. It was as it learning that Santa Claus had died. I know exactly what he means."

—Patti Smith

~~~

"My first memories of John Olguin stem from Juan Cabrillo Day at Cabrillo Beach. My mom was a teacher for many years and my uncle was a lifeguard, so they both knew John over the years. Then when I got the opportunity to go whale watching with some students in elementary school, there he was again, sharing with us all the amazing things about whales and the ocean. He was so enthusiastic that you couldn't help but feel excited about these amazing creatures. I love Cabrillo Beach, it's my place of reflection and many amazing memories. I can't help but think that a lot of that is because of this special person named John Olguin. Even after years of not seeing him, when we would cross paths, he would look at you and speak to you as if he really remembered you out of all those thousands of kids he impacted! What a cool guy John Olguin is and his love for San Pedro will continue to touch others forever!"

—*Kirstin Inlow Baldonado*

~~~

"Walking my children to White Point Elementary usually included a stop at Mr Olguin's trees to see what little gifts he left ... pretty seashells, all sorts of sea themed trinkets; it made the walk to school more interesting and educational. We also always enjoyed the grunion runs at Cabrillo Beach and dancing like jellyfish. Mr. Olguin is now teaching the Angels in Heaven how to dance like jellyfish. Mr. Olguin you will be missed."

—*Carmen Hill*

~~~

"I feel so privileged to have met this wonderful humanitarian. John Olguin had been instrumental in developing ways for children and their families to learn not only about the whales, but all marine life. He has touched the lives of thousands of people over the years and ... provided them with life long memories."

—*Staci Kaye-Carr*

~~~

"This is John Olguin's front door. I am sure that each and every thing that is mounted on this door has a special story that goes along with it. And if John were here to tell you each story, he would do just that. He always made time to be with his friends and especially to tell a story. Like this door, anyone who knew John had a story, at least one, and most likely many, to tell about their experiences or time shared with this amazing man."

—*Nanci Morris*

~~~

"I remember him coming once in a while to 15th Street School when I was in Grade 2 and meeting him at the Cabrillo Marine Aquarium, always full of happiness and would stop what he was doing to tell us kids a story, and he did do the jelly fish dance ... he will be missed greatly."

—*Abisai Garcia Quen*

~~~

"The first time I met John was at the Old Spaghetti Factory as we and he were attending a play written by a friend (Margaret Rector). I knew I had met someone very special and unique. That was 32 years ago and we have known each other ever since. What an amazing man. Like a ripple on a pond, he influenced many thousands of lives."

—*Gayle Fleury*

~~~

"If more real men were like him, the world would be a much better place."

—*Tony Lafferty*

~~~

"I remember hatching grunion eggs at 5, walking the tide pools with him at 10, Whalewatching each year my whole life, working as a docent and an intern at the museum, swapping LA City Rec and Park lifeguarding stories. Big events for the Whale Festival and the Light House Restoration. He literally led the way into all my best life experiences. He used to regale my mom with stories of rushing home for the good shoes and tie so he could take his girl out. He learned from hardship to be forgiving and generous, and we all have benefited from his generous and infectious heart. He stood up in church almost every Sunday to offer a prayer of Thanksgiving for some act of kindness he had witnessed in our little town."

—Linda Gillingham Sciaroni

~~~

"As a young girl the biggest thrill ... besides going to Cabrillo Beach on hot summer days ... was a chance to follow Mr. Olguin around the beach as he told stories and legends and gave us facts to remember ... that he would quiz us on the next time we met ... what a wonderful example of a mentor and life coach for all of San Pedro's children (and its visitors) Thank you Mr. Olguin for wonderful days and memories that will last a lifetime.... You will be Missed and Remembered by many!"

—The Dodson Famly

~~~

"He taught us about love: of the ocean, of its creatures, of our town, of one's family, of one's spouse, of sleeping outdoors, of floating on one's back like a sea otter, and of life. He enriched my childhood immeasurably. I hope he knows how much he was loved and by how many. There will never be anyone just like him, but if people strive to be as close to him as they can, think of what our world would be like."

—Christiana Dominguez

~~~

What an inspiration! He was my neighbor for 7 years and I loved every minute of it! A loving, thoughtful man who gave to his community every day of his life."

—Marcus Johns

Bibliography and Further Reading

An Illustrated History of Los Angeles County, California. Chicago: Lewis Publishing Company, 1889.

Bancroft, Hubert Howe. *The Works of Hubert Howe Bancroft: History of California: vol. I, 1542–1800.* San Francisco: A.L. Bancroft, 1884.

Behrens, June, and John Olguin. *Whalewatch!* Chicago: Childrens Press, 1978.

Black, Nancy A., and Southwest Fisheries Science Center (U.S.). *Killer Whales of California and Western Mexico: A Catalog of Photo-Identified Individuals.* Silver Spring: U.S. Dept. of Commerce, National Oceanic and Atmospheric Administration, National Marine Fisheries Service, 1997.

Branco, Castelo F. "Cabrillo's Nationality," *Academia de Marinha* (1987).

Bulloch, David K. *The Whale-Watcher's Handbook: A Field Guide to the Whales, Dolphins and Porpoises of North America.* New York: Lyons & Burford, 1993.

Cabrillo Historical Association. *Cabrillo's World: A Commemorative Edition of Cabrillo Festival Historic Seminar Papers.* San Diego: Cabrillo Historical Association, 1991.

Chapman, Charles E. *A History of California: the Spanish Period.* New York: Macmillan Co., 1921.

Crane, J.M. "The Response of Male Grunion to a Wiggling Stick," *Bulletin of the Southern California Academy of Sciences* 68, no.3 (1969): 191–93.

Eder, Tamara, and Ian Sheldon. *Whales and Other Marine Mammals of California and Baja.* Edmonton: Lone Pine Publishing, 2002.

Finegan, Peter. "Discovery of California by Juan Rodriquez Cabrillo," *Cabrillo College Voice* (Aptos, CA), November 20, 1995 and December 04, 1995.

Fleming, Standish M. "King of the Boundless Sea," *Orange Coast Magazine,* January 1979.

Gaffey, John T., II. "The Town of San Pedro, 1882," *The Shoreline* 26, no. 2 (October 1998).

Guinn, J.M. *A History of California and an extended History of Its Southern Coast Counties, also containing biographies of well-known citizens of the past and present.* Los Angeles: Historic Record Co., 1907.

Houston, John M. "First Cabrillo Discovery of San Pedro Celebration – 1920," *The Shoreline* 13 (October 1986).

Hoyt, Erich. *The Whale Watcher's Handbook*. Garden City: Doubleday, 1984.

Idyll, Clarence P. "Grunion, the Fish that Spawns on Land," *National Geographic* 135 no. 5 (1969): 714-23.

Kelsey, Harry. *Juan Rodriguez Cabrillo*. San Marino: Huntington Library, 1986.

Marquez, Ernest, and Veronique De Turenne. *Port of Los Angeles: an Illustrated History from 1850 to 1945*. Santa Monica: Angel City Press, 2008.

Mathes, Michael W. "The Discoverer of Alta California: Joáo Rodrigues Cabrilho or Juan Rodriguez Cabrillo?," *The Journal of San Diego History* 19, no. 3 (1973).

McKinzie, Joe. *San Pedro Bay*. Charleston: Arcadia Publishing, 2005.

Reupsch, Carl and Cabrillo Historical Association. *The Cabrillo Era and His Voyage of Discovery*. San Diego: Cabrillo Historical Association, 1982.

Schaadt, Mark. *Cabrillo Beach Coastal Park*. Edited by Ed Mastro and Cabrillo Marine Aquarium. Charleston: Arcadia Publishing, 2009.

Schaadt, Mike and Ed Mastro. *San Pedro's Cabrillo Beach*. San Francisco: Arcadia Publishing, 2008.

Silka, Henry P., Irene M. Almeida, and San Pedro Bay Historical Society. *San Pedro: A Pictorial History*. San Pedro Bay: San Pedro Bay Historical Society, 1984.

Verge, Arthur C. *Los Angeles County Lifeguards*. Charleston: Arcadia Publishing, 2005.

Wagner, Henry, and California Historical Society. *Juan Rodriguez Cabrillo, Discoverer of the Coast of California*. San Francisco: San Francisco Historical Society, 1941.

Walters, Mark J. *The Dance of Life: Courtship in the Animal Kingdom*. New York: Arbor House/W. Morrow, 1988.

Wright, Bertram C. *The 1st Cavalry Division in World War II*. Tokyo: Toppan Printing Co., 1947.

DR. STEFAN E. HARZEN

Dr. Stefan E. Harzen serves as Chairman and CEO of the Taras Oceanographic Foundation and concurrently as the Executive Director of Blue Dolphin Research and Consulting, Inc. and the Director of the Sustainability Office of Balam Investments/The Balam Escape.

His expertise has long expanded from marine mammals to conservation, management, green technology and consulting. He is an advisor to community and business leaders on a wide range of future and sustainability issues, and an accomplished scientist, writer, photographer and musician.

Widely regarded a man of culture and knowledge, Stefan is a Fellow of the renowned Explorers Club and has been included in the pages of *Adventurous Dreams, Adventurous Lives*, together with 120 other outstanding individuals, representing a "Who's Who" of international exploration.

DR. BARBARA BRUNNICK

Dr. Barbara Brunnick is the Director of the Palm Beach Dolphin Project where she continues to follow her passion of studying whales and dolphins that began at the Cabrillo Marine Museum. Over the years, she has worked on various research projects, most notably studying Atlantic Spotted dolphins in the Bahamas, producing novel insights into the social organizations of these animals.

Currently she is the Research Director of the Taras Oceanographic Foundation, and as such she continues her work with wild marine mammals by actively compiling a catalogue of bottlenose dolphins in Palm Beach, Florida.

Over the last decade she has developed advanced spatial analysis techniques and a new generation of maps many expect will change how we see the world.

Barbara is also Fellow of the renowned *Explorers Club* and has been similarly included in the pages of *Adventurous Dreams, Adventurous Lives.*

MIKE SCHAADT, DIRECTOR,
CABRILLO MARINE AQUARIUM

Mike Schaadt, a life-long Southern Californian, is Director of Cabrillo Marine Aquarium, which is owned by the City of Los Angeles, Recreation and Parks Department. Mike has been involved in formal and informal marine science education for more than 30 years. He graduated with a Bachelor's degree in Marine Biology and a Master's degree in Biology from California State University Long Beach. Mike has taught biology at local community colleges and brings to his job a strong background in science education. He has a keen interest in finding novel ways to motivate people to learn about and care for the ocean. His research interest is the natural history of plankton with special emphasis on deep-sea forms. He has been a SCUBA diver for over 30 years and is an avid ocean swimmer, spending many of his lunch hours swimming at Cabrillo Beach.